The
HEBREW
PROPHETS

James D. Newsome, Jr.

John Knox Press
ATLANTA

Library of Congress Cataloging in Publication Data

Newsome, James D. (James DuPre), 1931–
. The Hebrew Prophets.

Includes bibliographical references.
1. Bible. O.T. Prophets—Introductions. I. Title.
BS1505.5.N48   1984   224'.06   84-760
ISBN 0-8042-0113-7

© copyright John Knox Press 1984
10 9 8 7 6 5 4 3
Printed in the United States of America
John Knox Press
Atlanta, Georgia 30365

For our parents
Hildred and Lollie
James and Brantley

Contents

1
The History of Prophecy in Israel Before Amos

The Roots of Hebrew Prophecy

When someone mentions the phrase "Old Testament prophet," most of us who have been raised in the traditions of the Christian church reflexively think of one or more of the great Hebrew prophets of the classical period: Isaiah, who spoke of God's gift of a special child, or Jeremiah, who lamented the impending doom of his nation, or Ezekiel, whose bizarre visions were sometimes matched by his equally bizarre behavior. It is not inaccurate to think in terms of such personalities. Indeed, it is almost inevitable, because these are among the towering Old Testament individuals whose personal experiences of God have helped to shape and to inform the religious experiences of Jews and Christians for more than two thousand years. However, if we think of the Old Testament prophets *only* as those for whom biblical books (the records of their utterances) have been named, we overlook the contributions of countless other persons without whom the work of these great "canonical" prophets[1] might not have been possible. Although the material in this book is largely devoted to prophets who were active during and after the eighth century, it is necessary, in order to understand their significance, first to examine the history of prophetic activity which preceded them.

---

[1] In this book the terms "canonical" prophets and "classical" prophets are used interchangeably to refer to those prophets whose words are recorded in books of the Old Testament canon which bear their names. These prophets are also sometimes referred to as the "writing" prophets, although that term (which will be avoided here) is misleading in that it inaccurately implies that these prophets were in each case the direct authors of the biblical books associated with them.

In doing so, we become aware of the fact that not only do the familiar canonical prophets stand at the end of a long historical tradition, but also that that slice of time during which they worked was relatively brief when compared to the total sweep of the history of Israel.

If modern scholarship has established with certainty anything about the origins of the prophetic movement within Israel, it is that (1) these origins are complex, and (2) they are difficult to reconstruct in all of their detail. Perhaps the Old Testament itself gives us one of the best clues concerning the origins of Hebrew prophecy. In the narrative account of the coming to power of Israel's first king, Saul, there is this brief digression:

> (Formerly in Israel, when a man went to inquire of God, he said, "Come, let us go to the seer"; for he who is now called a prophet was formerly called a seer.) (1 Sam. 9:9)

The text says, in effect, that at an early period in Israel's history the office of seer and that of the prophet were not identical, but that with the passage of time the functions of the seer were taken over by the prophet so that the seer ultimately disappeared.

What were the nature and the functions of this seer (literally: the one who sees)? Scholars now know that the office of the seer existed among a number of ancient people. In Mesopotamia, for example, that area to which the earliest Hebrews were most closely related (Gen. 11:28), the seer was an important person, often a priest attached to the temple of some deity, whose task it was to make known truths hidden from ordinary men and women. This frequently involved determining the will of the deity and, therefore, the outcome of the events which were important to the king, to the nation, and to individual men and women. Such things as the success or failure of the harvest, the results of warfare, the consequence of infection or disease were all of concern to the seer. According to the literature of the Sumerians and Akkadians, primary civilization builders of Mesopotamia, the seer arrived at an understanding of these and other crucial questions by means of the ability to interpret dreams and visions (the seer's own as well as those of others) and by the ability to "read" the movements of heavenly bodies (see the story of the "wise men from the East" in Matt. 2:1–12), the patterns of birds in flight, and the entrails of certain animals. Baked clay models of sheep livers have been found by archaeologists in certain Mesopotamian centers with "maps" drawn upon them to indicate the omens each part of the liver was supposed to represent.

If we return to the story about Saul in 1 Samuel 9:1—10:16, we can discover how similar were the Hebrew and Mesopotamian perceptions of the nature of the seer. Saul was searching for his father's strayed livestock when, after repeated failure, he accepted the suggestion of his servant that they inquire of a man of God who lived in the vicinity. After making sure that they had adequate resources with which to pay the seer for his services, they approached him for guidance in finding the lost animals. What Saul did not know is that the seer, who was Samuel, had previously been told by God to be on the lookout for the man who was to become Israel's first king. The story ends as Samuel tells Saul to forget about the livestock, which had been found, and to prepare for anointing as Israel's first prince (1 Sam. 9:1–27). It therefore seems that in ancient Israel, as well as in ancient Mesopotamia, the task of the seer was to inform ordinary men and women of truths they themselves could not know and to do so by means of special, divinely bestowed powers of clairvoyance.

Clairvoyance was a gift which other prophetic individuals in ancient Israel enjoyed. The blind prophet Ahijah recognized the wife of King Jeroboam in spite of her efforts to conceal her identity and foretold the death of her and the king's son (1 Kings 14). Elisha "saw" an encampment of enemy soldiers and saved the army of Israel (2 Kings 6:8–10). A short time later, the prophet successfully petitioned God that the gift of clairvoyance be extended to one of his servants (2 Kings 6:17). Isaiah informed King Hezekiah of the disaster about to overtake the invading Assyrian army (2 Kings 19:32–36).

Ecstasy is the second of the two roots of classical Hebrew prophecy suggested by the text of 1 Samuel 9:9. Again, the context of this verse assists us in understanding the nature of the phenomenon. After having anointed Saul as prince of Israel, Samuel, in his capacity as clairvoyant, "sees" an impending encounter between Saul and a band of traveling ecstatics. He tells Saul that he will "be turned into another man," that is, that he will become "infected" by the ecstatic state of mind. Later that day Saul does meet these prophets and under the power of their ecstasy "the spirit of God came mightily upon him, and he prophesied among them" (1 Sam. 10:1–13).

The ecstatic prophet, therefore, was a person who, like the seer, was usually closely identified with the worship of God (the ecstatics whom Saul met in 1 Sam. 10 were returning from a "high place" [vs. 5], that is, a shrine of worship) and who, under the influence of a trance-like state of mind, uttered divine oracles. Ecstatic experiences could be either violent or calm, but they need not be thought of as occasions when all self-control was lost. Rather, they were moments when, to the frequent accompaniment of music-making, singing, dancing, or more bizarre forms of behavior, the concentration of the individual or of the group was focused upon the divine presence in such a manner that the will of God became known. Ecstasy helps to explain Saul's behavior before Samuel in Naioth when he "prophesied before Samuel, and lay naked all that day and all that night" (1 Sam. 19:24). Ecstatic behavior is also engaged in by the court prophets of the Israelite King

Ahab who falsely promised success in battle to him and to Judean King Jehoshaphat (1 Kings 22:10–12). And ecstasy can be identified in a number of the actions of Ezekiel, such as the curious manner in which he shaves his head and beard to accompany an oracle from God (Ezek. 5:1–12).

As in the case of the seer, the activity of the ecstatic prophet was by no means confined to ancient Israel. One example of ecstatic seizure among the Canaanites comes from an Egyptian document of the eleventh century B.C. which describes the journey of a certain Wen-Amon to Phoenicia (the Phoenicians were a branch of the Canaanites). While Wen-Amon is involved in negotiations with the prince of the Phoenician town of Byblos, one of the prince's servants falls into an ecstatic trance in which he delivers an oracle which provides divine vindication of Wen-Amon's mission.[2] The Old Testament itself gives us a later description of the ecstatic behavior of certain Canaanite prophets of Baal. In their contest with Elijah on Mount Carmel "they cried aloud, and cut themselves after their custom with swords and lances, until the blood gushed out upon them. And as midday passed, they raved on . . ." (1 Kings 18:28–29). Furthermore, records from ancient Mari on the Euphrates, a Semitic city-state which was a rival in the eighteenth century B.C. to the Babylon of King Hammurabi, contain references to oracles delivered by prophetic figures under the influence of ecstasy.

These examples demonstrate that ecstatic prophecy was not unique to the ancient Hebrews. Like the power of clairvoyance enjoyed by the seer, it was a faculty associated with divine worship in a number of ancient societies. Such differences as existed between the two offices were small and many ancient peoples may have made no distinction between seer and ecstatic at all. Both relied upon abnormal powers to ascertain the divine will, both employed visions, and both uttered oracles. If the ancient Hebrew seers drew upon their inspired intuition, while ancient Hebrew prophets took recourse to altered states of mind, that distinction had been sufficiently erased by the time of the writing of 1 Samuel 9:9 that the Hebrew author of that text felt it necessary to provide a historical footnote. However, to say that the offices of the seer and of the ecstatic prophet were known outside Israel is by no means to suggest that there were no important differences between prophecy as it developed in Israel and related phenomena among other ancient peoples. Old Testament prophecy is unique in that nowhere outside Israel were there to be spokespersons for God of the stature of Amos, Jeremiah, and the Second

---

[2] James B. Pritchard, editor, *Ancient Near Eastern Texts Relating to the Old Testament*, Third Edition with Supplement (Princeton: Princeton University Press, 1969), p. 26. This volume is hereafter referred to as ANET. For purposes of simplification, brackets and other marks which indicate that the text has been conjecturally restored by the editors have been dropped from some of our quotations from ANET. Students should consult ANET itself in order to determine the full extent of these restorations.

Isaiah, to name only a few. This distinctive nature of Old Testament prophecy will become clear on the pages which follow.

Prophetic Guilds

It is clear from our discussion that much prophetic activity in ancient Israel was carried on by groups of prophets. Indeed, it should be stressed that for an extended period of Old Testament history group prophecy was the norm, while individual prophets who worked alone were the exception. One of the important developments in the history of Hebrew prophecy is the increasing tendency, with the passage of time, for individuals to step forward to speak a word from Yahweh. But Old Testament prophecy cannot be fully understood apart from some appreciation of the prophetic guilds within Israel which, to a certain extent, would ultimately nourish and sustain the individual prophet.

The evidence within the Old Testament points to the prophetic guilds as being frequently organized around some central figure who served as both spiritual mentor to his followers and as the arbiter of custom and discipline. Samuel was such a personality. We find him presiding over the activities of his band of ecstatic followers (1 Sam. 19:20), and even extending to the whole nation his multiple authority as prophet, priest, and judge (1 Sam. 7). In fact, of all the Old Testament prophetic figures it is perhaps Samuel who demonstrates most clearly the several responsibilities of the leader of the prophetic guild.[3] Elijah presided over a prophetic guild (often called the "sons of the prophets" [2 Kings 2:7]), and the ritual by which he transferred spiritual authority to his disciple Elisha (2 Kings 2) is also to be understood as a transfer of leadership within this particular prophetic guild. The cycle of Elisha stories preserved by the deuteronomistic historians provides us with one of our best insights into the daily life within a prophetic guild (2 Kings 4:38–41). Here we see the band of prophets carrying out the instructions of their leader for the preparation of the communal meal. When it is discovered that one of the members of the guild has unknowingly introduced a toxic substance into the pottage, appeal is immediately made to the leader, the

---

[3] Abraham (Gen. 20:7), Moses (Hos. 12:13), and Aaron (Exod. 7:1) are also called prophets. The book of Deuteronomy goes so far as to identify Moses as the example of what a Yahweh prophet should be (Deut. 18:15–22). Some scholars have felt that these references are anachronisms, the shifting back into an earlier time of a term which came into common use only later. The suggestion here is that these persons were called prophets because, like Samuel and others, they were revealers of God's will. However, it is clear that both "seer" and "prophet" (or similar terms) were used in the ancient Near East at a very early date, and thus there is no fundamental reason why the words should be denied to Abraham, Moses, and Aaron.

"man of God" of verse 40. The crisis is met when the leader, Elisha, neutralizes the toxin by the addition of some kind of flour or meal. That a miraculous act is implied in this text is made clear by Elisha's activity in the very next pericope (2 Kings 4:42–44).

However, one should not think of life within these guilds as tightly structured as was, say, life within some medieval Christian monastic communities. The individual "sons of the prophets" were free to come and go, and they often maintained other responsibilities in addition to those directed toward their prophetic guild. One of Elisha's followers was also a husband and father (2 Kings 4:1), a distinction enjoyed by other prophetic figures, as well, who seem to have lived in their own houses (1 Kings 13:11) and possibly to have earned a livelihood by means of some "secular" pursuit.

Many of the prophetic guilds may have taken pains to identify themselves by means of distinctive clothing or other marks. Elijah wore a tunic of animal skin gathered at the waist by a leather strap (2 Kings 1:8; see also Mark 1:6). Isaiah, in at least one period of his life, wore similarly crude garments (Isa. 20:2). And a very late passage, dating from the postexilic era, suggests that a tunic of animal skin or woven animal hair was the means by which a prophet was to be recognized (Zech. 13:4).

Other texts imply that some prophets used additional means of identification, such as a distinctive mark on the forehead, perhaps a letter or word representing the divine name Yahweh. This would help to explain how King Ahab recognized the anonymous prophet of 1 Kings 20:35–43 when the man removed the covering from his face (note similar marks upon the forehead in Gen. 4:15; Ezek. 9:4; and on the hand in Isa. 44:5 [note also Rev. 13:1]). Other prophets may have shaved their heads as signs of distinction (2 Kings 2:23).

There were two important types of prophetic guilds in ancient Israel, the cult prophets and the court prophets. We have already noticed that both the seer and the ecstatic were closely associated with the worship of God. When we also remember that formal religious worship in Israel was a much older institution than the monarchy, we are probably justified in concluding that of the two major types of prophetic guilds that of the cult prophet was the older.

In the years before the centralization of worship in the Jerusalem Temple (and, for that matter, even after) these guilds were often attached to the various shrines at which the worship of Yahweh was conducted. They probably not only functioned there as prophets in the sense that they delivered oracles from God, but they also undoubtedly served in the priestly capacity of offering sacrifices and of receiving the people's petitions to God. In very early times, in fact, the difference between priest and cultic prophet was probably very subtle (again the example of Samuel may be pointed out), and as late as the time of Jeremiah and Ezekiel priestly families produced major prophetic figures.

Samuel and his prophetic guild were closely attached to the sanctuary at Shiloh until its decline or destruction at the hands of the Philistines. Then Samuel seems to have transferred his activities to the shrines at Mizpeh and Naioth, while other members of the guild moved to Nob (1 Sam. 19, 21, 22). Elijah was associated with the shrine on Mount Carmel (where there was, of course, a competing guild of Canaanite cult prophets [1 Kings 18]), an association Elisha continued after his master (2 Kings 4:25). Following the establishment of Yahweh worship in Jerusalem by David and its enshrinement in Solomon's Temple, a prophetic guild also flourished in this place. The suggestion is that here the cult prophets in time came to have special responsibility for the poetical and musical aspects of the liturgy, and many scholars view certain of the Psalms of the Old Testament as having been composed by the cult prophets attached to the Jerusalem Temple. The author of the books of Chronicles, writing after the Exile, lists certain guilds of Temple singers who had close priestly connections (1 Chron. 6:31–48), and these may represent the final task at which the guild of Temple prophets arrived. In fact, some scholars point to this process of "ritualization" of prophetic utterances as one of the signs of prophecy's decline toward the end of the Old Testament period. One may wish to compare the concern for the restoration of Temple worship which consumes much of the energies of two of the later canonical prophets, Haggai (1:4) and Zechariah (1:16), a concern which is a far cry from the attitudes of Amos (5:21–24) and Jeremiah (7:1–15).

In earlier times the attachment of a certain guild of cult prophets to its center of worship was often loose, for we find prophetic bands sometimes roaming the countryside or perhaps going from one shrine to another. Both Elijah (1 Kings 17:19) and Elisha (2 Kings 4:8–10) are described as having special rooms set aside in people's houses where they ate and stayed as they traveled. This condition probably endured in the Northern Kingdom until the time of its collapse before the Assyrian army in 722 B.C. In the Southern Kingdom, however, as worship became centralized in the Jerusalem Temple, cultic prophecy ultimately tended to be limited, especially after the Exile, to this single shrine.

The other type of prophetic guild within ancient Israel was that of the court prophets. The evidence which would enable us to understand the origins of the guilds of court prophets is missing from the Old Testament, but it seems likely that this group grew out of, and in some respects was an extension of, the prophetic guilds associated with the cult. With the rise of the monarchy under David the cult received a certain amount of royal protection and patronage. David, of course, moved the Ark of the Covenant to Jerusalem and gave it a place of honor there, and in the next generation Solomon built a Temple for the worship of God, a shrine which was, to a certain degree, considered to be an extension of the royal palace and a special chapel of the king (see also Amos 7:13 where the Bethel temple is described as "the king's sanctuary"). It would not be surprising, under those conditions, for certain of the cult prophets to be pressed into special service by the king. This may have happened primarily on special occasions, as when the king needed advice about the conduct of a war (see 1 Kings 22:6). Or the court prophets may have functioned on a more permanent basis and in this manner became distinguished in the popular understanding from those prophets whose duties were primarily cultic. The episode related in 1 Kings 22 provides us with the best Old Testament "window" by which we may look into the world of the court prophet. Kings Ahab of Israel and Jehoshaphat of Judah are in need of advice concerning the wisdom of a military campaign against their enemy Syria. A group of prophets is summoned who affirm unanimously that the military campaign has the blessing of Yahweh. Jehoshaphat, however, suspects their counsel and asks for an independent judgment. A certain Micaiah is brought forward, a prophet about whom we have no information except in this passage. Micaiah delivers a judgment which contradicts that of the band of court prophets, an act for which he is beaten and thrown into prison (1 Kings 22:1–28).

The incident tells us some important things about the court prophets. First, there were sometimes large numbers of them, four hundred in 22: 6. Second, we are given some idea of the pressures put on the court prophets to flatter the king and to say things which he and his advisers wanted to hear. Ahab initially does not want to consult Micaiah ("I hate him, for he never prophesies good concerning me, but evil" [vs. 8]) and does so only at Jehoshaphat's insistence. When Micaiah finally is allowed to speak the truth, both the regular court prophets (vs. 24) and the king (vss. 26–27) vilify him. We will see that some of the great canonical prophets, notably Amos and Jeremiah, are to be subjected to similar treatment. Third, we have here a very important example of a prophetic figure who steps out of the crowd or who sets himself apart from the guild in order to deliver an independent assessment of God's will. This is, as we have pointed out, one of the crucial elements in the nature of prophecy within ancient Israel.

Perhaps the single most important court prophet in the Old Testament is Nathan, who was counselor and adviser to David. Another prophet, Gad, is also mentioned as important to David's life and career. We will discuss Nathan in some detail below, but we should notice here that Gad is called "David's seer" in 2 Samuel 24:11; 1 Chronicles 21:9; and 2 Chronicles 29:25, whereas Nathan's title is simply, "the prophet." Whether this implies a closer connection between Gad and David than between Nathan and the king is impossible to say. We do know, however, that Gad had been close to David from the time of the latter's days as a fugitive and that on at least one occasion (1 Sam. 22:5) he had given him important advice in his flight from Saul. Gad's most celebrated prophecy, however, has to do with David's census and the building of the altar on the threshing floor of Araunah, the Jebusite (2 Sam. 24; 1 Chron. 21). The Chronicler gives us the information that David indicated this spot as the site of the Temple altar (1 Chron. 22:1).

In summary, it may be said that the court prophets were probably derivative from the cult prophets and that at times (especially when the king's grip upon the cultic apparatus was strong) the two groups may have been virtually identical. Various monarchs may often have manipulated their prophets so as to have them give a divine sanction to what the king planned to do. But figures such as Nathan, Gad, and Micaiah are evidence that on some occasions, at least, even the court prophet courageously spoke the truth of God, although the king and his less forthright subjects often did not want to hear it.

The Nature of the Prophets' Religious Experiences

It is difficult for many of us today to appreciate the encounters with God which the ancient Hebrew prophets report, encounters which resulted in the prophetic word from God. The powers of clairvoyance and of the ecstatic trance are not phenomena to which we easily relate, and there are at least two important reasons why this is so. First of all, unlike the Hebrew prophets, we live in an intellectual environment which has been deeply influenced by science and the scientific method. Because of this we tend to think of the sacred and the secular as somewhat mutually exclusive spheres of reality. The entrails of sheep may tell us something about the anatomy of that animal or, if they are diseased, may even contain important information concerning epidemiology, but we do not expect them to tell us the will of God or whether there will be another World War. However, there was no concept of the secular among the ancient Hebrews (or other ancient peoples, for that matter). All things were sacred in the sense that nothing existed and no event happened which did not somehow reflect the presence of the Deity. Sequences of events which would be explained by us in terms of cause-and-effect might be seen by them as expressions of the mind of God. (For example, compare the difference between the manner in which Freud viewed dreams and the manner in which they are understood by Joseph in the book of Genesis.)

Another important factor which makes it difficult for many of us to enter the experiential world of the Hebrew prophets is that that human individual or group who, in our time, claims to have some private revelation from God is often (and quite rightly!) suspected of being emotionally unbalanced or of attempting to perpetrate a fraud. Too much unhappiness has been caused by such people in our century for most of us to take them at their word. The tragic case of Jim Jones and the Jonestown community of several years ago is a dramatic example of the destructive power of one who claims some special word from God. From a different era, the Salem witch trials are a similar example.

Yet such differences should not cause us to reject the prophetic experience of God out of hand, for the Hebrews themselves struggled with the problem of the destructive power of those who pretended magic and of those who falsely claimed to be spokespersons of God. Rather, we must understand that the prophetic experiences of God, while conditioned by the world view of those who underwent them, were deeply rooted in the conviction that God had a will for the world, and especially for the people Israel, and in the conviction that God was concerned enough about the human race to communicate that will.

The experience of Isaiah at the time of his call to be a prophet provides us with a revealing insight into the nature of the prophetic awareness of God (Isa. 6). Three phenomena are reported here of which at least the first two are common to many other prophetic accounts. First, Isaiah had a vision, that of an exalted God. Second, there was an experience of audition when Isaiah heard the voices of the cherubim, then also that of God. Third, there was a sensation of feeling, that of being touched upon the lips by the coal from the altar. In other words, the text conveys the impression that the prophet's total being was overwhelmed by the presence of God. Even so, that is not the main emphasis of this account. The most important features of the passage are God's call to Isaiah to assume the prophetic role and God's communication of the message which Isaiah must bear. The media through which the prophet becomes aware of God's presence are only of limited importance in themselves. The crucial aspect of the experience was the word which God was summoning the prophet to speak.

There is some evidence within the Old Testament that, as time passed, this content of the revelation to the prophet received more and more emphasis at the expense of less crucial features of the prophetic experience. The disappearance of the office of the seer may be seen in this light. The Old Testament Hebrews knew of the destructive power of those who practiced magic (Exod. 22:18), and when they were faithful to their own highest spiritual insights, they banned magicians, soothsayers, and witches from their midst (1 Sam. 28:3). Because the person who foretold the future often flirted dangerously with magic (a fact with which the Hebrews must have been impressed as they watched their Canaanite neighbors), the seer fell into disrepute in Israel. To be sure, the great prophets of the classical period often talk of events which are to take place in the future, but such oracles are almost always based upon what they know of the nature of a holy God and of a sinful, arrogant people. For example, God will destroy Jerusalem *because* of the wickedness of the people (Amos 2:4–5). Or God will not destroy the nation *if* the people repent (Jer. 3:12). Or *because* of God's love for Israel and *because* the nation has paid for its sin God will restore the nation (Isa. 40:1–5).

Unlike the decline in importance of clairvoyance, ecstasy continued to be a prominent feature of the prophetic experience throughout the classical period. During the Exile Ezekiel prophesies under the power of ecstasy (Ezek. 1), and in the postexilic period Zechariah experiences the word of God through both the dream (Zech. 1:8; 4:1) and the ecstatic trance (5:5). But, as in the case of Isaiah's experience of his call, it is the *content* of the divine message not the nature of the medium through which it is channeled which receives the most attention.

False prophets also experienced ecstasy, and in the account of the prophet Micaiah (1 Kings 22) there is an intriguing comment on the distinction between true and false prophecy. Micaiah describes how Yahweh permitted a "lying spirit" to influence the oracle of the false court prophets, while Yahweh told Micaiah and only Micaiah the truth. In other words, true prophecy was to be distinguished not by the quality of the ecstasy which accompanied it but by the content of the oracle. This again emphasizes the importance of the oracle in contrast to the relative unimportance of that ecstasy which accompanied it. It also emphasizes the difficulty involved in detecting whose prophecy was true. Unless one could evaluate the prophet on the basis of the validity of previous oracles, one was forced to wait to see how a given oracle squared with events. This is not unlike the problem faced by modern men and women who are often subjected to many persons who claim to speak for God and yet who say quite contradictory things.

In summary, although it is difficult for us fully to understand the nature of the prophetic experience, it is important that we realize that the main concern of the Hebrew prophets was not *how* they received a word from God, but *what* that word was. They, like we, were often confronted by magic which pretended to be prophecy and by persons who spoke false and misleading oracles. They did their best to suppress the former and to reveal the latter for the frauds they were.

Three Important "Pre-canonical" Prophets

Before concluding this discussion of the history of prophecy in Israel before the time of the "canonical" prophets, we will do well to examine in some detail the life and service of three prophetic figures who helped to shape

the course which prophecy of the classical period was to follow. We have
spoken of each of them several times already, but this section will permit us
a brief overview of the life and times of each.

Nathan (literal Hebrew: "he gave") was, as we have observed, one of at
least two court prophets active during the reign of David. He first comes to
our notice in 2 Samuel 7:1–17. Here he tells David that it is not the Lord's
will that he (David) build a temple (house) for the Lord, but that the Lord
will establish a perpetual dynasty (house) for David. Two important characteristics of the prophet are prominent here which are consistent with other
things we know about Nathan. The first is that he doesn't shrink from telling
David that what the king hopes to do (in this instance, to build Yahweh's
Temple) is contrary to God's will and should not be done. The second characteristic of Nathan which this passage reveals is his strong interest in the
fortunes of the Davidic kingdom. In fact, 2 Samuel 7:1–17 became an important theological and political document within the Jerusalem community,
God's covenant with David almost obscuring that with Moses in the mind of
some individuals.

Nathan's second appearance in the Old Testament is one of the more
electrifying moments in all the Bible. David has committed adultery (perhaps
rape—the text is ambiguous) with the beautiful Bathsheba and has caused
her husband Uriah to be killed in battle (2 Sam. 11). In a bold and forthright
manner Nathan then steps forward to confront the king with his wrongdoing
(notice that in 2 Sam. 7:2 David asks for the advice of Nathan, but here
[12:1] Nathan acts because Yahweh has "sent" him). He entraps the king by
telling a story which is sure to arouse David's righteous indignation (12:1–4)
and then by pointing out to David that he is the guilty party (12:7). Nathan's
"you are the man" is one of the important moments in Old Testament prophecy, for by means of this denunciation Nathan reminded his monarch that not
even the king was above the moral law of God. Nathan could have been
beaten, imprisoned, or even killed for his words, but he spoke them nevertheless. And it is to the credit of David that he accepted the accusation and
cast himself upon the mercy of God (12:13).

A third and final appearance of Nathan allows us to see him actively
involved in the struggle over who would succeed the aging David. In order
to·head off a successful *coup* by David's son Adonijah, Nathan prompts Bathsheba to speak a good word for her son Solomon, a commendation which
Nathan himself affirms before the king (1 Kings 1:5–31—there seems to
have been some kind of special relationship between Nathan and Bathsheba,
perhaps going back to the events of 2 Sam. 11—12). The strategy results in
the collapse of Adonijah's efforts and in the ultimate coronation of Solomon
as king with Nathan in attendance (1 Kings 1:32–53).

These three episodes portray a court prophet of·unusual courage and skill.

If Nathan was a member of some prophetic guild at court, he certainly does not let himself be bound by that relationship. Rather, he courageously affirms the word of God in spite of great danger to himself and actively involves himself in the affairs of the kingdom. In doing these things Nathan helps to create a model which many of the later "canonical" prophets are to use.

A second important "pre-canonical" prophet is Elijah (literally: "Yahweh is God") whose story is told in 1 Kings 17—2 Kings 2. There is much more information in the Old Testament about Elijah than about Nathan, yet some of it must be evaluated carefully, since it does not all seem to be of equal merit. There appear to have circulated various cycles of stories about Elijah which were inserted by the deuteronomistic historians into their account of the history of King Ahab. These Elijah stories have an anecdotal flavor (unlike most of the later literature associated with the "canonical" prophets), and not all of these anecdotes ring with the same authenticity.

The reign of King Ahab (c. 869–850, and therefore the times in which Elijah lived and worked) seems to have been marked by a sharp polarization within the society of the Northern Kingdom. Ahab was married to the Phoenician princess Jezebel, a marriage which seems to have been for the purpose of cementing a political alliance between Israel and the rich maritime center of Tyre. This alliance helped to foster increasing prosperity within Israel, but it seems to have been a prosperity which benefited primarily the governing mercantile classes, while the bulk of the peasants remained quite poor. This polarization was made worse by the aggressive efforts of Jezebel to promote the worship of Baal within Israel, and it may have been that most of her converts were from the same socio-economic stratum which enriched itself through the lucrative trade with Tyre. If so, Israelite society became increasingly divided between the wealthy classes (who professed or at least tolerated Baalism) and the peasants (many of whom remained loyal to Yahweh).

Of the several incidents from Elijah's life which the Old Testament recounts, three are of special interest. The first of these is the contest with the prophets of Baal on Mt. Carmel (1 Kings 18:20–40), an incident to which we have already referred. It should be noticed here that the challenge for the contest is issued by Elijah in order to demonstrate to Ahab that it is not he (Elijah) who is the "troubler of Israel," as Ahab had alleged (18:17), but the king himself. We cannot be quite sure of all of the causes for Ahab's wrath, but they undoubtedly had to do with Elijah's opposition to Ahab's policy of religious tolerance and perhaps to his poor record of "human rights" as well (see below). The point to be taken here is that Elijah, like Nathan, did not hesitate to set himself in opposition to the political establishment. Unfortunately for Elijah, however, he did not enjoy his sovereign's sufferance. As far as the contest itself is concerned, it is one of several occasions during Elijah's ministry when the prophet exercises miraculous powers. But the important thing in the mind of the author of this incident is not the miracle itself, but the message which the miracle conveyed, namely, that Yahweh, not Baal, is the God of Israel. (One of the reasons for considering some of the other anecdotes relating to Elijah to be less elevated in mood is their apparent preoccupation with the element of the miraculous as, for example, 2 Kings 1:9–16.)

A second memorable event in the ministry of Elijah is the theophany on Mt. Horeb (1 Kings 19). Elijah flees for his life following the slaughter of the Baal prophets at the conclusion of the Mt. Carmel contest, and he takes refuge far to the south on the mountain associated with the giving of the law to Moses (Horeb was the name used among the Northern tribes for Mt. Sinai, the latter name being preferred by Southern writers). This story reflects a feeling among some prophetic individuals that Israel's "golden days" had been the period of its wandering in the wilderness and that its subsequent settlement in Canaan had resulted in a prostitution of its faith and morals. The commission from God which follows the theophany sets the stage for the work of Elijah's disciple and successor, Elisha (1 Kings 19:15–18).

A third significant event in Elijah's prophetic ministry is his confrontation with Ahab over the matter of Naboth (1 Kings 21). The manner in which the peasant Naboth is deprived of his land and of his life is probably symptomatic of the disregard with which many in the ruling classes treated the ordinary citizenry. The tension between Ahab and Jezebel, on the one hand, and Naboth, on the other, may also represent the tension between the worshipers of Baal and those of Yahweh. Elijah's denunciation of Ahab (vss. 20–24, although mitigated to some extent by vss. 27–29) reveals the deep hostility between this man of God and the grasping, devious monarch.

In Elijah, therefore, we may identify a number of elements which came to characterize certain of the prophets of the "classical" period. Fearless before even the most powerful men and women, zealous for undivided loyalty to Yahweh, insistent that even the simplest people of the land had rights which not even the king could abrogate, Elijah spoke with the authority of one who bears a message from God. Although his oracles were never given canonical status in the same way as those of Amos and Hosea, two other prophets active in the North, Elijah's memory was preserved in a special manner by subsequent generations of both Jews and Christians. In the late prophetic tradition, his return was expected before the final outpouring of God's judgment (Mal. 4:5). And among the earliest Christians he was identified with John the Baptist (John 1:21) and even with Jesus (Matt. 16:14).

A third prophetic figure who deserves to be mentioned is that of Elisha (literally: "God is salvation"), the follower and successor of Elijah. Many readers of the Old Testament have expressed the feeling that the stories of Elisha ring with less authenticity than do those associated with his master.

This is because the cycle of Elisha stories is so heavily weighted with miraculous elements that there sometimes seems little room left to portray the kind of spiritual and moral zeal which characterized Elijah (notice the crudeness of the miracles in 2 Kings 2:23–25 and 6:1–7). In addition, some of the stories about Elisha seem to be duplicates of those told about Elijah (compare the similarity in structure and content between 1 Kings 17 and 2 Kings 4). Nevertheless, there is at least one important incident which does give us an insight into the nature of the prophetic role as exemplified by Elisha. In 2 Kings 9 there is related the manner in which Elisha inspires a revolt on the part of an army commander, Jehu, which succeeds in toppling the throne of King Joram, the son of Ahab and Jezebel who continued the policies of his parents. The bloody uprising and the violent overthrow of Joram not only signaled the violent suppression of Baalism in Israel, but it also took the form of a peasants' rebellion in that it marked the overthrow of the rich and powerful by the poor people of the land.

Elisha, then, is an example of a prophet who was not content simply to speak a word from God, but who was also willing to go to great lengths to shape historical forces in order to bring them into harmony with what he considered to be God's will. (Compare his similar role in the affairs of Syria [2 Kings 8:7–15].)

2
AMOS

Date of Amos' Work: c. 760 B.C.
Location: The Northern Centers of Bethel and Samaria.
Central Theological Concept: God will destroy Israel because
   of its sinfulness.
An Outline of the Book of Amos will be found on p. 22.

Amos: The First of the Canonical Prophets

With the work of Amos a new era begins in the history of Hebrew prophecy. For the first time the words of a prophetic individual are preserved and
gathered together into a kind of anthology. This is different, of course, from
the manner in which the work of such figures as Nathan, Micaiah, Elijah,
and Elisha was preserved, that is, as historical reminiscence. In the case of
Amos an effort is made to preserve the words of the prophet in the very
literary forms in which they were originally uttered. It is the first step in the
long process which ultimately leads to the inclusion of the book of Amos in
the canon of the Old Testament and, beyond that, to the whole phenomenon
of a corpus of prophetic writings. It should be emphasized that the focus of
this literary activity is upon the prophetic message. Sometimes a given prophetic collection will include some biographical information about the prophet
as well as references to contemporary events, but always the spotlight is on
the prophetic word and on the divine message the human words are intended
to convey.

What led to this important new way in which Israel was to remember its
prophets and their words? No one can be quite sure. One suggestion is that
the radical, uncompromising nature of Amos' preaching demanded a new
kind of literary medium, one which went beyond the old method of anecdotal
reminiscence. Another suggestion, not entirely contradictory to the first, is
that Amos considered himself to be a new departure from the old prophetic
ways. His statement in Amos 7:14 may suggest that he had never belonged
to any prophetic guild and that he therefore felt there was a divine immediacy

to his words which was not true of more commonplace "professional" prophets. This sense of departure with respect to his calling may have caused Amos' followers or perhaps the prophet himself to record his words in a fashion which had not been the case in Israel before Amos' time. A third possible explanation is that, since the destruction of Israel did not take place immediately after Amos' ministry (Samaria did not fall until 722, or almost forty years after Amos preached there and at Bethel), some of Amos' contemporaries may have wished to preserve his words in written form so that the next generation, who had not known the prophet, would have a record of his words and of God's promise to judge the nation. This would be similar to the writing of the Gospels at the time when the first generation of Christians, those who had either known Jesus or known Jesus' original followers, was growing old. Whatever the reason, that which began with Amos soon became the norm, and to the collection of Amos' oracles were ultimately to be added those of Hosea, Micah, Isaiah, and many others.

The Historical Context of Amos' Work

The editorial notice in Amos 1:1 identifies the Southern King Uzziah (c. 783–742) and the Northern King Jeroboam II (c. 786–746) as the monarchs in whose reigns the work of Amos took place. Amos' prophetic activity seems to have been of short duration, perhaps only a year, and scholars date the time of that activity at about 760. If we knew more about the earthquake mentioned in 1:1, our dating could be more precise. The book of Amos also makes it clear that, while the prophet was a southerner (1:1), his work was done in the Northern Kingdom (7:10).

The Northern Kingdom of Jeroboam II was a proud and prosperous nation. The Old Testament itself tells us very little about this king or about the nature of his rule. What scanty information we do have is contained in 2 Kings 14:23–29, and this implies that Jeroboam II was an aggressive monarch who successfully extended the borders of Israel toward the north at the expense of the Aramean power centers of Damascus and Hamath and toward the south as far as the Dead Sea (the "Sea of the Arabah").[4] This military expansion is confirmed by the book of Amos which refers to the capture of the cities of Lo-Debar and Karnaim, both to the east of the Jordan (6:13).

---

[4] 2 Kings 14:25 mentions a prophet named Jonah the son of Amittai. This otherwise unknown individual seems to have been a court prophet who, perhaps in order to flatter Jeroboam, foretold grand victories in battle (compare the manner of the court prophets of 1 Kings 22). It was probably by design that this nationalistic prophet becomes the subject of the book of Jonah, an example of Old Testament literature that is anything but nationalistic. See the discussion of the book of Jonah, pp. 196–200.

The times were ripe for Israel to flex its military and economic muscle. The great Assyrian empire to the northeast had subdued Israel's frequent enemies, the Arameans. A stone fragment of the royal archives of the Assyrian king Adad-nirari describes the humiliation to which he subjected the Aramean city-states around 800.

> I shut up Mari, king of Damascus in Damascus, his royal residence. The terror-inspiring glamor of Ashur, my lord, overwhelmed him, and he seized my feet, assuming the position of a slave.[5]

Adad-nirari then lists the impressive booty which he forced the Aramean king to deliver. So thorough was the defeat of Damascus and other cities in the region that nearly half a century later they appear to have offered no effective resistance to the territorial designs of Jeroboam II.

Nor was Assyria itself prepared to challenge Jeroboam. Adad-nirari was followed upon the throne by a succession of weaker kings, so that Assyria does not trouble the area of Syria-Palestine again until the campaigns of the fierce Tiglath-Pileser III (745–727). The kingdom of Judah also does not appear to have interfered with the expansionist policies of Jeroboam. The book of Amos, which would likely have been sensitive to any such tensions, betrays no sign of hostility between North and South at this time.

Israel's military and political power under Jeroboam II resulted in increased commerce and wealth. Yet it was not wealth which was equally shared among all classes in society. Amos' words portray an economic polarization which produced a very wealthy class of merchants and rulers who "feel secure on the mountain of Samaria" (6:1) but who "oppress the poor" and "crush the needy" (4:1) even as they enjoy their own luxuries.

It is interesting that, under these circumstances, religious activity was strong. The book of Amos suggests that the old cultic centers of Bethel and Gilgal were often thronged with worshipers who led bleating sheep toward the sacrificial altars (4:4; 5:5; 5:21–24), but it was worship supported by a view of God which was inadequate and, in the end, destructive. The present prosperity was viewed as God's blessing and approval upon the nation, while Israel's obligation in return for this divine favor was considered to be that of lavishness in its worship. Also, there was little or no thought given to the moral responsibility which each person should have felt toward his or her neighbor.

In addition to the self-serving spirit in which Yahweh was worshiped in the Israel of Jeroboam II, there is some evidence that the worship of the Canaanite deity Baal was also a persistent force. Inscriptions have been found

---

[5] ANET, p. 281.

which date from this period in Israel's life in which a number of personal names bear the divine name "Baal." Also, Amos himself mentions the worship of the Mesopotamian gods Sakkuth and Kaiwan (5:26).

The irony of all of this is that Jeroboam II was the great-grandson of King Jehu (842–815) who had gained the throne of Israel through a *coup d'etat* inspired by the prophet Elisha, a revolution which had the purpose of reestablishing the worship of Yahweh and of ending the oppression of the poor by the rich. Yet over the succeeding generations that lesson had certainly been lost upon the royal house of Israel and upon the people as well.

The Prophet and the Book

We have been given very little biographical information about Amos, but that which we have is quite interesting. Amos 1:1, the editorial introduction to the entire book, tells us that the prophet was a shepherd from the region of the Judean village of Tekoa, a few miles south of Jerusalem. Much of this land was rough and sparse and, as we know from the stories about young David, who was also a shepherd, it was capable of producing individuals who were as independent and tough as the conditions under which they lived. Amos 7:14 adds the information that Amos also tended sycamore trees, pinching their fruit so that it would ripen and become fit for eating. It seems likely that Amos was more than a day laborer, for his literary and oratorical skills imply some formal education and contact with other literate persons. So he may have been the owner of an agricultural enterprise of some kind, although it remains doubtful that he was a wealthy man. The order of Jeroboam II delivered through Amaziah (7:12) suggests that Amos' Judean roots were well known, and it is likely that at the conclusion of his prophetic work he returned to his native land.

At some point in his life Amos responded to God's call that he become a prophet, although he apparently had had no previous prophetic connections (7:14). The full meaning of his denial of prophetic status is uncertain, but it probably implies, as stated earlier, that Amos was associated with no prophetic guild. Some scholars have gone on to suggest that Amos even repudiated the idea that he was a prophet at all, although that interpretation remains dubious. In any event Amos traveled to the Northern religious center of Bethel, the most important shrine of Yahweh worship in the Northern Kingdom at that time. There and apparently also in the capital city of Samaria itself he delivered a series of oracles in which he promised the destruction of the nation. His reasoning was quite clear if not always convincing to those who heard him. Israel had repudiated Yahweh because it had turned from justice and righteousness and had oppressed the poor and helpless in its midst. Therefore, God would destroy the nation. There were probably some few who responded with sympathy to Amos' words, but the reaction of most is characterized by the hostility of the Bethel priest Amaziah who sought a royal commission to banish Amos from the land (7:10–13). We do not know how Amos reacted to this attempt at official interference with his prophetic mission, but it is a significant reading of the pulse of the religious establishment of the Northern Kingdom that such an attempt was made.

As stated above, we are ignorant of Amos' formal education, but his words betray an individual who was both knowledgeable of Israel's religious traditions and skilled in the literary and oratorical forms in which he cast his messages. Most scholars believe that, while the book of Amos has been worked over by one or more subsequent editors, much of its contents come directly from the prophet himself, and it is therefore from the words of the book that we infer important information about the mind of the man.

Several of the literary forms which Amos uses reflect his highly developed power with words. Amos 5:2, for example, is cast in the traditional form of the Hebrew lament, the *qinah*. This is the poetry of the funeral, of mourning, and it was often used by Hebrew poets to express their deep sorrow over their or the nation's loss. Portions of the book of Lamentations, for example, are written in this same form with its traditional 3 + 2 meter which was the very soul of sorrow for ancient Hebrews. Amos skillfully uses this poetic device to strengthen the gloom of his lament over Israel:

> "Fallen, no more to rise,
> is the virgin Israel; . . ." (5:2)

Another effective means by which Amos animates his message is through the messenger speech. Here the speaker assumes the role of a herald from the king. The message is that of the sovereign, and the human speaker is merely the vehicle through which that message passes. Typically this oracle is prefaced by the words, "Thus says Yahweh . . . ," or it may be concluded with the phrase, "says Yahweh." Also, Yahweh is frequently represented in the first person in order to heighten the awareness of the hearers that the message is not that of the prophet, but that of God. Chapter 4 of Amos is a series of messenger speeches placed one after another in such a manner that they become a drumroll of Israel's guilt before God.

Amos' words also betray the fact that he was a master of climax and suspense in the art of oratory. The series of judgment speeches with which the book begins (1:2—2:16) probably should be thought of as a single sermon. Here Amos denounces Israel's neighbors one by one and promises the judgment of God upon them, a prospect most subjects of Jeroboam II would have found quite pleasant.[6] Then, however, the prophet turns with an unexpected vengeance upon Israel itself and in the most angry tones of all declares that God will punish the wicked nation (2:6–16). Some have suggested that this may have been the first sermon Amos preached upon reaching Bethel. If so, it would have proved an excellent means of first, gaining the attention of his audience and, then, driving home the word of the wrath of God.

Another passage in which Amos' words build a powerful climax is 3:3–8. A series of questions is asked to which the obvious answer is "yes." Many of these questions sound as if they come from Israel's wisdom tradition, for they reflect common-sense observations about the nature of life and human experience. Under the force of this arrangement the final question (vs. 8) has been answered even before it is asked: God has spoken and this human prophet has no choice except to relay these words. It is felt by many scholars that this passage reflects a situation, not unlike that of 7:10–13, in which Amos is forced to defend the authenticity of his prophetic calling.

Yet a third passage which builds to a climax is 7:1–9. This text is a record of three visions, each of which begins with the introductory formula "the Lord Yahweh showed me" (vss. 1, 4) or "he showed me" (vs. 7). After the visions of the locusts and the fire the prophet intercedes for the people. His prayers and the response of Yahweh are virtually identical (vss. 2b–3 and 5–6). After the climactic third vision, however, that of the plumb line (vss. 7–9), there is no prayer by the prophet and no announcement of grace by Yahweh. The implication is clear: Amos has given up hope that Israel will repent, and the judgment of Yahweh is now assured.[7]

There are other evidences of the skills of Amos the writer and speaker. The verbal images which he uses are fresh from the daily life of the people and forcefully portray the various aspects of his message to the nation. We have just referred above to the symbols of the locusts, fire, and plumb line. The first two, of course, represent the judgment which God intends for Israel, while the third is emblematic of the righteousness of God which is the standard by which Israel's unrighteousness becomes apparent.

The passage 5:18–20 employs a different set of images to portray the unexpected nature of God's judgment. The background of this oracle is the Day of Yahweh (notice that the phrase is repeated three times in this brief passage). In the popular understanding this was to be an occasion of great

---

[6]The formula repeated here is "For three transgressions of . . . , and for four, I will not revoke the punishment." Four plus three equals seven, a number which the ancient Hebrews considered to be a symbol of completion or totality. The formula is thus a stylized manner of saying, "For all the vast sins of . . . I will not withhold the punishment."

[7]Some scholars have drawn attention to the fact that the first two of these visions and the vision of 8:1–3 reflect the sequence of the seasons, 7:1–3 having to do with an invasion by locusts of the tender spring growth, 7:4–6 a summer drought, and 8:1–3 the autumn harvest of fruits.

joy, a moment in history when God would demonstrate partiality by elevating Israel in some manner over its neighbors. The thrust of Amos' oracle is that the day of Yahweh will come, but it will be a day of wrath, not a day of grace. It is a day in which darkness prevails, not light. It will be the experience like that of a person who fled from a lion only to meet a bear, or who, in the sanctuary of one's home, was attacked by a serpent.

A deadly pun is employed in 8:1–3 to describe the overthrow of the nation. A basket of fresh fruit (*qayits*) becomes a reminder that Israel's end (*qets*) is near.

It is likely that a later editor or editors, rather than the prophet himself, is responsible for the structure of the book as it appears in the Old Testament.

> A. A Sermon Against the Nations (Principally Israel):
>   1:1—2:16.
> B. A Collection of Oracles on the Doom of Israel:
>   3:1—6:14.
> C. Three Visions: 7:1–9.
> D. A Confrontation with Amaziah: 7:10–17.
> E. A Fourth Vision: 8:1–3.
> F. Further Oracles and a Vision: 8:4—9:10.
> G. A Word of Hope Concerning Judah: 9:11–15.

In spite of the above arrangement some of the earlier oracles may indicate a rough chronological sequence in Amos' ministry. As we have already mentioned, some scholars see the material in 1:3–2:16 as reflecting the type of sermon Amos preached upon first reaching Bethel. This is followed by the collection of oracles which ends at 6:14 and which (although many individual oracles are in fragmentary form) represents the type of prophetic pronouncement which Amos delivered during his ministry there. It is within this collection of oracles, however, where we can see that style and subject matter, not chronology, were the organizing principles by which much of this material was editorially arranged. The oracles of 4:1–11 may have been placed together because of their common ending ("says Yahweh"), while those of 6:1–7 begin with the same word ("woe").

The hand of an editor is unmistakable in other ways as well. The concern of someone that later generations of readers view Amos' words in their proper historical context is expressed in 1:1. This person was probably a Judean, since the name of the King of Judah is placed before that of the King of Israel and this is so in spite of the fact that none of Amos' words seem to have been delivered in Judah. Some scholars have felt that this is one indication that it was among circles in Judah who were friendly to Amos that the collection of his oracles received their first written form. It may be that the same writer is responsible for the brief prose introductions to Amos' oracles in 3:1 and 5:1

and also provided the information in 7:10–17 in which we are told of the angry confrontation between the prophet and the priest Amaziah.

A number of scholars have concluded that some of the oracular material attributed to Amos is also the work of later writers who were sympathetic to Amos' basic message and who wished to expand it or in some manner to apply it to their own times. There is disagreement among these scholars concerning how much material of this kind is contained in the book of Amos, but many would contend that at least the oracles against Tyre (1:9–10) and Edom (1:11–12) should be considered as later editorial expansions because they seem to reflect a situation which existed after Amos' lifetime. They would also view the oracle against Judah (2:4–5) as a subsequent addition made by a Judean writer, perhaps to guard against the misunderstanding on the part of some fellow citizens that the South was somehow morally superior to the North and thus immune to God's justice. The final oracle of the book (9:11–15) seems to be out of place in Amos' time, since it speaks of "the booth of David that is fallen" (vs. 11), and many scholars would thus view this as a word of hope (intended to balance Amos' words of judgment) written at a time after the Southern Kingdom had been destroyed by the Babylonian army (587 B.C.). We should not think of these additions to the words of Amos as being made in a false or deceptive spirit by persons who counterfeited the prophet's words. Our modern concepts of literary authorship were not shared by people in the ancient world, and these expansions are the work of those who honored the prophet as a spokesperson of God and who wished to give his words new force in the midst of situations which the prophet himself did not live to see.

The Theology of Amos

Amos' sermons are not essays in theology, but are communications to the people of God delivered in the white heat of prophetic passion and, as such, they are shaped so as to have maximum impact upon Amos' hearers. However, it is possible to infer something of the overarching concepts about God and about God's will for Israel which drove Amos to respond to the call of the Lord, in the first place, and, in the second, to declare God's mind and heart. Amos' theology may be thought of as being based on the following principles.

A. *Yahweh, Israel's God, is sovereign over the world*. Yahweh, the creator of the world, "forms the mountains, and creates the winds" (4:13), made the starry constellations, divided the day from the night, and summons the rain (5:8). Many of those who lived in the Northern Kingdom were tempted

by the worship of Baal which was closely associated with rain and the fertility of the earth, and so Amos wished to leave no doubts on this point: "Yahweh is his name" (5:8). Yahweh is even responsible for the annual rise and
fall of the Nile River in Egypt (9:5).

Because Yahweh is sovereign Lord, the presence of Yahweh is inescapable. Amos 9:2 is remarkably similar to Psalm 139:8, part of a great hymn
to the power and presence of God.

"Though they dig into Sheol from there shall my hand take them; though they climb up to heaven, from there I will bring them down." (Amos 9:2)	If I ascend to heaven, thou art there! If I make my bed in Sheol, thou art there! (Ps. 139:8)

Psalm 139:1–12 may be seen as an expression of a view (similar to that of
Amos) of the God who inhabits all of human life.

Because God's presence is inescapable, the destinies of all nations are in
God's control. Damascus, Gaza, Ammon, and Moab are all mentioned in the
long oracle of judgment in 1:3—2:16. Assyria and Egypt, the two great
power centers of Amos' time, are under Yahweh's authority (3:9). So are the
Ethiopians, the Philistines, and the Arameans/Syrians (9:7).

Yahweh's power is matched by the holiness and righteousness of Yahweh.
The first of these terms implies a quality which we might call transcendence
or "otherness" while the second, which is often linked with the word "justice," denotes a moral integrity and predictability on the part of Israel's God.
These aspects of God's nature are connected to the burning passion of God
that all peoples, especially Israel, should display a similar integrity. God "has
sworn by his holiness" (4:2), insists upon free-flowing justice and righteousness (5:24), and yearns for "good, and not evil" (5:14) and for "justice in the
gate" (that is, in the councils of the village elders—5:15).

B. *Yahweh has a special relationship with Israel.* Nowhere does Amos
use the word "covenant," a term which many other Old Testament writers
employ to designate God's election of Israel, the chosen people. Nevertheless, the idea of the covenant is implicit in Amos' thought. "You only have I
known of all the families of the earth" (3:2) refers to this special relationship
between God and Israel. This choice of Israel to be God's own people has
resulted in repeated acts by God through which Israel has been saved from
danger and destruction. Amos 2:9–11 reflects an awareness that without the
grace of God Israel would not even exist but would have long ago been
destroyed by its enemies. Even the extended litany of Israel's continuing
rejection of God and of God's repeated efforts to win the nation back (4:6–
11) is an expression of God's grace for, in Amos' mind, if God did not love

Israel in a special manner, Israel would not have been wooed so persistently by God. Yahweh is "your [Israel's] God" (4:12) and Israel is "my [God's] people" (8:2).

There is a twofold sense in which Amos uses the word "Israel" and in which he views this special relationship between God and Israel. Like other Old Testament writers Amos sometimes means by "Israel" the whole Hebrew people who came into the land of Canaan and who, after conquering the inhabitants ("the Amorite" of 2:9,10), settled in to till the land and to populate the cities. God's special relationship is with this larger nation, as the references to the Exodus, the wilderness wandering, and the conquest in 2:10 and in 4:10 suggest. On the other hand, Amos' particular concern is with the Northern Kingdom and, as do other Old Testament writers, he frequently uses "Israel" to refer to this nation, which he also calls "Samaria" (3:9), "Joseph" (5:6), "Jacob" (7:2), and "Isaac" (7:9). God's special relationship extends to this Northern Kingdom and upon it Amos levels God's words of judgment (see C. below). Why Amos has nothing to say about God's relation to the Southern Kingdom (assuming with many scholars that 2:4–5 and 9:11–15 are from the hand of a later editor) it is impossible to know. Perhaps he simply felt that Judah's depravity was not as great as that of Samaria.

C. *Because Israel has broken this relationship, God will destroy the nation.* The history of God's dealings with this people is a long story of God's love and of Israel's rejection of that love. Repeatedly God has chastened the people in order to win them back, but it has all been to no avail (4:6–11). Over and over God's mercy has been expressed so that, while they have been punished for their sin, yet they have not been destroyed (7:1–6). But now God's patience is exhausted and the destruction of the Northern Kingdom is inevitable (7:7–9). Occasionally, it seems that Amos believes there is still time for Samaria to repent and to escape the just consequences of its waywardness (5:4–7, 14–15). But most of Amos' prophetic messages reflect his despairing belief that the nation will never turn from its evil ways. Under such circumstances God has no choice but to destroy Israel (2:13–16; 3:9–11, 13–15; 5:18–20; 7:11; 8:1–3; 9:2–4). Some students of Amos have identified the brief oracle in 3:2 as the summary of Amos' preaching concerning God's election of Israel and Israel's destruction:

> "You only have I known
>   of all the families of the earth;
> therefore I will punish you
>   for all your iniquities."

The reason for the severity of God's judgment was related, in Amos' view, to the nature of Samaria's sin. It was not simply that the North was a prosperous nation. Amos might even have agreed with some other Old Testament writers who believed that prosperity was a sign of God's blessing (see Deut. 7:12–14; Prov. 3:9–10). But the Northern Kingdom had responded to God's blessing with shallow and perfunctory worship (4:4–5). What is more, the North had used its prosperity to purchase laziness and indolence (6:4–7). And perhaps worst of all the North had gained its prosperity, in part at least, by dishonesty and fraud (8:4–6) and by the oppression of the poor and needy (4:1). Therefore, says Yahweh,

> ". . . they shall take you away with hooks,
>   even the last of you with fishhooks." (4:2)

> "the high places of Isaac shall be made desolate,
>   and the sanctuaries of Israel shall be laid waste,
>   and I will rise against the house of Jeroboam with the sword." (7:9)

> "The songs of the temple shall become wailings in that day," . . .
> "the dead bodies shall be many;
>   in every place they shall be cast out in silence." (8:3)

We do not know if Amos lived to see the fulfillment of his violent promises, but when Samaria fell to the advancing Assyrian army in 722, many must have remembered his words and interpreted the destruction of the nation as the consequence of its sin.

A Key Text: Amos 5:21–24

Many interpreters of Amos have pointed to this text as one of the more important things Amos had to say. There is nothing specific here either about God's special relationship with Israel or about God's judgment which is coming upon the Northern Kingdom. But there is something said about what God expects from men and women, and for that reason this passage may have more relevance to modern readers of Amos than other passages which deal directly with the historical situation in the eighth century B.C.

> [21]I thoroughly repudiate your religious festivals
>   and I will not tolerate your assemblies of worship.

> [22]Although you offer me your whole burnt offerings, . . .

> None of your offerings will I accept,
>   and your religious feasts upon fat meat I will disregard.

> [23]I cannot bear to listen to the noise of your songs,
>   and my ears are closed to the music of your harps.

> [24]But pour forth justice like water,
>   and righteousness like an inexhaustible torrent![8]

---

[8]Author's translation.

Before proceeding to discuss the passage as a whole, let us look at important features of each verse.

Verse 21: The passage is a poem composed of five units of two lines each. In the first line two strong verbs are placed side by side in the Hebrew text which might literally be translated "I hate, I reject." The literary impact of such an arrangement is to emphasize the force of the speaker's emotion. The speaker is Yahweh, of course, and although there is nothing like the familiar formula "thus says Yahweh," this passage is clearly a judgment speech in which the prophet considers himself to be the medium through which Yahweh's message is relayed. The religious festivals in question may have been the three great annual pilgrimage festivals of the Hebrew year, Passover (also called Unleavened Bread), Weeks (both of which were in the spring), and Booths (in the autumn). These festivals are described in several places in the Old Testament, among which are Exodus 23:14–17 and Deuteronomy 16:1–17.

In the second line of verse 21, the Hebrew verb which we have translated as "tolerate" literally means "to smell." It is a very old word which, along with similar words in other ancient languages, referred to the reaction of God (or the gods) to human worship. The idea behind the word was, of course, that the deity smelled the aroma of the sacrificial smoke and was thus appeased. Genesis 8:21 expresses this idea in even more graphic form than Amos 5:22.[9] It is safe to say that Amos did not think that God smelled the sacrificial smoke in a literal sense. Rather, the occurrence of this word here reflects the fact that many times the Old Testament uses the language of an older mythology but in such a manner that the mythological content has been removed.

Verse 22: The second line of verse 22 is missing, and scholars have been at some pains to decide if it was lost at some point in the transmission of the Hebrew text of Amos or if someone other than Amos added line one to the prophet's words. Since the verse begins with "although," the first of these two explanations seems the more likely (because something else is needed to balance the "although" phrase). The whole burnt offerings were acts of sacrifice in which virtually the entire animal was laid on the altar and completely consumed by the flames. Unlike some other forms of sacrifice, no portion of the whole burnt offering was given to the priest or the people to eat. What is more, the animal sacrificed was usually one of the more valuable animals the worshiper possessed. Although the second line of verse 22 is missing, we

---

[9]Compare Genesis 8:21 to the following lines from the Gilgamesh Epic which describe the reaction of the gods to the sacrifice offered by Utnapishtim, the hero of the Mesopotamian flood story:

> The gods smelled the savor,
> The gods smelled the sweet savor,
> The gods crowded like flies about the sacrificer. ANET, p. 95.

may conclude that it declared in some manner that Yahweh would have nothing to do with such sacrifices.

In the second part of verse 22 a Hebrew word is used (which we have translated "offerings") which is general in meaning and which refers to all kinds of sacrifices. The "religious feasts" referred to here were a type of community banquet which often concluded an occasion of worship. The fatted animals upon which the people feasted had been sacrificed to Yahweh after portions had been set aside for the people to eat. This was a regular procedure in the worship of ancient Israel (Deut. 12:7), but one can sense a mockery in Amos' voice at this point. Perhaps he is placing the "fat meat" in the same category of self-indulgence as the "beds of ivory," the "lambs," and the "calves" of 6:4, the "idle songs" of 6:5, and the "finest oils" of 6:6.

Verse 23: The "noise" which Yahweh wishes to put away is a word used in other places in the Old Testament to refer to the rumbling of chariot wheels (Jer. 47:3) and the tumult of an encamped army (1 Sam. 14:19). The obvious implication is that the songs of worship sound to Yahweh like so much grating unpleasantness. The Hebrew word for "harps" is the same as a word meaning "pitcher" or "jar." This type of harp was therefore characterized by a jug-like cavity in its frame which amplified the sound, and specimens of such instruments have been discovered by archaeologists in several ancient Near Eastern sites.

Verse 24: This verse forms the climax to the oracle. The focus here is upon the two Hebrew words *mishpat* ("justice") and *ts^edhaqah* ("righteousness"). The first of these is related to the Hebrew verb "to judge," and it therefore finds its setting in the court of law, specifically within the council of village elders who adjudicated legal matters in the ancient Hebrew community. It was the responsibility of these elders to maintain the social equilibrium within the community by ensuring that proper relations prevailed among the members of the community. As a part of that responsibility it was their task to defend by means of the law those who were too poor or weak to defend themselves. In 5:10 one sees Amos' conviction that here, within the smallest community unit of the Northern Kingdom ("in the gate"), this responsibility was not being carried out. In other words, right relationships among men and women were being destroyed because the moral law of God was being ignored, and this destruction was being carried out at the very "grass roots" of Samaria's life.

In Amos' view *ts^edhaqah* was closely associated with *mishpat* (see Amos 5:7). *ts^edhaqah* refers to the moral posture of that man or woman who attempts to maintain a right relationship with his/her neighbors in the community or who helps to restore relationships which have been broken. Like *mishpat*, *ts^edhaqah* is thus relational in nature. It is the foundation of all right relationships without which there could be no *mishpat*. These terms were understood to apply not just to human relationships, but to God as well, and many times the writers of the Old Testament refer to God as "righteous" (Ps. 7:9) or "just" (Deut. 32:4). The main verb in the first line of verse 24 ("pour forth") literally means "to roll" and is used in other parts of the Old Testament to refer to the act of rolling a stone (Prov. 26:27) or rolling up a scroll (Isa. 34:4). Therefore, the meaning here seems to be something like "to tumble" or "to cascade." The "torrent" of the second line of this verse is a reference to the streams or wadis of Palestine which gush with water after the rain, but soon dry up. The stream of righteousness and justice for which Amos appeals, however, is inexhaustible.

Verse 24 seems to break the thread of Amos' images which, up to this point, have been associated with sacrifice and worship. But there is at least one occasion in the Old Testament where water is described as a sacrificial element (see 2 Sam. 23:16 with its interesting phrase "poured it [the water] out to Yahweh"), and this may be the link which, in Amos' mind, connects the "water" and the "torrent" of verse 24 to the other images of worship and sacrifice in the passage.

There has been considerable discussion among scholars as to whether Amos is here condemning ancient Hebrew worship as such or is only denouncing the superficiality and extravagance of the forms of worship which he witnessed at such northern cultic centers as Bethel and Gilgal (4:4). Some of those who claim that Amos is opposed to the ancient Hebrew cult on principle point to his statement in 7:14 in which Amos denies an affiliation with a prophetic guild. Because the guilds were often closely associated with cultic centers, Amos' rejection of any association with them may imply a rejection of the cult itself. It is more likely, however, that Amos intends to denounce what he sees as a *perversion* of worship as it is carried on in the Northern Kingdom. That worship seems to have been characterized by the same ostentatious display of wealth and pomp which was true of other aspects of the nation's life. When that reality is added to the nation's disregard of the moral implications of its faith in Yahweh, the result is a seething anger in Amos' heart. Amos would have been aware of a long tradition within Israel that the validity of worship depended upon the attitude of the worshiper.

> Who shall ascend the hill of Yahweh?
> And who shall stand in his holy place?

> He who has clean hands and a pure heart,
> who does not lift up his soul to what is false,
> and does not swear deceitfully. (Ps. 24:3–4)

It is precisely this spirit which is being violated, and Amos' purpose is to remind his hearers that God will not tolerate an empty shell of religious faith, especially when that shell is gilded with pretense.

3
HOSEA

Date of Hosea's Work: c. 750–725 B.C.
Location: The Northern Kingdom, probably the cities of
  Samaria, Bethel, and Gilgal.
Central Theological Concepts: Israel has broken the covenant
  which God established with the nation by responding to
  the faithful love of God with faithlessness. Therefore,
  God will destroy the nation.
An Outline of the Book of Hosea will be found on p. 35.

The Historical Context of Hosea's Work

The final three decades of the life of the Northern Kingdom, roughly the period of Hosea's ministry, are characterized by two different moods: one of tranquility and prosperity, the other of political instability and violence. Each of these moods is reflected in the words of Hosea who felt them both to be destructive of the nation's well-being. As is so often the case in the history of the Old Testament period, the transition from one mood to another is marked by a change in political rulers, in this case a change which involved not only the death of the King of Israel but also the coming to power of a new and energetic King of Assyria.

Hosea's ministry began about 750, during the final years of Jeroboam II (786–746). As we have already discussed in connection with the ministry of Amos, Jeroboam's administration gave to Israel a period of great wealth and peace. This was partly the result of the weakness of Israel's neighbors, primarily the Aramean kingdoms around Damascus and Assyria, whose rulers during Jeroboam's lifetime were relatively weak. Many of Amos' words indicate that this was a time of prosperity in Israel and, although it was a prosperity which that prophet viewed with great concern, it was the result in large measure of the political stability which Jeroboam had been able to achieve.

This mood of stability and peace, however, was shattered around 746 when Jeroboam died and was succeeded by his son Zechariah (not to be confused with the prophet of that same name). After a reign of only six months, the new king was assassinated by a certain Shallum, who was perhaps a jealous army officer or royal official. Within a month of this political murder, however, Shallum himself was killed by another conspirator, Menahem, who placed himself upon Israel's throne (745–738). Menahem seems to have been an especially violent man who did not hesitate to slaughter his own people when they stood in his way:

> At that time Menahem sacked Tappuah and all who were in it and its territory from Tirzeh on; because they did not open it to him, therefore he sacked it, and he ripped up all the women in it who were with child. (2 Kings 15:16)

The story of this rapid succession of kings is briefly told in 2 Kings 15:8–16.

Another event which was to shatter the mood of stability and prosperity which characterized Jeroboam's reign was the accession to power of the Assyrian monarch Tiglath-Pileser III, whom the Old Testament calls Pul (745–727). The new king was ambitious and aggressive and he soon subdued the enemies who had sapped the energies of his predecessors. He was thus able to turn his attentions to the west, toward Syria, Israel, and Judah. Menahem joined other rulers in Syria-Palestine in offering tribute to Tiglath-Pileser, and the brief record of Israel's submission to Assyria in 2 Kings 15:19–20 states that the money used to placate the Assyrians was taken in liberal amounts from those Israelites who had grown prosperous during the days of Jeroboam. But for the moment, at least, the nation was spared destruction.

Menahem was succeeded by his son Pekahiah in 738. However, Pekahiah was soon murdered by one of his officers, Pekah (737–732), who with the assistance of fifty armed soldiers from Gilead placed himself upon the throne (2 Kings 15:25). This *coup d'etat* may have been motivated by Menahem's policy of appeasing the Assyrians, for Pekah set himself to the task of forming a coalition of powers intended to defy Tiglath-Pileser. His chief ally was Rezin, King of Damascus, and in 734 these two rulers descended upon the kingdom of Judah with their armies when that nation's King Ahaz refused to join their coalition (the so-called Syro-Ephraimitic War described in 2 Kings 16:5–9). Instead of submitting to Pekah and Rezin, Ahaz appealed to Tiglath-Pileser for help and the powerful Assyrian responded in force. Tiglath-Pileser's treatment of the Northern Kingdom is recorded in this manner in the Assyrian royal archives:

> As for Menahem I overwhelmed him like a snowstorm and he . . . fled like a bird, alone, and bowed to my feet. I returned him to his place and imposed tribute upon him, to wit: gold, silver, linen garments with multicolored trimmings, . . . great . . . I received from him. Israel . . . all its inhabitants and their possessions I led to Assyria. They overthrew their king Pekah and I placed Hoshea as king over them. I received from them 10 talents of gold, 1000 talents of silver as their tribute and brought them to Assyria.[10]

---

[10] ANET, pp. 283–84.

The fact that still another royal murder had taken place is confirmed by 2 Kings 15:30 and the new Israelite king, Hoshea (732–724), took the throne as a puppet of the Assyrians. Tiglath-Pileser himself died in 727, however, and Hoshea seized this opportunity to renounce his vassalage to the Assyrians, probably in the hope that the Egyptians, who also hated the Assyrians, would come to his aid (2 Kings 17:3–4). The new Assyrian monarch, Shalmaneser V, laid siege to the city of Samaria, a military stalemate which lasted for three years (2 Kings 17:5). Before the siege of Samaria was over Shalmaneser had died and had been succeeded by his son, Sargon II (722–705), who destroyed the city and carried the people into exile, thus bringing the Northern Kingdom to an end.

Hosea's ministry spanned most of these years (it seems to have come to a close just before the fall of Samaria in 722). The prophet was therefore an eyewitness to both the stability and wealth under Jeroboam II and the instability and violence of the several rulers who followed. Each period offered to Hosea different evidence for the same fundamental fact: Israel had failed to return Yahweh's love. It was an apostasy for which the nation would be punished.

The Prophet and the Book

We know almost nothing about Hosea or about the personal circumstances under which he received and carried out God's call to be a prophet. The brief introduction to the book of Hosea (1:1) tells us that he was the son of an otherwise unknown Beeri. It also contains the information that his ministry took place during the reigns of the Judean kings Uzziah, Jotham, Ahaz, and Hezekiah and during the reign of the Israelite king Jeroboam II. As mentioned above, most scholars consider the material contained in the book of Hosea to reflect the period from about 750 (near the end of the reign of Jeroboam II) to just before the fall of Samaria in 722.

Unlike the similar introduction to the book of Amos, Hosea 1:1 gives us no help in locating Hosea's home nor are we told the places where he delivered his sermons. Nevertheless, it seems clear that he was a native of the Northern Kingdom (Hosea's favorite word for his nation is Ephraim) and that his oracles were probably delivered in the capital city of Samaria and in the sanctuaries of Bethel and Gilgal. This would mean that he followed closely in the footsteps of Amos, although there is little in the book of Hosea to indicate that he was directly influenced by the prophet from Tekoa.

The most intriguing and baffling aspect of Hosea's personal life is his relationship with the woman Gomer. In obedience to the command of God

Hosea married a prostitute and by her fathered three children (1:2–9). On the basis of the prominent place which the Canaanite worship of the fertility deity Baal played in the thought of Hosea (in a negative manner), it would seem that Gomer was one of the many cult prostitutes associated with that worship. Another section, 3:1–5, written as an autobiographical account from the prophet himself, describes how Hosea purchased a woman who was "a paramour and an adulteress" and took her into his home.

The theological significance of these texts is obvious. Hosea was convinced that, in tolerating the worship of Baal in its midst, Israel had "played the harlot" (4:15) before God, a prominent theme in his preaching to which we will return. But the manner in which these two texts relate to the life of the prophet himself is a matter of great debate.

There are basically two questions neither of which yields an easy answer. First, is the unnamed woman of 3:1–5 the same as the Gomer described in 1:2–9, or is she another woman (one must remember that some Israelites still practiced polygamy in Hosea's day)? Furthermore, if she is Gomer, is 3:1–5 an account from the prophet himself of the manner in which he married her, and thus the same incident which is related by someone else in 1:2? Or (still assuming the woman of 3:1–5 to be Gomer) did Gomer at a time subsequent to the birth of the three children leave Hosea, thus making it necessary that the prophet reclaim her, a reclamation described by him in 3:1–5?

The second question involves the manner in which 1:2 should be understood. It has seemed unlikely to some scholars that Hosea would believe that God actually wanted him to marry a prostitute, an act which under normal circumstances would have been utterly repugnant to someone with Hosea's spiritual commitment. Therefore, the suggestion has been made that perhaps Hosea married a woman who *later* turned to cultic prostitution and that he therefore grew to see in his relationship to her a paradigm of God's relationship to Israel. Other scholars have put forward the proposal that the material in 1:2–9 and 3:1–5 should not be taken literally at all but should be thought of as having the nature of parables. Yet a third group of interpreters feels that Hosea's marriage to a woman who was *already* a prostitute should be taken quite literally and that the very outrageous nature of the deed caused Hosea's prophetic words to contain that much more force.

The view adopted here is the last of these and it is the belief of this writer that it was precisely the shocking nature of Hosea's action, when matched to the shocking nature of his words, which caused his oracles to be remembered and preserved. It is also the understanding here that 3:1–5 is an autobiographical account of the manner in which Hosea first won Gomer and thus fulfilled the command of God recorded in 1:2. It should be stressed, however, that these conclusions are far from certain.

There is nothing else which we know of Hosea the man. Since his oracles do not seem to reflect the fall of Samaria in 722, he may have died shortly before that catastrophe. Or he may have made his way to Judah and found a home among friends and sympathizers there. It is certain that it was in the Southern Kingdom that his oracles were preserved and edited, and he may have received hospitality there from the same persons who treasured and shared his words.

As an orator and poet Hosea shares certain things in common with Amos. When he speaks, it is often clear that the real speaker is Yahweh and that the human prophet is merely the bearer of the Deity's words. Also, his oracles are frequently framed in poetry, and many of the words and poetic forms relate to other areas of the people's life. For example, Hosea uses a Hebrew word (*rib*) which is translated "controversy," "contention," or (in its verbal form) "to contend." This is the language of the law court and suggests that Yahweh is the plaintiff (and sometimes the judge) who has brought Israel before the bar of justice. Hosea 4:1–19 is an example of this law-court imagery (note especially vss. 1 and 4).

Yet Hosea's style is different from that of Amos in many ways. Although it is obvious that Yahweh is the speaker in many of Hosea's oracles, Amos' familiar "thus says Yahweh" is almost never used. Instead Hosea relies upon the first person pronoun (in Hebrew, the first person verb form) to let his hearers know that the words are those of Yahweh. Hosea 6:4–6 is an interesting example of this style.

However, it is undoubtedly in the use of simile and metaphor that Hosea excels. If Amos used the device of climax to engage the attention of his hearers, Hosea seems to have achieved the same effect by means of his word pictures most of which portray either the nature of Yahweh or the condition of Israel before its God.

Yahweh is like: a husband (2:2)
              a father (11:1)
              a physician (7:1)
              a fowler (7:12)
              a lion (5:14)
              a leopard (13:7)
              a she-bear (13:8)
              the dew (14:5)
              the dawn (6:3)
              the rain (6:3)
              a cypress (14:8)
              a moth (5:12)
              dry rot (5:12)

Israel is like: a wife (2:2)
  a sick person (5:13)
  a silly dove (7:11)
  a trained heifer (10:11)
  a luxuriant grapevine (10:1)
  grapes (9:10)
  the early fig (9:10)
  a lily (14:5)
  an olive tree (14:6)
  a woman in labor (13:13)
  an unborn son (13:13)
  an oven (7:4)
  a cake of bread (7:8)
  a bow (7:16)
  morning mist and dew (13:3)
  chaff blown from the threshing floor (13:3)
  smoke that rises from the window (13:3)

There is almost no area of daily life from which Hosea has not drawn some image by which to convey his message.[11]

An overview of the book of Hosea suggests the following outline:

A. Texts Relating to Hosea's Domestic Life and
the First Collection of His Sayings: 1—3.
B. The Second Collection of Sayings: 4—11.
C. The Third Collection of Sayings: 12—14.

These three sections of the book probably reflect the sequence in which the book was composed. Many scholars feel that the first section, 1:1—3:5, began with the prophet's own account of the manner by which he won the woman (Gomer?), 3:1–3, and with an early collection (again, perhaps the prophet's own) of Hosea's sayings, 2:2–15. To this material a subsequent editor added the biographical information in 1:1–11 and other prophetic fragments, 2:1, 16–23. Ultimately, chapters 1—3 were used to form an introduction to the entire book.

The second section, 4—11, seems to contain oracles delivered during the final years of the peaceful reign of Jeroboam II (4:1—5:7) and during the tumultuous, frequently bloody events associated with Kings Menahem and Pekah (5:8—6:6 seems to echo the Syro-Ephraimitic War).

The third section, 12—14, is judged by many scholars to contain the

---

[11]We are indebted for this list to Hans Walter Wolff, *Hosea*, p. xxiv. Translated by Gary Stansell. Hermeneia. Philadelphia: Fortress Press, 1974.

prophet's words spoken during the reign of King Hoshea, when a brief decade of tranquility preceded the final collapse of the Northern Kingdom.

The precise manner in which all of this material was brought together into its present shape is, of course, a matter of conjecture. However, there is a scholarly consensus which feels that the final editors were Jerusalemites who did their work after written records of the prophet's speeches (and perhaps the prophet himself) were brought south following the collapse of Samaria in 722. At many points, the Hebrew text of the book is garbled and these distortions may reflect the chaotic final days of Hoshea's reign and the efforts of Hosea's sympathizers to escape the onslaught of the Assyrian army.

Although a rough chronological sequence is evident in the text of the book of Hosea, each of the three major collections of sayings also appears to have been brought together on the basis of something approaching the same thematic plan. This is perhaps best seen in 2:2–15 which, as noted above, may be the written form executed by Hosea himself of a spoken sermon or series of sermons. Here an accusation (vss. 2–5) is followed by a pronouncement of judgment (6–13) which is in turn followed by an announcement of salvation (14–15). Again, the court of law is the background, especially the local tribunal presided over by the elders who sit at the city gates (the word *rib* is used in vs. 2 [RSV: "plead"]). Something of the same general framework may be identified in the second and third collections of sayings in which a series of oracles combining accusation and judgment are concluded by major announcements of salvation (11:1–11; 14:1–8).

The Theology of Hosea

Several important postulates characterize the preaching of Hosea, among which are the following:

A. *Israel is the people of Yahweh*. This fundamental belief of Hosea upon which all of his other theological statements are based is more often assumed in his oracles than explicitly stated. Yet there are significant clues to its presence in virtually every passage of the book. One of the more important of these clues is Hosea's preference for using the personal name for Israel's Deity, Yahweh (RSV: the LORD), instead of the more general designation, *'elohim* (God). The use of this name implies the intimacy of a close personal relationship which existed between God and Israel. Some scholars even point to 1:9 as a reference to the burning bush episode of Exodus 3 in which the name Yahweh is connected to the verb "I am" (vs. 14) and in which a new era begins in the relationship between God and the people Israel.

However, there are more specific ways in which God's election of Israel is expressed by Hosea, and many of these are references to the nation's past.

Hosea possessed an unusually profound appreciation for the historical traditions of Israel and he did not hesitate to cite these in his effort to remind his people of their spiritual responsibilities. He refers to God's covenant with Adam (6:7) and to the story of the patriarch Jacob (12:3–4). There are several allusions to Israel's experience in Egypt (2:15; 11:1; 13:4) and Moses' role in the Exodus earns for him the designation "prophet" (12:13). The giving of the law is referred to (4:6; 8:1, 12), as is the period of Israel's wanderings in the wilderness (2:3; 9:10; 13:5). These and other incidents from Israel's past are not cited simply for the purpose of historical reminiscence but in such a manner as to remind the people that they were chosen as Yahweh's own (Yahweh was Israel's "first husband"—2:7) and they were cared and provided for over the years.

B. *Israel has rejected Yahweh's love and has broken the covenant.* Hosea could be quite specific in his preaching to the people concerning their sin, and he identified three areas of their moral and spiritual irresponsibility. First, they have violated the covenant with Yahweh by disregarding its laws. While Hosea does not mention Mt. Sinai specifically, we have just seen that he knew of the events described in Exodus 19—20. What is more, he understood that the establishment of the covenant and the giving of the law were closely linked in that faithfulness to the law was to be a primary means by which Israel honored and preserved Yahweh's covenant. However, each of Hosea's allusions to the law is negative, in that the law is mentioned only to point to Israel's disobedience of it (4:6; 8:1, 12). Hosea 4:2 almost reads like a tragically distorted recital of the Ten Commandments: "there is swearing, lying, killing, stealing, and committing adultery."

A second manner in which Israel has rejected Yahweh's love is to be seen in the history of the monarchy. From a very early time there was a deep suspicion of the office of the king on the part of some Israelites. In the period of the Judges, Gideon refused the crown of Israel on the grounds that a human king would compromise the authority of Israel's only true king, Yahweh (Judg. 8:23). Later Samuel, when confronted by the people's demand for a king, is reported to have replied in a similar vein (1 Sam. 8:10–18; cf. 8:7. For a different point of view read 2 Sam. 7:1–17.). This view of the king as one who violates the relationship between Yahweh and Israel finds strong support from Hosea, and he frequently reminds his hearers of the sins perpetrated in the name of the monarchy.

The bloody revolt of Jehu which wiped out the preceding dynasty of Omri and which made possible the accession of the family of Jeroboam II is denounced as an offense for which Israel will suffer (1:4; cf. 2 Kings 10). Going back to the origins of Israel's monarchy under Saul, the very words with which the people request a king are quoted in derision (13:10; see 1 Sam. 8:6, 19). And Gilgal, where Saul was first acclaimed as king by the people, is described as the place where "I [Yahweh] began to hate them [the kings]" (9:15; see 1 Sam. 11:15).

It will be remembered that many of Hosea's oracles were spoken in the period following the death of Jeroboam II, and there is no doubt that his view of monarchy was influenced by the current political intrigue and instability which the prophet viewed as further evidence of the people's sin.

> By their wickedness they make the king glad,
>   and the princes by their treachery.
> . . .
> All their kings have fallen;
>   and none of them calls upon me. (7:3, 7)

There are other passages, however, which suggest that it was more than the present immorality and bloodshed connected with the struggle for the monarchy which Hosea found offensive. Like Gideon, he seems to have felt that the institution of the monarchy was evil of itself and a violation of God's will.

> They made kings, but not through me.
>   They set up princes, but without my knowledge [consent]. (8:4; see
>   also 13:11)

A third manner in which Israel had broken Yahweh's covenant is by means of its false worship, and it is to this sin that Hosea devotes a great deal of his prophetic energies. Part of the problem here has to do with simple idolatry, and the calves erected in Samaria by Jeroboam I (1 Kings 12:28) are singled out for special scorn (8:6; 13:2). But Israel's most serious apostasy had to do with its worship of the Canaanite fertility deity Baal, and Hosea's denunciation of this false commitment surfaces time and again in the literature associated with him.

The worship of Baal had been carried on in Canaan long before the arrival of the Hebrews and it was closely associated with the cycles of weather and of agriculture. It was Baal who provided for the fertility of the earth by sending the rains in their seasons and, therefore, Canaanite farmers went to some pains to insure his benevolent attitude. Because of Baal's role as the sustainer and reproducer of life, his worship often involved the sexual union of men and women (sacred prostitutes) which was performed for the purpose of reminding Baal (a word which means "husband") of his role in making the earth fertile. The temptation to join the celebrations for Baal, with their emphasis upon the sensual and material and their absence of moral demand, must always have been very real for the Hebrews. But in the Northern Kingdom the accession of King Ahab's Queen Jezebel, a Canaanite (c. 870), marked a new and ominous turn, for the queen was a zealous advocate for her god. Jehu's revolt had subsequently suppressed much popular support for the Baal cult, but it is clear that this apostasy had reemerged as a genuine danger during the lifetime of Hosea.

In the face of this threat to the integrity of Yahwism Hosea denounces the Baal cult and recalls Israel to a right relationship with Yahweh. Seizing upon the image of the sacred prostitute, Hosea charges Israel with harlotry, and the phrase "you have played the harlot" (5:3; 9:1; cf. 4:10) must have been heard often upon his lips. It is in this connection that the personal references in 1:2–9 and 3:1–5 assume a theological perspective. It is unclear whether Hosea became aware of Israel's harlotry before God because of his own pain at his wife's prostitution, or if his personal experience was fashioned into an object lesson for the people because he was already tragically aware of Israel's waywardness. Either way, the point of these two passages is clear and, in order to underscore the message, the names of the three children born to Hosea and Gomer bear word of the anger of God: Jezreel, where the murders of Ahab and his family had taken place (1:4), Not Pitied (1:6), and Not My People (1:9). When viewed against this background, the words of 2:2 become not just a plea to Gomer, but to Israel that the nation forsake its false and destructive devotion to Baal:

> "Plead with your mother, plead—
> for she is not my wife,
> and I am not her husband—
> that she put away her harlotry from her face,
> and her adultery from between her breasts;" (2:2)

In attempting to remind Yahweh's people of their true allegiance, Hosea applies to Yahweh certain terms and concepts which were in current use in the cult of Baal. Upon the lips of someone else these words might have seemed dangerously near to a compromise with the Baal worship, but with great skill Hosea applies them to the task of calling Israel back to its senses. Yahweh has a partner, as does Baal in the goddess Anath. However, Yahweh's betrothed is not a goddess but Israel (2:19). Yahweh is Israel's "first husband" (2:7, 16). It is Yahweh, not Baal, who causes the earth to yield its food, "the grain, the wine, and the oil" (2:8, 9, 22). Yahweh is a green tree (a frequent symbol for Baal) which produces edible fruit (14:8).

Just as the rulers of Israel had been targeted for special scorn because of their role in the nation's evil, the priests are likewise singled out for judgment because of their role in Israel's prostitution. Yahweh's lawsuit (*rib*) is with the false priests (4:4) who are no better at practicing their loyalty to Yahweh than the wicked people (4:9). Priests are grouped with the king as those who lead Israel astray (5:1). Priests are like robbers and murderers because of what they do in the royal sanctuary at Shechem (6:9).

In summary, Hosea is convinced of the nation's sin. Israel is a sick patient

(5:13), a "dove, silly and without sense" (7:11), "a stubborn heifer" (4:16), a half-baked cake of bread (7:8), among other things.

C. *Yahweh is calling for Israel to come back*. It is not Yahweh's will that Israel should continue in its sin or that the covenant between them should remain broken. The same love which led to Israel's election in the beginning still compels Yahweh to woo this wayward people. The brief autobiographical fragment, 3:1–5, portrays Yahweh as a jilted lover who yearns for the beloved Israel in spite of its faithlessness and adultery. Here the prophet responds to the divine imperative by purchasing the harlot (Gomer?) from her partner in adultery and claiming her as his own. The act is interpreted as a paradigm of the nature of God's love for Israel: "even as Yahweh loves the people of Israel, though they turn to other gods and love cakes of raisins" (3:1).

The grounds for the restoration of the covenant as enunciated by Hosea are strikingly similar to those expressed by Amos, yet they are more inclusive. There are several places in the text of the book of Hosea where those principles by which Israel is to live are proclaimed. The table on the opposite page allows us to see these at a glance.

(1) *chesedh* (RSV: "steadfast love," "kindness," and "love") is the most consistently expressed principle. It is a term used frequently in the Old Testament to refer to God's covenant love, the enduring, persistent commitment which Yahweh has for Israel and which is exercised in good times and in bad. Hosea's continued reference to this term demonstrates his concern that Israel reciprocate this same loving loyalty to Yahweh.

(2) *mishpat* ("justice") and *tsedheq/tsedhaqah* (two forms of the same word root for "righteousness") occur twice each, once in the same text (2:19). One will remember the discussion of these terms which were so important in the theology of Amos (pp. 28–29). As did Amos, Hosea demanded that a quality of right moral and legal relationships within the community of Israel should prevail as a reflection of these same right relationships which God has extended to the people.

(3) *da'ath 'elohim* ("knowledge of God") also occurs twice and a similar phrase ("you will know Yahweh") once. The verb "to know" is frequently used in the Old Testament to refer to the sexual union of a man and a woman. In this sense the above phrases underscore Hosea's condemnation of Israel's "harlotry" and demand pure faithfulness to Yahweh alone. A second meaning of the verb "to know" is to be found as a reference to the law. To know God is to know God's commandments and, of course, to obey them.

(4) *'meth/'emunah* (related words meaning "faithfulness") refer to a consistency in personal commitments which is the basis of all lasting relationships. This quality has been notoriously absent from Israel's relationship to

2:19–20	4:1	6:6	10:12	12:6
chesedh steadfast love	*chesedh* kindness	*chesedh* steadfast love	*chesedh* steadfast love	*chesedh* love
mishpat justice				*mishpat* justice
tesedheq righteousness			*ts^edhaqah* righteousness	
	da^cath ^эelohim	*da^cath ^эelohim*		
(compare with "you will know Yahweh")	knowledge of God	knowledge of God		
^эemunah faithfulness	*^эemeth* faithfulness			
rachamim mercy				

Note: the English words and phrases above are keyed to the RSV text. The italicized words are the Hebrew originals.

God and its restoration is seen by the prophet as a condition for the renewal of Yahweh's covenant with Israel.

(5) *rachamim* (RSV: "mercy") is a sense of compassion, especially for those in need.

When seen together, these key words and phrases portray a conviction on the part of Hosea that only a return by Israel to right relationships within the community and to a right relationship to Yahweh can result in the continuation or renewal of the covenant. God is willing to resume the role of Israel's husband and savior, if Israel will only permit it.

> for it is time to seek Yahweh,
> that he may come and rain salvation upon you. (10:12)
>
> Return, O Israel, to Yahweh your God, . . . (14:1; see 6:1; 12:6)

D. *Israel will be punished.* Hosea was a man of hope, but he was not an unrealistic optimist. In spite of Yahweh's openness to the people's return, there was little evidence that they would do so. In fact, as the serene years of Jeroboam II gave way to the violent and chaotic time which followed, Hosea must have often grown very doubtful that any shock to the nation's life, no matter how severe, would ever result in a change of Israel's heart. And so he frequently spoke of God's judgment upon the nation.

At times the prophet describes this judgment in general terms. Yahweh will have "no pity" (the same word root as "mercy" above) on this people who have become "not my people" (1:9). Yahweh is to them like a "moth" and like "dry rot" (5:12), or like the fowler who snares Israel with a "net" and who brings them down like "birds of the air" (7:12). In an extended use of similes, Hosea describes fickle Israel as being "like the morning mist," "the dew that goes early away," "the chaff that swirls from the threshing floor," "smoke from a window" (13:3). In the face of this fickleness Yahweh will exercise vengeance "like a lion," "a leopard," "a bear robbed of her cubs" (13:7–8).

In other places Hosea is more specific and his references are to the cult which Israel has desecrated. The places of false worship will be destroyed (10:2). And the productivity of the earth, upon which both humans and animals depend, will be taken away, the same productivity which Israel has tried to insure through its observance of the fertility rites associated with Baal.

> "Therefore I will take back
> 　my grain in its time,
> 　and my wine in its season;
> and I will take away my wool and my flax,
> 　which were to cover her nakedness." (2:9; see 4:3, 10)

It is also in terms of military conquest that Hosea sees Yahweh's judgment.

> therefore the tumult of war shall arise among your people,
> 　and all your fortresses shall be destroyed, . . . (10:14)

> they shall fall by the sword,
> 　their little ones shall be dashed in pieces,
> 　and their pregnant women ripped open. (13:16; see 10:1–2; 11:6;
> 　13:9–11)

In this connection, the period of servitude in Egypt is recalled, and Hosea promises an exile in which the armies of Assyria will play the role of Pharaoh of old.

> They shall return to the land of Egypt,
> 　and Assyria shall be their king,
> 　because they have refused to return to me. (11:5; see 9:3, 6; 10:6)

E. *In Yahweh's love, Israel will someday be restored.* Hosea's conviction of the indestructibility of Yahweh's love is so great, however, that he believes that not even Israel's sin can snuff it out. We have noticed above how each major section of the book of Hosea ends with the promise of restoration, and this editorial arrangement must surely reflect the nature of Hosea's preaching. Like a scorned lover, Yahweh continues to woo Israel and, just as the nation was brought out of Egypt long ago, it will be won over by Yahweh once again (2:14–15). In an amazing statement, this struggle with Israel becomes an internal conflict within Yahweh. The result of this strife is that

Yahweh cannot utterly destroy this people since to do so would be a violation of Yahweh's own being (11:8). Israel's faithlessness is contrasted with God's abundant love, and the blight of past judgment will become the fruitfulness of God's redemptive grace.

> They shall return and dwell beneath my shadow,
> > they shall flourish as a garden;
> they shall blossom as the vine,
> > their fragrance shall be like the wine of Lebanon. (14:7)

4
MICAH

Date of Micah's Work: Some time just prior to 701 B.C.
Location: Jerusalem.
Central Theological Concept: Because injustice has become a
    way of life, God will destroy Jerusalem and Judah.
An Outline of the Book of Micah will be found on p. 48.

Considered chronologically, Micah and Isaiah (who will be discussed in the next chapter) follow Amos and Hosea in the tradition of the "canonical" prophets, yet with the work of these younger contemporaries the prophetic movement witnesses a pair of significantly new developments. First, the focus of prophetic activity shifts from the Northern Kingdom to the Southern. This is not an especially surprising development for, although Amos and Hosea delivered their oracles in Samaria, the Northern capital, and in the Northern cultic centers of Bethel and Gilgal, there were many persons in the Jerusalem community who would have known and admired their work. It will be remembered that Amos was a native of the Judean village of Tekoa and it was probably to this region that he returned after his turbulent days in the North. It is also possible, as we have suggested, that Hosea fled to the South shortly before the fall of Samaria in 722. And it is certain that the collected oracles of both men were preserved and edited in the South and that they would have been well-known among certain circles there. The extent to which the work of Amos and Hosea influenced that of Micah and Isaiah is a subject of debate, but with the work of these latter two individuals the scene of prophetic activity moves permanently to the Jerusalem community (even Ezekiel, who is far removed from Jerusalem in a physical sense, considered himself to be very much a Jerusalemite).

The second new development which the work of Micah and Isaiah inaugurates is what might be termed a "living prophetic tradition" associated with each of these prophetic figures. The nature of this tradition and the details of the manner in which it was perpetuated are unclear, but it is evident that each prophet inspired a group of followers who not only preserved the words of the prophet but also supplemented them after (in some cases, long after) the prophet's death. We have already observed a tendency in this direction in the manner in which the oracles and other material associated with Amos and Hosea were treated editorially. With the work of Micah, however, and to an even greater extent with that of Isaiah, a school of prophetic activity is begun which, one might say, allowed the spirit of the prophet to live on and to speak to issues in a subsequent period. As we have said previously, this activity should in no manner be considered as literary or theological deception. Those who engaged in it were as convinced that they spoke the words of God as was their prophetic master, a conviction which both Jewish and Christian experience has confirmed. Whether the activities of this "living tradition" were purely literary or also involved public preaching we do not know. (The material associated with the Second Isaiah would suggest at least some of the latter.) Also uncertain is the extent to which this activity involved groups of persons (was there, for example, a guild of Micah prophets?) or relatively isolated individuals. Nevertheless, the material in the book of Micah makes clear and that in the book of Isaiah confirms that words continued to be issued in the names of these prophets long after their own times.

The Historical Context of Micah's Work

The editorial introduction to the book of Micah (1:1) states that the prophetic activity of the prophet took place during the reigns of three Judean kings—Jotham (742–735), Ahaz (735–715) and Hezekiah (715–687)—which would require a span of two decades at least. However, for a number of important reasons, the oracles which have been preserved from the prophet himself seem most at home in those uncertain and turbulent years of Hezekiah's reign, specifically those months just preceding the Assyrian invasion of Judah in 701. This does not necessarily mean that the information in 1:1 is incorrect, for Micah may have had a very long period of activity of which only a portion is reflected in his surviving words. Also, it must be admitted, his oracles are frustratingly difficult to date with any precision because of the almost total absence within them of specific historical references. Nevertheless, there is considerable cogency to the view that the words of Micah contained in the book which bears his name reflect the Assyrian crisis of Hezekiah's reign. (Cf. Jer. 26:18 which, when referring to the ministry of Micah, dates it only by reference to Hezekiah's reign.)

At the time of the collapse of the Northern Kingdom in 722 the Assyrian army also imposed itself upon the Southern Kingdom. There was a fundamental difference, however, in the manner in which the two Hebrew nations were treated for, whereas Samaria was politically destroyed, Jerusalem was spared, perhaps not only because of the South's previous attitude of cooperation with the Assyrians during the Syro-Ephraimitic War but also because the Judean kings Ahaz and Hezekiah were willing to pay substantial tribute to insure the survival of their nation. This was not a burden which Judah bore gladly, however, and over the years there seems to have been a growing eagerness to repudiate the nation's vassalage to Assyria. The details are sketchy, but it is apparent that Hezekiah, encouraged by Egypt, Assyria's enemy, revolted about the year 705. The climax of this insurrection is described in some detail in 2 Kings 18—19 where we are told that the Assyrians laid siege to the city of Jerusalem after conquering the surrounding countryside. Following an unsuccessful attempt by Assyrian emissaries to intimidate Hezekiah, the king appealed to the prophet Isaiah for help, an appeal to which Isaiah responded by pledging in God's name that the city would not be destroyed. 2 Kings 19:35–37 (cf. Isa. 37:36–38) describes a sudden and vast decimation within the Assyrian ranks (a plague?) and, quite suddenly, the siege is lifted. Although this dramatic moment is described very tersely in the Old Testament, it was to be remembered long afterward and was to become in the minds of many people a strange distortion of Isaiah's promise, for they came to interpret this incident as a sign from their God that *never* would Jerusalem be destroyed (cf. Mic. 2:6).

Many scholars feel that it was in these unsettled times that Micah worked and that the period just prior to Sennacherib's invasion and its spectacularly disastrous conclusion is the background for the words of the prophet which have been transmitted to us. (Note the phrase "to the gate of Jerusalem" in 1:12 [see also 1:9] which many believe refers to Sennacherib's siege.) There is some suggestion, since Micah had foretold the destruction of Jerusalem, that the lifting of the siege may have discredited him in the eyes of some. But others perceived that the truths expressed by the prophet were of an enduring nature and they, and perhaps the prophet himself, preserved his words. When Jerusalem was destroyed more than a century later the prophetic words of Micah undoubtedly claimed an even wider hearing than they had enjoyed during the prophet's own lifetime.

The Prophet and the Book

The book of Micah tells us very little about the personal life of the prophet. We do learn that he was a citizen of Moresheth (1:1; cf. Jer. 26:18), a pleasant village about twenty-five miles southwest of Jerusalem. Moresheth, also referred to as Moresheth-gath (1:14), lay in the Shephelah, the foothills which separate the hill country proper from the fertile coastal plain. As an inhabitant of this region, Micah would have been aware not only of the natural beauty of his homeland with its hillsides of grain and abundant fields of olives and grapes but also of its history as an arena of battle. The gentle surface of the land had served from ancient times as a natural highway for marching armies, especially the armies of Egypt to the south and those of its several foes to the north and east. The Shephelah also offered itself as the logical route of access into the central hill country, and it is not surprising that, of the fortifications built by King Rehoboam (c. 920), as described in 2 Chronicles 11:6–10, five of the sites are no more than a half dozen miles from Moresheth. Thus Micah would have been aware that great natural beauty and deep human tragedy are often found in close proximity.

We are given no record of the prophet's call from God, but in a brief autobiographical statement Micah does affirm his consciousness that what he does and says is from Yahweh:

> But as for me, I am filled with power,
>   with the spirit of Yahweh,
>   and with justice and might,
> to declare to Jacob his transgression
>   and to Israel his sin. (3:8)

No prophet ever stated a sense of vocation in more unequivocal terms, and if Micah ever suffered from the doubts which burdened Isaiah (Isa. 6:5) or Jeremiah (Jer. 1:6), his words which have been preserved show no sign of it. His total commitment to the prophetic calling compels him on at least one occasion to resort to bizarre behavior, if the words of 1:8 are to be taken literally. If he truly walked the streets of Jerusalem "stripped and naked" as a sign of the coming judgment, he would have performed a feat similar to that of his great contemporary, Isaiah (Isa. 20:2–4), two events which may, in fact, be related.[12]

There can be little doubt that it was in Jerusalem that Micah's prophetic ministry was carried out. In this respect he was remarkably like his country-man Amos whose home town of Tekoa was only a few miles distant from Moresheth. Although both men were at home in the village, they traveled to the centers of power in order to gain the widest possible audience for their words: Amos to Bethel and Samaria, Micah to Jerusalem. Yet Micah did not lose his sense of identity with the peasants of the countryside, and because of the oppression which they had sustained at the hands of the Jerusalem establishment, the latter was opposed by the prophet. Jerusalem's leaders are "those who devise wickedness" and who "work evil upon their beds" (2:1).

The suggestion has been made by some scholars that Micah was a local

---

[12] There are a few points of correspondence between the books of Micah and Isaiah, such as here and a duplicate of Micah 4:1–3 in Isaiah 2:2–4, but the extent of any real influence by one prophet upon the other is not known.

official in Moresheth, one of the "elders of Judah" who participated in the administration of justice within the village and who, on occasion, also took part in the deliberations of the king's court. The primary reason for such a conclusion is that it was within this group that, almost a century later, the memory of Micah was preserved (Jer. 26:17). Such a suggestion is attractive for it would help to explain not only Micah's keen sensitivity to the many miscarriages of justice which he saw but also the context in which he carried his complaint and his warnings of judgment to the religious and political establishment in the capital city. Nevertheless, such a conclusion must remain hypothetical for there is no concrete evidence in the book of Micah that the prophet exercised the duties of this office.

Just as we do not know the precise time when Micah began his prophetic activity, we also do not know the circumstances of its conclusion. Many scholars feel that with the easing of the Assyrian crisis of 701 Micah returned to his home. As stated above, some feel that he may have been discredited in the eyes of many of his hearers because his declarations concerning Jerusalem's destruction did not come true, at least not immediately. But the "elders of the land," who are contemporaries of Jeremiah, have a different interpretation. They cite the reforms of King Hezekiah as a sign of the repentance which caused Yahweh to withhold the destructive judgment (Jer. 26:19). Yet it is doubtful that Micah would have agreed with them. Just as Jeremiah was later to suspect that the reforms of King Josiah were only "skin deep" and did not involve a true change of the people's hearts, so Micah would have been perceptive enough to make a similar judgment with respect to Hezekiah's reforms. It is likely (but by no means assured) that, following the lifting of the Assyrian siege of Jerusalem, Micah returned to Moresheth convinced that his words were true, but that the time for their full realization was not yet at hand.

A simple outline of the book of Micah takes the following form.

> A. Micah's Oracles of Judgment upon Jerusalem: 1—3.
> B. Oracles of (Primarily) Salvation from a Later Hand: 4—5.
> C. A Third Stratum of Prophecies (these deal with the nation's fate before God as well as with the principles by which the godly life is to be lived): 6—7.

Modern scholarship is virtually unanimous in viewing the bulk of chapters 1—3 as the words of Micah himself. (In addition to the editorial introduction in 1:1, a number of scholars consider 1:2–7 and 2:12–13 as secondary.) As stated above, it is believed that these texts represent the preaching of Micah to his Jerusalem audience during or just prior to the Assyrian crisis of 701. In contrast to the preaching of Amos and Hosea which employed certain oratorical and/or literary devices to achieve maximum effectiveness, that of

Micah appears to be relatively blunt and straightforward. In fact, the very crudeness of his metaphors may have caused them to fall with greater impact upon the ears of his hearers, as in his description of the viciousness with which the powerful prey upon the poor of the land:

> you who hate the good and love the evil,
> who tear the skin off my people,
>   and their flesh from off their bones;
> who eat the flesh of my people,
>   and flay their skin from off them,
> and break their bones in pieces,
>   and chop them up like meat in a kettle,
>   like flesh in a caldron. (3:2–3)

Other word pictures could be less bloody, but equally effective, as in 1:4 and 2:12.

This is not to say that Micah was insensitive to the more subtle effects to be achieved by means of words. In 1:10–16, where he describes the destruction which is to come to the land, the prophet engages in series of deadly puns which the translation of James Luther Mays has effectively rendered into English (words in parentheses are added):

10 In the streets of Beth-aphrah roll in the dust (ʿaphar).

11 The Shophar (horn) they sound for you, community of Shaphir. . . .

13 You harness the chariot to the team (larekesh), community of Lachish.[13]

Alliteration, or the repeated use of the same sound, is employed in 1:16, while the cry of "woe" in 2:1 engages the imagery of ritual mourning to dramatize the tragedy that is to overtake the land.

The second section, chapters 4—5, has furnished the material for a great deal of scholarly debate. The reason, of course, is that the theme of judgment, so prominent in chapters 1—3, is replaced here by one of redemption and restoration, and scholars have been divided as to whether this change of mood represents a later stage through which the prophet himself moved or is the work of another person or persons writing at a later time.

This section contains several very interesting prophetic oracles. Micah 4:1–3 is virtually identical to Isaiah 2:2–4 and scholars have tried without complete success to determine which prophet (or prophetic tradition) borrowed from the other, or whether both prophetic traditions incorporated an already existing text into their respective bodies of literature. With its familiar words about "swords into plowshares" and "spears into pruning hooks"

---

[13] For the full translation and discussion of this text, see James Luther Mays, *Micah*, Old Testament Library (Philadelphia: Westminster, 1976), pp. 48–60.

the passage has endeared itself to generations of war weary men and women because of its promise of peace.[14]

Another passage of importance within this section is 5:2–4. The immediate meaning of this text has been widely discussed among scholars, many of whom compare it to similar exilic and postexilic texts which look for the restoration of the fallen Davidic dynasty in the person of a new ruler of that line (cf. Ezek. 34:23–24; Hag. 2:21–23; Zech. 6:11–14). However that may be, it is clear that the early Christian community saw this text as an oracle concerning Christ, Matthew 2:6 quoting most of verse 2 as evidence that it was to be in Bethlehem that the Christ child would be born. And for subsequent generations of Christians it is in this sense that the passage has found its fulfillment.

These and other texts from chapters 4—5 suggest that they were composed at some time subsequent to the fall of Jerusalem in 587 (and may, in fact, represent the latest material in the book). These two chapters reflect the faith of many who lived through that dark period believing that God had not utterly destroyed the people, but would someday restore them to their land. The broad strokes with which they painted the future held truths which even they did not recognize, for God's dealings with Israel would be climaxed not by the restoration of the king in a political sense, but in the coming of the King of Kings, the ultimate Davidic monarch, Jesus Christ. In order to balance Micah's own oracles of judgment in chapters 1—3 and to help place them in perspective, the promises of redemption in chapters 4—5 were incorporated into the Micah tradition by persons who treasured and kept alive the words of the prophet from Moresheth.

The final section, chapters 6—7, contains texts reflecting contrasting moods. Generally speaking, 6:1—7:6 is a collection of texts which speak of the alienation between Yahweh and Israel, while 7:8–20 describes the restoration of the broken relationship (7:7 acts as a bridge between these passages). Micah 6:1–5 has as its setting the court of law, the word *rib* occurring three times in verses 1–2 (RSV: "plead," "controversy," "controversy").[15] The point is that Yahweh has brought Israel before the bar of justice to answer for its waywardness.

Micah 6:6–8, one of the most profound passages in all the Old Testament, asks and then answers the question concerning the nature of true dedication to God. A detailed discussion of this text will be found at the end of the chapter. Micah 7:1–6 is another "woe" saying, reminiscent of 2:1–5, except that the subject ("I" of vs. 1) appears to be the city of Jerusalem which is in anguish over the judgment pronounced in 6:9–16.

---

[14] Cf. Joel 3:10, p. 187.

[15] The reader may wish to refer to the discussion of this word above on p. 34.

The mood of the final section turns, as noted above, at 7:7 and becomes an affirmation of the goodness of Yahweh. The climax to this section, indeed to the entire book, is achieved in 7:18–20 which is an essay on the wonder of God's mercy. The question with which this passage begins, "Who is a God like thee?" is considered by many to be a play on the literal meaning of Micah's name, "Who is like Yahweh?"

There is a sense in which the structure of chapters 6—7 recapitulates the judgment-turned-to-redemption arrangement of chapters 1—5. Although many important scholars see some words from Micah himself contained in several texts within this section, others believe the section to be an additional stage in the growth of the Micah tradition and would date most, if not all, of the material contained in it to a time after Micah's death, perhaps as late as the postexilic period.

The Theology of the Book of Micah

To speak of the theology of the *book* of Micah, as distinguished from that of the prophet himself, is to acknowledge the contribution of the "living tradition" of those who came after Micah and, in addition to preserving his words, continued to speak in his name. It is as difficult to separate the thought of that "living tradition" from that of the prophet himself as it is to separate with precision the various materials contained in the canonical book. In fact, it is basically the same exercise. Moreover, both Jewish and Christian communities of faith have, over the centuries, affirmed that the Word of God is to be heard in the entire Micah tradition, that is, in all seven chapters of the book of Micah, and not only in those texts which modern scholarship can attribute with certainty to the prophet from Moresheth. Therefore, it is from this perspective that the theology of the canonical book of Micah is described.

A. *The nation stands in a posture of sinfulness before God.* This sinfulness assumes two basic forms. First, a love of power and money has caused the leaders of the nation to cheat and oppress common men and women. In this regard, Micah's complaint is summarized thus:

> They covet fields, and seize them;
>> and houses, and take them away;
> they oppress a man and his house,
>> a man and his inheritance. (2:2)

This expropriation may have taken place by quite legal means, but its effect upon its poor victims was nonetheless devastating, especially upon women and children (2:9). Those who lost their lands also lost their livelihood and were reduced to poverty, perhaps living the remainder of their lives as indentured servants. So the expropriators won in two ways—coming into possession of both the land and the people to work it—a lucrative prospect which often kept them awake through the night in anticipation (2:1).

This same greed leads merchants to cheat their customers with false scales (6:11) and officials, who are supposed to be impartial, to hold out their hands for a bribe (3:11; 7:3). The manner in which the leaders defraud the people is so flagrant that Micah compares them to cannibals who eat the flesh of their victim (3:1-3). There is a sense in which the above texts from Micah may be thought of as descriptions of those horrors which ensue when men and women flagrantly violate the Tenth Commandment.

Second, this covetousness, in addition to infecting the political and judicial leaders of the land, has infected the religious leaders as well as many of the flock whom they lead (perhaps the same persons as the corrupt officials described above). "Priests teach for hire," complains Micah, and "prophets divine for money" (3:11). They proclaim soothing words to those who pay them well but call down fire and brimstone on those who do not (3:5). And soothing words are just what far too many people want to hear. To a person like Micah who proclaims a true although disturbing word from God, they object, "one should not preach of such things" (2:6). Such people deserve a preacher who utters "wind and lies," who avoids social sins by saying, "I will preach to you of wine and strong drink" (2:11) and who quotes hymns of the Temple in order falsely to assure the people of the protection of Yahweh (2:7 uses words similar to Ps. 86:5). Yet this hypocritical religion is nothing new, for it has been going on from Israel's very beginning. In a passage reminiscent of Hosea the history of God's people is briefly reviewed and evidence is produced, going as far back as the time of Moses, that Israel has answered God's love with indifference (6:1-5).

B. *Because of the nation's sin, Yahweh will destroy it.* When Micah speaks of the destruction of the nation, his language tends toward the symbolic. Unlike Jeremiah at a later time who was quite specific in naming the Babylonian army of King Nebuchadrezzar as the instrument Yahweh would use to judge the people, Micah is more circumspect. However, if the generally accepted reconstruction of Micah's time is correct, the avenging agent of Yahweh is the Assyrian army. Even so, what is going to happen is to be Yahweh's work, and no one should mistake that fact. In highly colorful imagery, the prophet portrays Yahweh as emerging from the Jerusalem Temple and striding across the landscape like an avenging angel (1:2-7). Before him the mountains will melt "like wax before the fire" (vs. 4) and the idols of the false gods will be shattered (vs. 7). At that time,

> Zion shall be plowed as a field;
> Jerusalem shall become a heap of ruins,
> > and the mountain of the house [of Yahweh] a wooded height. (3:12)

Yahweh will

> ". . . make you a desolation, and your inhabitants [an object of] a
>   hissing;
> so you shall bear the scorn of the peoples." (6:16)

In that terrible day Israel's children

> "shall go from you into exile" (1:16).

Special words of judgment are reserved for those two groups who have offended Yahweh most, the rulers and the clergy. As for the first group, those lands which they stole from others in turn will be taken from them by the conqueror (2:2–5). Also, in the day of destruction the treacherous priests and prophets will seek light from God, but will find only darkness (3:5–7).

C. *In spite of their sin, Yahweh will restore the people*. Exile may be the fate of the wayward people of God, yet even there God will not forget them. Instead they will be called together as a shepherd summons a flock and will be restored to God. God will perform for the weak and powerless a task which they could not hope to accomplish for themselves (4:6–7). Even in Babylon[16] this people will not be beyond God's love and protection.

> There you shall be rescued,
>   there Yahweh will redeem you
> from the hand of your enemies. (4:10)

The return from Exile, however, will not be the simple restoration of the people to their land. As of old, a Davidic king will rule over the flock of Yahweh as the undershepherd of God, and all the earth will be in awe of him (5:2–6). The city of Jerusalem will become the center of justice ("law") and faith ("word of Yahweh").

> and many nations shall come, and say:
> "Come, let us go up to the mountain of Yahweh,
>   to the house of the God of Jacob;
> that he may teach us his ways
>   and we may walk in his paths."
> For out of Zion shall go forth the law,
>   and the word of Yahweh from Jerusalem. (4:2; cf. 7:11–12)

The reason for this great redemption is not because of any superior strength or skill on the part of God's people. Rather, it is a reflection of the nature of Yahweh, Israel's compassionate and loving Lord.

---

[16] In this text the mention of Babylon, which did not emerge as a military power until almost a century after the time of Micah, is considered to be evidence that this passage is from the "living tradition" of Micah, rather than from the prophet himself.

Who is a God like thee, pardoning iniquity
and passing over transgression
for the remnant of his inheritance?
He does not retain his anger for ever
because he delights in steadfast love.
He will again have compassion on us,
he will tread our iniquities under foot.
Thou wilt cast all our sins
into the depths of the sea.
Thou wilt show faithfulness to Jacob
and steadfast love to Abraham,
as thou hast sworn to our fathers
from the days of old. (7:18–20)

A Key Text: Micah 6:6–8

There are few, if any, more incisive passages than this in all the Bible, for it answers the most profound question a person can ask: "How may one find peace with the ruler of the universe?" The answer is disarmingly simple and straightforward and, although it enunciates principles which are not readily achieved, those principles are nevertheless comprehensible to anyone who goes to the trouble to take them seriously.

It seems certain that the passage is a self-contained literary unit, structurally unrelated to the material which both precedes and follows it. The reader who is also familiar with the book of Amos will immediately be struck by the similarity between Micah 6:6–8 and Amos 5:21–24. In both texts the ancient Hebrew sacrificial system is rejected as a means of establishing a complete relationship with God in favor of a response which involves more far-reaching attitudes and actions on the part of individual men and women. Although Amos' rejection of the cult seems more total (and bitter) than that of Micah, that difference may be one of appearance only, and our discussion of the various questions raised by the Amos passage should be recalled here.[17] That there were other similar prophetic deliverances upon the relationship between sacrifice and "true" faith is confirmed by 1 Samuel 15:22; Psalm 40:6–8; and Psalm 51:16–17.

Although Micah 6:6–8 was originally an independent literary unit, it has been placed in our canonical book of Micah with an eye upon 6:1–5. That passage, it will be remembered, is a *rib* speech, the type of accusation one might hear in a tribunal of law such as that composed of the village elders. Here the defendant is Israel who is summoned before Yahweh, who acts as

---

[17] See pp. 26–29.

both plaintiff and judge, to account for its long history of faithlessness. Micah 6:1–5 offers Israel a means by which to restore the broken relationship with God, namely, to "remember" God's saving deeds of love (vs. 5). Verses 6–8 have been attached to 1–5 as a means of explaining in specific terms how Israel's act of remembering is to be carried out. Therefore, the passage makes good theological sense when it is read as a part of a larger section, verses 1–8, as well as when it is treated independently. Because the latter approach permits the passage to have a more universal appeal (that is, it allows the passage to transcend its specific setting in Israel's history and to speak to all humankind), it is the one usually taken by modern preachers and interpreters.

Verse 6a: The fundamental issue with which this text is concerned is raised by means of a two-line question which employs the time-honored device of Hebrew poets, synonymous parallelism (the second line repeats the essential meaning of the first). The question is asked in terms of material gifts to God because that is the manner in which Israel had been taught to think of correct worship. "None shall appear before me empty-handed" (Exod. 23:15) was the ancient injunction associated with the spring festival of Unleavened Bread, because to worship Yahweh on that occasion without proper sacrificial gifts would have been an act of ingratitude to the One who made possible the spring harvest of life-sustaining grain (and also an act of ingratitude for the people's deliverance from Egypt, since Unleavened Bread was also the occasion of the Passover celebration).

The verb in the first line of verse 6a (RSV: "come before") may also be translated "encounter" or "meet," implying that the relation between Yahweh and the individual is a personal one. The verb in the second line (RSV: "bow myself"), however, moves in the opposite direction because it has the meaning of "submit" or "surrender oneself" to a supreme being, a mood which is emphasized by the fact that God is "on high." Thus the two lines balance and complement one another and affirm that the encounter between God and humankind is intimate, yet it is a relationship between two emphatically unequal partners.

The use of the first person "I" in verse 6a (in Hebrew, the first person verb form), as well as in 6b and 7, indicates that the urgent question under consideration has to do not with Israel, as such, but with every individual human being. (This is, as we have noted, one of the factors which distinguishes 6–8 from the preceding section, 1–5.)

Verses 6b–7: The initial effort to answer the question raised in 6a consists of a listing of possible objects of sacrifice, the connection between answer and question being made by the repetition in 6b of the first of the two verbs of 6a, "come before." The list of sacrificial objects is "shaped" like a pyramid in that it begins with a quite common type of sacrifice, the whole burnt offering of a year-old calf and ends with the very uncommon and astonishing thought that perhaps Yahweh would be pleased with the sacrifice of a human child.

The whole burnt offerings mentioned in 6b were actually one among many different types of sacrificial offerings in ancient Israel. Here the entire animal was completely consumed by the flames, in distinction to other types of sacrifice in which portions of the meat (if it was the sacrifice of an animal) were set aside to be eaten by the priests or by the people or by both. The whole burnt offering of a year-old calf or other animal was a relatively routine occurrence in ancient Israel.

In the first line of verse 7 the "ante" is raised dramatically. If Yahweh will not be pleased with an ordinary sacrifice, perhaps an extraordinary one will be accepted: a thousand rams accompanied by ten thousand rivers (that is, an infinite quantity) of oil, the latter to be poured on the altar in an effort to enhance the value of the total sacrifice. The author of this text may have had in mind the example of King Solomon, the epitome of the extravagantly pious Hebrew. Solomon is reported to have sacrificed a thousand burnt offerings at Gibeon (1 Kings 3:4) and, at the Temple dedication, 22,000 oxen and 120,000 sheep (1 Kings 8:63).

However, in the event that Yahweh will not be pleased even with such an expensive offering, there is still something else more costly: the first-born child of the worshiper, "the fruit of my body for the sin of my soul." Child sacrifice was practiced occasionally in the ancient Near East, including Israel. The Hebrew Judge Jephthah sacrificed his daughter in fulfillment of a vow (Judg. 11:34–40), and the Judean Kings Ahaz (2 Kings 16:3) and Manasseh (2 Kings 21:6, cf. the action of the King of Moab, 2 Kings 3:27) sacrificed sons. One will also remember the account of Abraham's willingness to sacrifice Isaac (Gen. 22:1–19). Yet child sacrifice was expressly forbidden in Hebrew law (Lev. 18:21; Deut. 18:10), Leviticus 20:2–5 going so far as to say that the person who practices it is to be put to death. And the prophets were especially vehement in their denunciations of this bizarre form of worship (Isa. 57:5; Jer. 19:5; Ezek. 16:20). The idea would have been just as repugnant to the author of our passage, but he raises the possibility nonetheless as one which embodies the ultimate and most costly gift the worshiper could present to God.

Verse 8: There is an important structural shift here, for the speaker is no longer the questioning worshiper, but the prophet and also, by implication, God. The first two lines of verse 8 declare that the answer to the question asked in 6a is about to be given, and the phrase "O man" reflects the repeated first person pronouns of verses 6–7. The answer has three parts which move toward a climax in a manner somewhat similar to the "pyramid" of sacrifices in verses 6b–7. It says, in effect, that Yahweh does not yearn for material sacrifices at all, but for a quality of inner commitment: justice (*mishpat*), kindness (*chesedh*), and a humble walk with God.

Justice (*mishpat*) was one of the demands of Amos, and it will be remembered from our discussion of Amos 5:21–24[18] that in ancient Israel the term described the wholesome relations which exist within a community when the rights of individuals are honored and preserved. Kindness (*chesedh*) was a favorite term of Hosea[19] and implied more than simple benevolence. It too is a relational term and means something like "faithfulness to others within the community." The word is often used of God's covenant faithfulness to Israel, but here it probably means something like "a concern for others within whose midst one lives" or even "returning to God the same constant affection which God has shown for the people."

The phrase "to walk humbly with your God" is not found elsewhere in the Old Testament, although Deuteronomy 10:12 comes very near it with its injunction: "to walk in all his ways." Deuteronomy means by this not only obedience to the law, but also an inner commitment to God, for "to walk in all his ways" is coupled with "to fear Yahweh your God" and "to serve Yahweh your God with all your heart and soul" (cf. Mark 12:28–30 and parallels). The Hebrew word translated "humbly" is rare in the Old Testament, occurring only here and (in a different form) in Proverbs 11:2 where it is contrasted with "pride." Seen in this light, "humble" does not mean some quality of passivity or self-abasement (as the English word sometimes implies), but rather the ability to view oneself in a proper relation to God, that is, to be aware of one's need of, and openly to acknowledge one's dependence upon, God.

And so the movement within verse 8 is something like this: God seeks from the worshiper justice (*mishpat*), or right relationships with one's brothers-and-sisters-in-community; kindness (*chesedh*), or a compassionate faithfulness toward others-in-community; and a humble walk with God, or the loving commitment of all that one is to the Almighty. Human relationships are listed first but are climaxed and embraced by one's relationship to God.

This entire discussion, which began as a quest for the proper possession to present to God, ends on a radical note. God wants not *what we have* but *who we are*, ourselves and nothing else. It is not surprising that the prophets often provoked the anger of those who felt that God could be bought off or manipulated. Nor is it surprising that Micah 6:6–8 has sketched a pattern for human faith and conduct which has only once found its flesh-and-blood fulfillment—in Jesus Christ!

---

[18] See above, pp. 26–29.

[19] See discussion on pp. 40–41.

5
ISAIAH

Date of Isaiah's Work: c. 742–701 B.C.
Location: Jerusalem.
Central Theological Concepts: A just and holy God demands
   righteousness and trust from the people. Although the people
   will be judged, a remnant will be preserved. Furthermore,
   God will raise up a universal king from the line of David.
An Outline of the Book of Isaiah (chaps. 1—39) will be found
   on p. 68.

We have already discussed the view held by modern scholars who understand the materials in the book of Micah to be more than the product of a
single individual and to include the work of a "living prophetic tradition"
which continued long after the prophet's death and which, to a greater or
lesser extent, was carried on in his name. The materials in the book of Isaiah
represent a similar process, except that here the quantity of the written material is much greater and the history of the "living tradition" more complex.
In the case of the Isaiah tradition modern scholarship has been able to identify two additional prophetic personalities beyond that of Isaiah of Jerusalem
who made significant contributions to the Isaiah tradition and to the literature
which represents it. Because we do not know their names, they are referred
to simply as the Second Isaiah (who lived in Babylon near the end of the
Exile) and the Third Isaiah (who was active shortly after the restoration of
Jerusalem).[20] And, of course, it is possible to detect the work of a number of
other writers and editors who over the years helped to bring the canonical
book of Isaiah into its present form.

Because each of the three major prophets whose work is represented in
the book of Isaiah is important individually, we will devote a chapter to each
one. In the case of the material associated with the Second Isaiah (Isa. 40—
55) and the Third Isaiah (Isa. 56—66), an attempt will be made to explain
the reasons for treating this material differently from that associated with
Isaiah of Jerusalem (Isa. 1—39). Moreover, because those who were respon-

---

[20] As the discussion of the Third Isaiah points out (pp. 170–79), there are some scholars who
believe that this "individual" was actually a group of prophetic figures.

sible for the final, canonical shape of the book of Isaiah brought their material together on the basis of certain theological principles, the chapter on the Third Isaiah also contains a section entitled "The Theological Unity of Isaiah 1—66" (pp. 176–79). The present chapter will therefore limit its discussion to the work of Isaiah of Jerusalem.

The Historical Context of Isaiah's Work

It is possible to determine the dates of Isaiah's work with some certainty. Isaiah 1:1, a brief editorial introduction to the book, tells us that the prophet's ministry was carried out during the reigns of the Judean kings Uzziah, Jotham, Ahaz, and Hezekiah. If we understand with most scholars that Isaiah 6:1–13 is a record of Isaiah's call to be a prophet, the first year of his ministry would thus coincide with the last year of King Uzziah's life, or c. 742. (It is debated whether the statement in 6:1 means that Isaiah experienced his call after Uzziah died and possibly in some way as a consequence of his death or that the experience simply occurred in the same year, perhaps before the monarch's death.) There seems to be no activity by the prophet after the Assyrian crisis of 701, which would agree with the time frame described in 1:1. Thus, the period of Isaiah's active life as a prophet extends for approximately four decades, an unusually long span of time and one which embraced a number of decisive events in Judah's life. And it is evident from reading the material associated with Isaiah that he was deeply influenced by the political, military, and economic crosscurrents of his world.

The student will already be familiar with the historical contours of the years 742–701 from our discussions of the contexts of the ministries of Amos, Hosea, and Micah. With that information as a background let us look at the affairs of the four Judean kings mentioned in 1:1, an appropriate procedure in light of Isaiah's close involvement with the Judean court.

The first of these kings, Uzziah, is also called Azariah in the Old Testament (the difference in names involves only a single consonant in Hebrew). The generally accepted years of his reign, 783–742, parallel closely those of his great counterpart in the Northern Kingdom, Jeroboam II, who ruled from 786–746, and many of the same conditions of political stability and material wealth which prevailed in the North were also true of the South. The attention paid to Uzziah by 2 Kings is slight (14:21–22; 15:1–7), but more information is provided in 2 Chronicles 26:1–23.

Uzziah came to the throne of Judah as a lad of only sixteen years after his father Amaziah had been murdered by a group of unnamed conspirators (2 Kings 14:19–21; 2 Chron. 26:1). The Chronicles account of Uzziah's reign portrays an aggressive monarch who took every advantage of the same military vacuum which had favored the expansionist policies of Jeroboam to extend the borders of Judah. 2 Chronicles 26 mentions campaigns against the Philistines, the Arabs, and the Ammonites (vss. 6–8), which would imply that Uzziah pushed the sphere of Judean control in both southerly and easterly directions. A seal bearing the name of Uzziah's son Jotham, which was found by archaeologists in the ruins of Elath (Ezion-geber) gives credence to the report of 2 Kings 14:22 = 2 Chronicles 26:2 that during Uzziah's rule the ancient port of King Solomon at the head of the Gulf of Aqabah was reclaimed for Judah. 2 Chronicles 26 also reports the construction of fortified towers both in Jerusalem and "in the wilderness" (vss. 9–10), the latter phrase perhaps referring to the same southerly and easterly territories mentioned above. In addition, Uzziah's army is said to have been large and well-equipped. Although it is impossible to be sure, one may surmise that relations between Uzziah and Jeroboam II were peaceful, presumably because it was in the best interests of both monarchs that they remain so.

The result of Uzziah's political and military strength was a period of tranquility at home which allowed commerce to flourish and which permitted the mercantile class to accumulate large resources. And much of the same economic polarization which characterized the Northern Kingdom of Jeroboam II must have been true of Uzziah's Judah.

Toward the end of his life Uzziah contracted leprosy, a condition which resulted in his sharing political power with his son Jotham who became co-regent about the year 750. Uzziah perhaps continued to be an important political power even after this time. About 742 he died and Jotham claimed sole ownership of the throne.

The full accession of Jotham, who was to rule until about 735, ensured the continuity of the policies of Uzziah, and the account in 2 Chronicles 27:1–9 and, to a lesser extent, that in 2 Kings 15:32–38, confirm Jotham's interest in maintaining the military and political strength of the nation. The king was an energetic builder (2 Chron. 27:3–4) and a victorious warrior (vss. 5–6), and there can be little doubt that Judah's favorable economic position was perpetuated, as was the optimistic mood of the people.

Jotham's son, Ahaz, who was to rule Judah from about 735 to 715, was not as fortunate as his father and grandfather with respect to the military forces arrayed against his land. Shortly after Ahaz' accession, the Assyrian army of Tiglath-Pileser III appeared in upper Syria, causing the authorities in both Damascus and Samaria to seek some means by which to defend themselves. We have already discussed how Kings Rezin of Damascus and Pekah of Samaria invaded Judah, the so-called Syro-Ephraimitic War of 734, in an effort to force Ahaz into an alliance with them against the Assyrians. The accounts of this war in 2 Kings 16 and 2 Chronicles 28 indicate that this struggle was extremely costly to the Southern Kingdom, both in terms of the loss of human life and in terms of forfeited territories. At this time many of the areas to the south and east of Judah which had been won by the armies of Uzziah and Jotham were lost.

In response, Ahaz appealed to Tiglath-Pileser for help (against the strong protest of Isaiah, as we will see). The Assyrian king responded by crushing Damascus and Samaria and, although Jerusalem was spared further ravages at this time, Ahaz became, to all intents and purposes, an Assyrian puppet. This subservience to Tiglath-Pileser is best symbolized by the construction of an Assyrian-type altar in the Jerusalem Temple, the plans of which Ahaz sent to Jerusalem from Damascus where he had seen firsthand (and doubtless participated in) the worship of the Assyrian deity Asshur (2 Kings 16:10–13). Other forms of sacrilege, including the sacrifice of one of Ahaz' own sons, are mentioned in 2 Kings 16 and 2 Chronicles 28.

Ahaz' son, Hezekiah, who ruled from about 715 to 687, received upon his father's death a throne which was precarious at best. However, under his strong leadership efforts were made to reestablish both the purity of the worship of Yahweh in the Jerusalem Temple and the political independence of the nation. The extent to which these two efforts succeeded is unclear because, although the attention given to Hezekiah in the historical portions of the Old Testament is extensive (2 Kings 18—20 and 2 Chron. 29—32), these records are not entirely self-consistent nor are they easily reconciled with contemporary Assyrian records.

Hezekiah's efforts to purify Judah's worship may have been motivated by spiritual concerns, or they may have been simply an extension of the king's overall political designs. In any event, the king removed offensive objects and practices from the Temple and reinstituted forms of worship which were distinctively Yahwistic (2 Kings 18:3–6; 2 Chron. 29:2—31:21). Among the restored observances mentioned in 2 Chronicles is that of the Passover which was celebrated with such pomp and gladness that "since the time of Solomon the son of David king of Israel there had been nothing like this in Jerusalem" (30:26). Chronicles also maintains that Hezekiah's reformation was extended to the peoples of the now fallen Northern Kingdom, although only a few received it gladly (30:1–12). It is interesting that, although this reformation would have taken place during the active lifetime of Isaiah, it is not known how the prophet responded to it.

Hezekiah's efforts to win the political freedom of Judah have already been discussed in connection with the historical background of the prophet Micah. As was pointed out there, the precise details are unclear, but it would appear that with the death of the Assyrian monarch Sargon II and the accession of his successor Sennacherib in 705, Hezekiah took advantage of widespread unrest against the Assyrians to renew his nation's hope for independence. He cooperated with the Babylonian Merodach-baladan, who defied Assyrian authority in southern Mesopotamia, by receiving a Babylonian delegation in Jerusalem (2 Kings 20:12–15; Isa. 39:1–2; 2 Chron. 32:31), an act for which he was denounced by Isaiah. A new and powerful Egyptian monarch also seemed to provide potential help against Assyria, and it was probably about this time that Hezekiah "rebelled against the king of Assyria, and would not serve him" (2 Kings 18:7).

Sennacherib responded by a vigorous campaign in Syria-Palestine in the year 701 which resulted in the destruction of most of the Judean countryside and in the resubmission of Hezekiah to the Assyrians. The description of the great wealth which Hezekiah was forced to surrender (2 Kings 18:13–16) is probably to be dated to this time. Although Sennacherib's efforts to subdue Jerusalem were not completely successful (it is not clear how 2 Kings 19:35–37 [Isa. 37:36–38] is to be reconciled with 2 Kings 18:13—19:13 [Isa. 36:1–22]), it appears that Hezekiah continued in a state of vassalage for the duration of his reign.

The Prophet and the Book

We possess very few facts about the life and affairs of Isaiah. Verse 1:1 advises us that he was the son of an otherwise unknown Amoz (not to be confused with the prophet Amos). Because his prophetic ministry began in the final year of King Uzziah, that is 742, and extended for some four decades after that time, he must have been born around the year 760. There is no direct evidence that he was born into a priestly family, but that possibility cannot be ruled out, especially since his call to be a prophet seems to have taken place in that part of the Jerusalem Temple which only the priests could enter (6:1–8). Also, on the basis of the ease with which he moved in the circles of the Judean royal court, it may be assumed that his was a family of some social and political standing in Jerusalem. He was certainly not an "outsider" in the sense in which Amos was, nor did he, as was true of Hosea, ever repudiate the theological importance of the office of the king. To the contrary, a number of his more important oracles reaffirm the office of the Davidic monarch and see in that office not a deviation from God's plan for Israel, but one of the more important instruments for that plan's fulfillment. Isaiah was married to a woman whom he calls simply "the prophetess" (8:3), and they were the parents of at least two children, sons who bore the theologically symbolic names of A-Remnant-Will-Return (Shear-jashub, 7:3) and The-Spoil-Speeds–The-Prey-Hastes (Maher-shalal-hash-baz, 8:1). Although Isaiah seems to be no longer active after the Assyrian crisis of 701, the Old Testament gives no hint of his fate. There is a tradition which is at least as old as the early Christian era that Isaiah was martyred by being cut in two during the bloody purges of King Manasseh (see Heb. 11:37), but there is no way to determine the authenticity of that tradition.

Many scholars divide the active life of Isaiah into four major periods, a chronological scheme based upon both direct and indirect evidence from the book of Isaiah and from 2 Kings. *The Early Ministry* (742–734) begins with the prophet's experience of God's call near the time of the death of King Uzziah (6:1) and ends with the Syro-Ephraimitic War during the reign of King Ahaz. The tone of Isaiah's oracles during this period is very similar to those of his great predecessors Amos and Hosea in that he indicts the nation for its arrogance and greed. This period coincides closely with the reign of King Jotham, a time, as we have noticed, of relative peace and prosperity for the Southern Kingdom. The extent to which Isaiah was directly influenced by Amos and Hosea is not known, but it is significant that during this period of his ministry conditions in the South, which were similar to those in the North, summoned from Isaiah prophetic pronouncements which have much in common with the two great prophets who had been active in Bethel and Samaria. Judah is an evil nation which has allowed its sinfulness to corrupt its true and right relationship with God.

> Ah, sinful nation,
>   a people laden with iniquity,
> offspring of evildoers,
>   sons who deal corruptly!
> They have forsaken Yahweh
>   they have despised the Holy One of Israel,
>   they are utterly estranged. (1:4)

The basic causes of this waywardness will be familiar to every reader of Amos, Hosea, and Micah: people, especially the upper classes, have become greedy and they have allowed their love of material wealth to lead to the suppression of the rights of the weak and defenseless. Isaiah would have been aware that the coronation of every Davidic king involved the imperative laid upon the monarch to protect the interests of the poor and powerless (see Ps. 72:1–4, 12–14). The failure of the king and those about him to fulfill this charge was loathsome in God's eyes.

> Your princes are rebels
>   and companions of thieves.
> Every one loves a bribe
>   and runs after gifts.
> They do not defend the fatherless,
>   and the widow's cause does not come to them. (1:23)

Those in power spend their energies piling up wealth in the form of silver and gold, horses and chariots. They allow the pure worship of God to be compromised by their awe of magicians and fortune-tellers and by their worship of false gods (2:6–8). There is drunkenness and debauchery (5:11–12, 22–23), and the sinfulness of the nation has caused even the proper rituals of worship to be repugnant to God (1:10–11, which sounds very much like Amos 5:21–24). Therefore, the nation will be judged by means of a fierce enemy who will be summoned to do God's bidding.

> He will raise a signal for a nation afar off,
>   and whistle for it from the ends of the earth;
> and lo, swiftly, speedily it comes!
> . . .
> And if one look to the land,
>   behold, darkness and distress;
> and the light is darkened by its clouds. (5:26, 30)

One of the most effective means by which Isaiah conveys his message of the people's sinfulness and Yahweh's response of judgment is the so-called Song of the Vineyard (5:1–7). A popular song, perhaps one sung by the workers as they harvested the grapes in the fall, has been transformed into a parable by the prophet. Its verdict is ominous and inescapable: like a choice vineyard from which its owner expected a sweet harvest, Judah should have returned Yahweh's love with devotion. Instead, Judah's fruit has been wild and bitter, and the Lord of the vineyard will have no choice but to root it out. The song ends with a play upon words which reminds the reader of the thundering statement of Amos 5:24:

> and he looked for justice (*mishpat*),
>   but behold, bloodshed (*mishpach*);
> for righteousness (*ts^{e}dhaqah*),
>   but behold, a cry (*ts$^{e^c}$aqah*). (5:7)

Yet even in the very first period of his ministry Isaiah affirms that God's dealings with Judah are not about to come to an end, for beyond the judgment there is to be an act of redemptive love. This emphasis upon the remnant of the people which is to be saved is most dramatically expressed in the name of his son, A-Remnant-Will-Return (7:3), but other texts speak of this saving act of God as well (10:20–27; 11:10–16).

As we have seen, the death of Jotham and the accession of Ahaz coincided with an important change in the political and military environment in which Judah lived, and these changed circumstances are reflected in the oracles of Isaiah. The Syro-Ephraimitic War of 734 was a crisis thrust upon King Ahaz soon after he claimed the throne of his late father, a crisis which filled the unfortunate monarch with such terror that "his heart and the heart of his people shook as the trees of the forest shake before the wind" (7:2). As we have noticed, Ahaz responded to this threat from his two northern neighbors by calling for help from the Assyrian king, Tiglath-Pileser. It was a policy to which Isaiah held fundamental objections, not for political or military reasons, but for theological ones, and it is to this point in his ministry that the material in chapters 7—8 is related.

To Ahaz' hope for help in an alliance with Assyria Isaiah responded by calling upon Judah to reaffirm its sense of complete trust in Yahweh. As for the two kingdoms whose invasion of Judah had provoked the crisis, they were not to be feared. In a dramatic encounter between the king and the prophet, Isaiah declared this message from God: "Take heed, be quiet, do not fear, and do not let your heart be faint because of these two smouldering stumps of firebrands" (7:4). The reason for which Ahaz may take courage is not, however, the strength of Assyria or any other human ally; it is rather the strength of Yahweh who loves Judah and who will provide for all its needs. In this strength the nation should quietly and confidently trust.

> "If you will not believe,
> surely you shall not be established." (7:9)

But the king, perhaps understandably from a human point of view, was not willing to rely upon only spiritual power to fight against swords and spears, and when he persisted in his foreign policy, Isaiah promised that it would lead to disaster. He compared the gentle waters of the nearby aqueduct of Shiloah to his own counsel of quiet trust, but he likened the sometimes turbulent Euphrates to the military solution proposed by Ahaz, and he said:

> "Because this people have refused the waters of Shiloah that flow gently, and melt in fear before Rezin and the son of Remaliah; therefore, behold Yahweh is bringing up against them the waters of the [Euphrates] River, mighty and many, the king of Assyria and all his glory; and it will rise over all its channels and go over all its banks; and it will sweep on into Judah, it will overflow and pass on, reaching even to the neck; and its outspread wings will fill the breadth of your land, O Immanuel." (8:6-8)

This crisis also called forth another oracle of Isaiah, one of his most distinctive and memorable utterances. Isaiah 7:10–17 promises a sign that what Isaiah has spoken is indeed the truth of God. This sign is to take the form of a royal son, perhaps a child of Ahaz himself. His birth is to be a symbol of assurance that the kings of Samaria and Damascus are only temporary threats and that God has a destiny in mind for Judah other than the one Ahaz fears. Whatever immediate meaning Isaiah may have had in mind when he spoke these words, in time they came to have enormous implications for the belief of the Christian Church, and because of their importance, special attention is given to them later in this chapter (see pp. 73–76).

Ahaz' failure to listen to Isaiah results in an action which marks the second important phase of the prophet's ministry, that of his *Retreat from Public Activity* (734–715). In a sense Isaiah follows the advice he had given to the king, for he reacts to the folly which he witnesses around him with a quiet reliance upon the working out of God's will. Isaiah 8:16–22 describes how, in the face of his public rejection, he entrusts his words to his followers, the "testimony" and "teaching" of verse 16. Perhaps this refers to some written form of the oracles of the prophet and may mark the beginning of the formation of our present book of Isaiah. These words plus the sermons embodied in the names of his two sons, A-Remnant-Shall-Return and The-Spoil-Speeds–The-Prey-Hastes, are to be a passive contradiction of the false teaching of those who shape the opinions of the king and the people (the "mediums and wizards who chirp and mutter" of vs. 19). In the end the bankruptcy of this false teaching will be evident even to those who now follow it so eagerly (vss. 21–22).

With the death of Ahaz and the accession of Hezekiah in 715 Isaiah comes forward in a public way once more (see 14:28), the period of his so-called *Middle Ministry* (715–705). The prophet's messages during these years are consistent with those of his Early Ministry, but are redirected because of the changed political and military circumstances. Damascus and Samaria have been crushed and Judah is now firmly held within the constellation of Assyria's vassal states. Egypt and its ally Ethiopia, however, appear to have fomented trouble against Assyria and to have done so by encouraging revolt on the part of those people whose lands formed a buffer between the southern limits of the Assyrian empire and the borders of Egypt, including the Philistines and the Judeans. In 711 the Assyrians crushed the Philistine stronghold of Ashdod, and Isaiah felt called upon to warn Hezekiah and the authorities in Jerusalem that rebellion on their part would result in similar humiliation and suffering (20:1–6). In order to reinforce his point Isaiah acted out the shame of a prisoner of war by going about naked and barefoot for a period of three years, a dramatic way of saying that this would be the fate of the people if they, instead of relying on the grace and power of God to deliver them, relied upon the weapons and instruments of war. The action was also intended as a warning to Egypt and Ethiopia that not even they were beyond the reach of Assyrian might. As for Hezekiah's pro-Egyptian counselor, Shebna, he would be overthrown by God and replaced by a certain Eliakim, who would be more responsive to God's will for Judah (22:15–25),[21] a prophecy whose fulfillment seems reflected in 2 Kings 18:18. It is probable that Isaiah's oracles concerning Ethiopia and Egypt in chapters 18—19 also date from this time.

Yet Isaiah was not blind to Assyria's ambivalent position in God's eyes. To be sure, this nation had become the instrument Yahweh used in the judg-

---

[21]The symbolism of the key in 22:22 may have suggested Jesus' remark to Peter in Matthew 16:19 as well as the comment about the "key of David" in Revelation 3:7.

ment of Israel, yet this was no credit to Assyria who did not acknowledge its role in the unfolding will of God, but acted only out of lust and cruelty (10:5–11). In time Assyria itself must answer to God for its callous and bloodthirsty deeds (10:12–19).

It is in the period of the Middle Ministry that many scholars date two of Isaiah's more important oracles, 9:1–7 and 11:1–9. In a manner not unlike 7:10–17, these passages seem to be directed to the immediate situation and to refer to the ruling Davidic dynasty, perhaps portraying the kind of peace which Judah will enjoy by quietly trusting in Yahweh, in contrast to the destruction which military revolt will ensure. But also like 7:10–17, these oracles contain far more important messages than those addressed to Isaiah's own contemporaries, and because of their role in helping to formulate the theology of the Christian Church, they also will be discussed in some detail below (pp. 76–78).

The final years of Isaiah's public life, the so-called *Late Ministry* (705–701), are marked by the crisis brought on when Hezekiah openly defied Assyrian rule. We have already noticed that the events of these years are not at all clear. However, it seems that in 705 the death of the Assyrian king Sargon II (who had succeeded Shalmaneser in 722) inspired Hezekiah to join others in attempting to cast off the Assyrian vassalage. It was probably about this time that Hezekiah received the delegation of Babylonians who were themselves in revolt against Assyria (39:1–2 = 2 Kings 20:12–13). Isaiah was uncompromising in his opposition to this alliance with the Babylonians and seems to have lost no time in telling the king of its consequences (39:3–8 = 2 Kings 20:14–19). Nor was Egypt, who continued to stir up trouble, to be trusted. Any alliance between Judah and the kingdom of the Nile would result only in Judah's humiliation and destruction (30:1–7). Isaiah mistrusted these alliances, which he called "a covenant with death" (28:15), just as he had earlier mistrusted Ahaz' alliance with Tiglath-Pileser, because he saw in them a turning away by the nation from its fundamental reliance upon Yahweh alone. Rather, he counseled,

> "In returning and rest you shall be saved,
> in quietness and trust shall be your strength." (30:15)

When Hezekiah went ahead with his plans to revolt, the result was the kind of destruction which Isaiah foresaw. Isaiah 36—37 = 2 Kings 18—19 pictures the terrible situation in which Jerusalem found itself after the Assyrian armies had devastated the surrounding Judean countryside and, in the words of an Assyrian annalist, had confined Hezekiah "in Jerusalem, his royal residence, like a bird in a cage."[22] In great fear Hezekiah called upon

---

[22] ANET, p. 288.

Isaiah for help and the prophet responded by promising the deliverance of the city (37:6–7).

When we turn to an outline of the major divisions within Isaiah 1—39 we discover that, in certain respects, the periods in Isaiah's prophetic ministry are reflected in those divisions. The structure of Isaiah 1—39 is extremely complex and questions of the date and authorship of various passages will occupy the attention of scholars for many years to come. The sketch below is only of the most prominent contours.

> A. Material relating to Isaiah's Early and Middle Ministries: 1—12.
> B. Oracles of judgment upon foreign nations: 13—23.
> C. The Isaiah Apocalypse: 24—27.
> D. Material from Isaiah's Late Ministry: 28—33.
> E. Two poems: 34—35.
> F. Historical narratives about Isaiah: 36—39.

The first section, 1—12, is our richest source of information concerning Isaiah's activity during the Early and Middle Ministries. The oracles are directed almost exclusively to the Jerusalem community and are combined with a record of Isaiah's call (6:1–13) and other autobiographical passages.

In the second section, 13—23, a number of foreign nations are identified as the objects of Yahweh's judgment. Some of this material is from Isaiah, some from later hands.

The third section, 24—27, is the so-called "Isaiah Apocalypse," a designation based upon the concern these chapters exhibit for God's final judgment ("that day" of 24:21; 25:9; 26:1). In spite of the generally negative tone of this section, it contains some beautifully written passages which speak of hope (25:1–5; 26:1–6, 19). Most scholars are of the opinion that this material was composed long after the time of Isaiah, probably during the postexilic period.[23]

The fourth section, 28—33, is material which relates primarily to the period of the prophet's Late Ministry. In these oracles, many of which begin with the word "woe," Isaiah denounces Hezekiah's policy of seeking a military alliance against Assyria and he affirms God's continuing love for Judah.

The fifth section, 34—35, consists of two poems, perhaps from the period of the Exile, which deal with Yahweh's treatment of Judah and "all the nations" (34:2). Many scholars have drawn attention to the fact that the material in chapter 35 is very similar in certain ways to the material in Isaiah 40—55 and may reflect the ministry of the Second Isaiah. The final section, 36—39, is adapted with some changes from 2 Kings 18:13—20:19.

---

[23]For a further discussion of chapters 24—27, see p. 176.

The Theology of Isaiah 1—39

The theology of Isaiah, when arranged systematically, demonstrates both this prophet's link with the prophetic tradition which preceded him and his own originality.

A. *Yahweh is a holy God who demands justice and righteousness from the people.* The account of Isaiah's call in chapter 6 embodies one of the most profound statements on the holiness of God in the entire Old Testament. The reader will wish to refer to the discussion of this passage below, but notice should be taken here of the chant of the seraphim in 6:3. The threefold repetition of the word "holy" is a form of the Hebrew superlative: "Most holy is Yahweh of hosts." This sense of the holiness of God is reinforced by the other images in the passage, for example, the "throne, high and lifted up" (vs. 1).

Holiness for Isaiah had at least two basic meanings. The first is a sense of physical separation and elevation. God is holy in the sense of being totally other than the creation. Yahweh made the world, including humankind, and presides over it as Lord: "In that day men will regard their Maker, and their eyes will look to the Holy One of Israel" (17:7). It is this deep awareness of the sovereignty of Yahweh which causes Isaiah to refer repeatedly to Yahweh as the "Holy One of Israel" (1:4; 5:19, 24; 10:17, 20).[24]

A second way in which Isaiah understands the holiness of God is in the sense of moral integrity.

> But Yahweh of hosts is exalted in justice,
> and the Holy God shows himself holy in righteousness. (5:16)

Perhaps Isaiah learned to connect holiness and moral purity from his prophetic predecessors (cf. Amos 4:2), but he affirms this conviction with a force which could have been generated only by his own inner commitment. What is more, to be aware of the holiness of God is to be aware of the reality of human sin. Isaiah's reaction to his experience of the holiness of God is to cry out in anguish over his sin and that of his people (6:5). When compared with other peoples, Judah might seem to be as morally responsible as anyone else, but when compared with the living God, Judah's selfishness and greed are revealed for what they are.

B. *Sin is rebellion against Yahweh.* The oracle with which the book of Isaiah opens and which many scholars believe comes from early in the proph-

---

[24]This emphasis on the holiness of Yahweh becomes, as we will see, one of the themes which lends unity to the entire book of Isaiah.

et's active life describes the sin of the nation in terms of disobedience to and defiance of Yahweh.

> "Sons have I reared and brought up,
>> but they have rebelled against me.
> The ox knows its owner,
>> and the ass its master's crib;
> but Israel does not know,
>> my people does not understand." (1:2–3)

As we have noticed in our preceding discussion, Isaiah is quite specific in his identification of certain sins. In his Early Ministry these included idolatry (2:8), as well as the greed which leads officials to accept bribes (1:23) and to oppress the poor and defenseless (3:13–15; 10:2). During the reigns of Ahaz and Hezekiah (the Middle and Late Ministries), however, Isaiah broadened his concerns to the political arena and denounced the nation's dependence upon military alliances because he was convinced that such a posture resulted in an absence of dependence upon Yahweh alone (28:14–22; 30:15–18; 31:1–3).

C. *Because of love for them, Yahweh calls this people to repentance and faith.* For Isaiah the traditional means of making amends for sin, the sacrificial system, is not enough (1:10–15). The nation must repent by recognizing its evil ways and reversing the pattern of its behavior.

> "Wash yourselves; make yourselves clean;
>> remove the evil from your doings
>> from before my eyes;
> cease to do evil,
>> learn to do good;
> seek justice,
>> correct oppression;
> defend the fatherless,
>> plead for the widow." (1:16–17; see also 1:18–19; 31:6)

What is more, the nation must have trust in Yahweh as the people's provider and sustainer. Isaiah's statement to Ahaz at the time of the Syro-Ephraimitic War emphasizes this point by means of a play upon words:

> "If you will not believe (*ta'aminu*),
>> surely you shall not be established (*te'amenu*)." (7:9)

In other words, both a willingness to redirect its life and a sense of absolute dependence upon Yahweh is necessary if the broken relationship is to be restored.

D. *The consequence of sin and rebellion against Yahweh is judgment.* God's displeasure at the sinfulness of the people is symbolized in the choice of Assyria as "the rod of my anger, the staff of my fury" (10:5; see also 5:26–30; 7:18–25). God will chasten this people and send them into exile (5:13), but this punishment is more than just an expression of Yahweh's anger. It has a purpose, and that is to purify the nation by removing the evil from its life in order that the good may flourish.

> "I will turn my hand against you
>   and will smelt your dross as with lye
>   and remove all your alloy.
> And I will restore your judges as at the first,
>   and your counselors as at the beginning.
> Afterward you shall be called the city of righteousness,
>   the faithful city."
> Zion shall be redeemed by justice,
>   and those in her who repent, by righteousness. (1:25–27)

E. *Beyond judgment a remnant will be saved.* The nature of God's attitude toward judgment, that is, to cleanse rather than to destroy, is perhaps at the root of Isaiah's concept of the remnant. As we have seen, this concept is most dramatically expressed by Isaiah in the name of his son A-Remnant-Shall-Return (Shear-jashub, 7:3). During the time of his retreat from public life, this son and his brother The-Spoil-Speeds–The-Prey-Hastes (Maher-shalal-hash-baz, 8:1), both of whom would have been visible in the daily affairs of Jerusalem, became quiet witnesses to the message of their father: the nation will be destroyed, but a purified remnant will return (8:18). Isaiah 10:20–23 and 11:11–16 express the same confidence in a restored remnant of the people.

F. *A Messiah of the line of David will be raised up by God.* The word "Messiah" is not used by Isaiah in connection with his oracles concerning the future of the Davidic dynasty. However, the three passages, 7:14–17, 9:1–7, and 11:1–9, have played such an important role in shaping the messianic faith of the Christian church that we are perhaps justified in using that word in reference to them. As the discussion below demonstrates, these passages are not without their difficulties, but they demonstrate that Isaiah, dissatisfied over the performances of the Davidic kings who were his contemporaries, looked forward to God's raising up a member of the house of David who would far surpass such kings as Ahaz and Hezekiah in both faith and power. To these texts and to the one which relates Isaiah's call we now turn.

Four Key Texts

A. 6:1–8

This passage, as we have noted, is an account of Isaiah's call to be a prophet, a record which has been preserved in the first person and which, therefore, may be considered to come from Isaiah himself. As a literary unity the call comprises all of chapter 6, but its most significant part is clearly verses 1–8, and it is to this that we will give our attention.

Verse 1: The fact that the narrative of the call begins with a statement concerning its date suggests that Isaiah composed this account some time after the actual experience, and some scholars have suggested that this later time was the occasion of Isaiah's retreat from active life about 734. If so, the call represents an introduction to chapters 6—8 which may have formed the first unit within what was to become the book of Isaiah. For the prophet to say that he "saw Yahweh" is astonishing, in view of the mortal consequences of such a vision (Exod. 19:21). Actually, the prophet means that he saw (and felt, vs. 4) the evidences of Yahweh's presence, rather than that he gazed on Yahweh's face as such. Nevertheless, it is clear that the prophet was overwhelmed by a reality which his senses could not appropriate nor his words describe. The throne upon which Yahweh sat is probably to be thought of as the Ark of the Covenant which rested in the Holy of Holies, the focal point of and most sacred room within the Jerusalem Temple. The visual image is thus that of Yahweh enthroned, the Deity shrouded in smoke (vs. 4), with the train of the royal robe spilling out from the Holy of Holies into the rest of the Temple. "High and lifted up" is a reference both to the majesty of the nature and to the physical elevation of Yahweh.

Verse 2: The seraphim are literally "the burning ones." Their number is not disclosed, but it does not follow from verse 3 (as is sometimes suggested) that there were only two of them. Why they were "burning" is not clear, but they were obviously supernatural beings who were charged with standing guard over the Deity, just as servants and bodyguards would surround a human monarch. Each seraph covers its face with one pair of wings in order not to risk gazing directly upon Yahweh, flies with another pair, and covers its nakedness ("feet" here being a euphemism for genitalia) with a third pair.

Verse 3: This song of the seraphim has influenced the language of worship in both Jewish and Christian traditions as have few other biblical formulations. The threefold repetition of the word "holy" is, as mentioned above, a form of the Hebrew superlative: "supremely holy is Yahweh." The meaning of the word "hosts" is debated, meaning perhaps "peoples of the earth," "heavenly bodies in great numbers," or "divine beings in great numbers." In any event, its use here portrays Yahweh as a God who presides not just over the people of Israel, but over all creation and its inhabitants, a thought reaffirmed by the second line of the seraphim's song. The Hebrew word behind "glory" may also be translated something like "radiant presence" and was a term by which the Hebrews, especially the priests, referred to God's indwelling in their midst (Ezek. 1:28). The force of this statement is that Yahweh's presence is not limited just to the Jerusalem Temple but fills "the whole earth."

Some scholars have pointed out that, whereas the first line of the seraphim's song speaks of God's nature as such, the second refers to God's relationship to the world.

Verses 4–5: When Yahweh speaks, the very building reverberates due to the majesty of this voice, and the effect is no less dramatic upon the prophet. This vision of God's holiness, majesty, and purity paralyzes Isaiah with the knowledge of his and his people's sinfulness. The fact that the prophet speaks of human sin in terms of "unclean lips" may be by way of contrast to the song of verse 3, which the seraphim *are* pure enough to sing. Or it may be in anticipation of Yahweh's prophetic call which Isaiah feels himself unworthy to speak. Either way, his awareness of his unclean lips is described as a direct consequence of the vision his eyes have seen: "the King, Yahweh of hosts."

Verses 6–7: One of the cherubim, doubtless acting upon the command of Yahweh, responds to the prophet's sinful condition. The act of absolution (touching the lips with a burning coal) is accompanied by the words of absolution: "your guilt is taken away, and your sin forgiven." (One should compare Jer. 1:9, also a record of that prophet's call. Another similar passage is Ezek. 3:1–3 where the newly called prophet is given a scroll to eat, symbolizing the prophet's internalizing [and thus his authority to speak] the word of God.)

Verse 8: Finally, there is the call of Yahweh to Isaiah, the act to which verses 1–7 have been leading. It comes in the form of a question to which the prophet responds and assents to go. There follows in verses 9–13 the content of the message Yahweh wishes Isaiah to proclaim.

Many of the elements of Christian devotion are embodied in these verses: the majesty and "otherness" of God; God's moral purity, on the one hand, and the sinfulness of the prophet and the prophet's people, on the other; the gracious act of God which nullifies the destructive nature of human sin and which calls the prophet into a new relationship with God; finally, the awful responsibility of living and speaking God's word to one's own generation. It is little wonder that many individuals have found in this passage words which describe their own spiritual pilgrimage: adoration, confession, forgiveness, and service.

B. 7:10–17

This is one of the most difficult passages to interpret in all the prophetic literature of the Old Testament simply because, on the one hand, it has played an enormously influential role in helping to shape the Christological belief of the Christian church (based on Matt. 1:23) and, on the other hand, because the text as it stands seems to say something quite different from the traditional

Christian interpretation of it. Let us see, first, what we can make of the text and, then, how that corresponds to Matthew 1:23.

Verses 10–13: Isaiah speaks directly for Yahweh in verse 10, evidence of his own confidence in his prophetic calling. Ahaz, however, who is anything but confident, refuses the invitation to request a divine sign. The setting for all of chapter 7, it will be remembered, is the Syro-Ephraimitic War of 734, and in consequence of 7:1–9 Isaiah offers a divine sign to the king as evidence that Yahweh's promise of deliverance from the kings of Damascus and Samaria is genuine. Ahaz pretends to be hiding behind the ancient belief that it is sinful to attempt to manipulate God by asking for a private revelation (see Matt. 12:38–42), but the king is actually attempting to conceal his own doubts and fears. To this Isaiah responds that the Lord will give a sign, nevertheless, and because Ahaz will not accept from God a sign of redemption, the sign imposed upon him will be, as it turns out, one of judgment.

Verses 14–15: The sign is to be the birth of a son to a young woman. It should be noticed here that the Hebrew word is 'almah, which is used of any young post-pubescent woman, whether she is married or not. It is not the Hebrew word for "virgin," which is bethulah. Had Isaiah meant to describe a supernatural birth, there would have been little reason for him to choose 'almah. The child's name is to be Immanuel, Hebrew for "God with us." The "curds and honey" of verse 15 are the food of the people, the ordinary produce of the land (cf. Exod. 3:8 which describes the Promised Land as "flowing with milk and honey"). His identification with the people of God is symbolized in the promise that, when the child is mature, that is, old enough to make moral distinctions, "curds and honey" will be his food.

Verses 16–17: The promise of judgment comes to a climax in these verses. By the time of the child's maturity the two kings whom Ahaz fears so greatly, Rezin and Pekah, will be gone. However, a new devastation will be upon the land, that of the cruel and destructive Assyrian army. It is probable that the last phrase of verse 17, "the king of Assyria," is a gloss added by a later scribe who wished to make explicit that which is implied in the preceding part of the verse.

The important question about this passage is, of course, one of interpretation. What does it all mean? It seems clear that Isaiah has in mind an immediate application of his words. The sign is to be one for Ahaz himself (and his counselors—"you" of vs. 14 is plural), and it is evident from the above discussion that the sign is to be a portent of judgment. But just who is the young woman and who is God-With-Us?

In response to these questions, the answers which have been given by scholars have generally fallen into three groups each of which presents its own difficulties: (1) The woman is Ahaz' own wife and God-With-Us is to be Ahaz' son, perhaps his successor Hezekiah. The difficulty here is that Hezekiah is already six or seven years old in 734,[25] and we know of no other son of Ahaz who gains the kind of notice in the Old Testament which one would expect of God-With-Us, the fulfiller of this prophecy. (2) Another suggestion is that the woman is Isaiah's own wife, the "prophetess" of 8:3, and that God-With-Us receives a symbolic name, similar to those of his brothers A-Remnant-Shall-Return and The-Spoil-Speeds–The-Prey-Hastes. The problem with this suggestion is that The-Spoil-Speeds–The-Prey-Hastes is born at about this time (see 8:1–4), and it also seems highly unlikely that Isaiah would have his own son in mind without saying so. (3) A final suggestion is that the young woman and her son are *any* representative Judean mother and child of the time. According to this view, by the time a typical Judean mother's son who is born at this juncture grows to maturity, the threat from Damascus and Samaria will be gone, and this typical mother will name her son God-With-Us in thanksgiving. However, the celebration will be premature because Yahweh will then bring judgment in the person of the Assyrian king. The difficulty with this proposal is that Isaiah appears to have in mind a specific mother and child.[26]

It is likely that Jewish interpreters of this passage before the Christian era were as perplexed by the above problems as are modern commentators. What is certain is that the Jews, who translated the Old Testament into the Greek version (the Septuagint) in Egypt in the third and second centuries B.C., introduced another dimension into the passage when they rendered the Hebrew *'almah* by the Greek word *parthenos*, a term which clearly means "virgin." Thus there was added to this text the element of the miraculous birth of God-With-Us, and it was this emphasis which the author of the First Gospel applied to his narrative of the birth of Jesus (Matt. 1:23) by using it to reinforce his portrait of Jesus' miraculous birth of the Virgin Mary.

It should be emphasized that to understand the problems associated with the interpretation of Isaiah 7:10–17 and to realize the history of this text which led to Matthew's use of it in his Gospel is by no means a threat to faith. First of all, Matthew did not twist the text to make it say something it did not say.[27] The interpretation of 7:14 which considered it to be a promise of a miraculous birth from a virgin mother was already in his tradition. He simply applied that interpretation to his understanding of what had happened

---

[25] Hezekiah was twenty-five years old when he began to rule in 715 (2 Kings 18:2), meaning that he was born about 740.

[26] To further complicate the picture, Ahaz himself is referred to as God-With-Us in Isaiah 8:8.

[27] "Matthew" in this discussion means the author of the First Gospel, who may not have been the same person as the disciple of that name.

in Nazareth and Bethlehem. Moreover, the Christian doctrine of the Virgin Birth of our Lord by no means rests upon Matthew 1:23 alone, but is reported in other ways by both Matthew and Luke (who does not refer to Isa. 7:14) and is also affirmed by the early church. And so Isaiah's oracle comes to have a meaning which the prophet himself seems not to have anticipated, one which is not contradictory to his original intention, but which surpasses it. The sign of judgment to the house of David becomes by God's grace a sign of redemption to all Israel and to all humankind. He is not simply *called* Immanuel, he *is* Immanuel, God-With-Us, Jesus Christ. It is possible, therefore, both to appreciate the complexities involved in interpreting 7:14 and to profess with confidence "I believe in Jesus Christ, who was . . . born of the Virgin Mary." As it turns out Isaiah, by the grace of God, spoke more wisely than he knew.

C. 9:1–7

This passage is a hymn of great joy over the victory which the King of Judah has won or is about to win over his nation's enemies. Because of its similarities to certain of the Royal Psalms in the Old Testament (Pss. 2; 18; 20; 21; 45; and the like) and to similar coronation liturgies from other ancient Near Eastern peoples, many scholars believe that Isaiah wrote this hymn to celebrate the coronation of one of his contemporaries, either Ahaz or, more likely, Hezekiah. It contains all of the affirmations one would expect of such a hymn: rejoicing over the accession of the new monarch, confidence that he will be blessed by God, and faith in his ability to do God's will.

Verse 1: This is a statement of confidence that the lands of the Northern Kingdom, as well as those "beyond the Jordan" (perhaps Ammon, Edom, Moab), will be reclaimed by the new king. The political and military background of this verse fits well into the Middle and Late Ministries of Isaiah.

Verses 2–3: Those who have been oppressed will rejoice. Images upon which the prophet draws are those of the dawn (vs. 2) and the harvest (vs. 3).

Verses 4–5: The reason for the rejoicing of the people is that Yahweh has delivered them from their bondage (the repeated pronoun "his" in vs. 4 refers in a collective way to the liberated people). The reference to Midian recalls the great victory won by Gideon in Judges 6:33—7:25.

Verse 6: This refers to the enthronement of the new king. Some interpreters have reported a connection between the "child" and "son" here (parallel references to the same person) and the "son" of 7:14, and that view cannot be ruled out entirely. More likely, however, the connection should be seen with such a statement as Psalm 2:7 where the newly enthroned king is described as having been adopted or appropriated as the son of God at the time of his coronation. To this affirmation of the king's special relationship to God is then added a list of his royal titles, a practice common among many ancient

Near Eastern peoples.[28] The first of these, Wonderful Counselor, is a reference to the divinely endowed wisdom which the king will exercise. The second, Mighty God, is unusually bold in that the Hebrews, unlike the Egyptians and some others, did not consider their king to be divine.[29] They did, however, consider him to be a special representative of God in their midst. The third, Everlasting Father, reflects a confidence in the perpetuity of the Davidic covenant (cf. 2 Sam. 7:13), not in the immortality of the king. "Father" was a common term for king throughout the ancient Near East. The final royal title, Prince of Peace, refers, of course, to the peace which Yahweh will bring to pass through the instrumentality of the new king and which has already been celebrated in verses 1–5.

Verse 7: This is another, more extended reference to the perpetuity of the Davidic dynasty. Notice the occurrence of the words *mishpat* ("justice") and *ts^edhaqah* ("righteousness"). We have noticed on several occasions the prophetic concern for the moral qualities which these words represent, but they were also very much at home in the royal ideology of Judah, as in Psalms 18:20–24; 45:7; and 72:1–4.

At a very early time this passage was understood by the Church to be a prediction concerning Jesus Christ and is referred to in that light in Matthew 4:15–16. Although Isaiah may have had a more immediate application in mind for his prophetic hymn, the fact is that no flesh-and-blood king of the Davidic line ever lived up to its high ideals and goals. And the earliest Christians, therefore, realized that only in Jesus Christ could the sweeping claims of the prophet find their fulfillment. Only he in his incarnation is Mighty God. Only he is the true Prince of Peace (Luke 2:14). And so the "child" of verse 6 was understood in a new way as the Child of Bethlehem and the "kingdom" of verse 7 was seen to be that kingdom which he has established in the hearts of all men and women who love him. Today in many churches this passage (or parts of it) is read as the Old Testament lesson for Christmas Day and is sung repeatedly throughout Advent and Christmas seasons as a part of George Frederick Handel's *Messiah*. In hearing it in this setting, as on other occasions, we are reminded that the prophets of the Old Testament spoke God's truth far more profoundly than even they sometimes realized.

D. 11:1–9

This passage is similar to 9:1–7 in that it too is considered by many scholars to be a royal hymn to one of Isaiah's contemporaries, perhaps Hezekiah.

---

[28] Compare the royal titles given David in 2 Samuel 23:1: "the man who was raised on high, the anointed (messiah) of the God of Jacob, the sweet psalmist of Israel."

[29] Psalm 45:6 may be, depending on the manner in which one translates the Hebrew, another instance in which the king is called God.

With 7:10–17 and 9:1–7 it forms a trio of passages from Isaiah in which the church has discovered profound Christological meaning.

Verses 1–5: The "shoot from the stump of Jesse" is an offspring of the Davidic royal family, as Hezekiah was an offspring of Ahaz. The new king will receive the "spirit of Yahweh" as did David (1 Sam. 16:13), a spirit which will endow him with a number of qualities beginning with wisdom and ending with the fear of Yahweh. The concern of the Davidic king with justice for the poor and oppressed (vs. 4) is also referred to in the Royal Psalm 72:1–4, 12–14. *Mishpat* ("righteousness") and *ʾemunah* ("faithfulness") will characterize his rule.

Verses 6–9: Here is a highly picturesque portrait of the kingdom of peace which the Davidic king will establish through the agency of Yahweh. It is not a peace only among humans, but extends to all of creation, so that even wild beasts are tame and docile. Furthermore, this kingdom of peace will be characterized by a universal acknowledgement of the rule of Yahweh over the whole earth. That the focus of this kingdom is to be Jerusalem is symbolized by "my holy mountain," that is, Mount Zion (vs. 9).

For many of the same reasons which caused 9:1–7 to be applied to Jesus Christ by the early church, so this passage was similarly interpreted at a very early time in Christian history. The moving portrait of the Davidic king as the one who sustains the helpless and who establishes a reign of universal peace speaks of a hope which Christians believe is established only by Christ. That hope is fulfilled in a partial, anticipatory manner now in the hearts of those who love Christ and will be fully established by him in the end of time.

6
ZEPHANIAH

Date of Zephaniah's Work: sometime between 640 and 622 B.C.
Location: Jerusalem.
Central Theological Concept: Yahweh will destroy Jerusalem
and all of humankind. However, a remnant will be saved.
An Outline of the Book of Zephaniah will be found on p. 82.

There are few more moving evidences of the relation between prophecy in the Old Testament period and the events which took place in the prophets' world than the long "dark period" between Micah and Isaiah, on the one hand, and Zephaniah, on the other. For some three-quarters of a century prophetic activity among the Hebrews was dormant, at least as far as the biblical record indicates, and this span of time corresponds with one of the most politically and spiritually oppressive periods in the history of Judah. The Davidic throne was occupied for most of this time by Manasseh (687–642) whom the Old Testament remembers as the most evil king ever to rule from Jerusalem and the most long-lived! Appropriately our study of Zephaniah begins with a discussion of this blighted era and then turns to the prophet's reaction to it.

The Historical Context of Zephaniah's Work

As noted in the previous chapter, Hezekiah, in spite of his efforts to win the political independence of Judah, probably remained a vassal of the Assyrian monarch Sennacherib for the duration of his (Hezekiah's) lifetime. The energetic Assyrian ruler was murdered in 681, however, and his son Esarhaddon claimed his father's throne. But before he could secure it, it was necessary for the prince to fight off rival claims among his brothers each of whom wished to preside over the vast Assyrian empire. Emerging victorious from this civil strife, Esarhaddon determined to extend Assyrian power into Egypt which, through its continuing efforts to foster revolt among the states of Syria-Palestine, constituted an ongoing danger to Assyria's western defenses. After encountering some reverses, the Assyrian army defeated the forces of Pharaoh Taharqa and occupied Lower Egypt. The Egyptians soon attempted to repulse the Assyrians, however, and in 669 Esarhaddon found it necessary to launch a new campaign against the kingdom of the Nile. On his way to Egypt Esarhaddon died and the successful completion of the campaign was left to his son and successor, Ashurbanipal, who in 663 destroyed the ancient city of Thebes, the political and cultural heart of the Egyptian nation.

Assyria was now at the height of its military power and this zenith coincided almost exactly with the midpoint of the reign of Judean King Manasseh. Manasseh had ascended the throne of David following the death of his father Hezekiah in 687 and it is not surprising that, with Assyrian power continuing to rise, he remained in the state of vassalage to that nation which he had inherited from his father. What may be surprising, however, is that he seems to have done so willingly and, unlike Hezekiah who was responsible both for spiritual reforms within his kingdom and for efforts to win its freedom, it seems that Manasseh was interested in neither. It was his efforts to overturn the spiritual advances for which his father had worked which caused the deuteronomistic historians to remember him as the worst descendant of David who ever lived (2 Kings 23:26–27 blames Manasseh for the ultimate destruction of Jerusalem some half century after his death).

The Old Testament record of Manasseh's reign is told in 2 Kings 21:1–18. Here we read of acts of sacrilege which included the building of altars to alien deities (many of which Hezekiah had previously torn down) even in the Jerusalem Temple itself. He introduced the worship of Mesopotamian astral deities and, what is more, "he burned his son as an offering, and practiced soothsaying and augury, and dealt with mediums and with wizards" (vs. 6). In part, these acts of religious apostasy may have been accomplished to please Manasseh's Assyrian masters, but he seems to have pursued these tasks with an energy which even his subservience to Sennacherib and Esarhaddon did not require. And in addition to his religious heterodoxy Manasseh committed murder on a grand scale (vs. 16). Just who the victims of his bloody purges may have been we have no idea, but they may have included his political as well as spiritual enemies, perhaps persons who tried to resist his reactionary policies. As noted in the previous chapter, one ancient story (not reported in the Old Testament) is that the prophet Isaiah was killed in these massacres.

Manasseh's influence lived on even after his death. In 642 he died and was succeeded by his son Amon who reigned for only two years. Amon, whose reign is described in 2 Kings 21:19–26 as similar to that of his father, was murdered by a group of palace conspirators who themselves were then executed by "the people of the land" (vs. 24). Amon's son Josiah, a boy of eight, was placed on the throne, but because of his tender years he was incapable of strong action for the moment. In time, as we will see, Josiah became the moving force behind a vigorous reformation in Judah's spiritual and political life, but during his youth the long shadow of his grandfather continued to be cast over the land.

Sometime during this period when Josiah was still young, a group of savage warriors fought their way across the horizon of Judah's world and left behind a memory of terror which was to persist for centuries. These were the Scythians and, while little is actually known about them, they seem to have come out of the Caucasus region intent upon enriching themselves by conquest and war, not unlike the Vikings of a later era. They appear to have struck an alliance with the Assyrians, so that the Scythians' attention was turned away from Mesopotamia and toward the west, that is, Syria and Palestine. Sweeping down the coastal plain, they overran the old Philistine cities and threatened Egypt until Pharaoh Psammetichus I paid them a large ransom to turn back. They were eventually defeated by the Medes, a group of hardy people who lived in the area of present-day Iran, but not before they sent shudders of terror through all of Syria and Palestine. So memorable was the Scythian horror that Paul, writing some seven hundred years later, uses the word "Scythian" as a synonym for barbarity (Col. 3:11).

The Prophet and the Book

The information we are given about Zephaniah, the individual, is very sparse. Zephaniah 1:1, a brief editorial introduction to the book, tells that he was active during the reign of King Josiah (640–609). On the basis of the character of the contents of the book we would judge that Zephaniah's prophetic ministry therefore took place sometime before the decisive reformation of 621, for the social and spiritual conditions suggested in this literature are more consistent with the period of Josiah's reign before rather than after that reformation. The further information is given that Zephaniah was a fourth-generation descendant of Hezekiah. We cannot be certain if this is a reference to King Hezekiah or to some common citizen who happened to have the same name, but if the king is intended, it means that Zephaniah was himself a member of the Davidic royal family.

Zephaniah was apparently a citizen of Jerusalem, for he refers to several places within the city (1:10–11). What is more, he is not averse to criticizing the royal administration (1:8; 3:3), although he does not condemn it as being an evidence of the nation's sin in the sense in which Hosea had done. On the other hand, he does not, like Isaiah, view it as a particularly beneficial force in the nation's life. Nor is he, as were some of his prophetic predecessors, motivated by a special concern for the poor and powerless, although he does identify *mishpat* ("commands"), *tsedheq* ("righeousness"), and *ʿanawah* ("humility") as moral ideals (2:3). On the basis of his concern for the purity of the cult, some have felt that he may have been a priest, although there is no confirmation of this fact in the book of Zephaniah. And some scholars have suggested that he may have been associated with those who were responsible for young Josiah's training, an education which would bear fruit in the great reformation of 621.

The book of Zephaniah is our only source of knowledge about the prophet. It is very brief, and because it contains almost no references to the events of the prophet's day, its passages are difficult to date with precision and to relate to contemporary events. The traditional interpretation of Zephaniah's ministry is that he was compelled into the prophetic role by the invasion of the Scythians whom he saw as the destructive agency which Yahweh was bringing upon Judah and its neighbors for their sinful ways. The primary evidence for this is the character of 1:10–18, which seems to describe the kind of carnage inflicted by the Scythians (1:18 has often been interpreted as a reference to the successful effort of Pharaoh Psammetichus I to bribe the Scythians into turning away from Egypt). Yet it must be admitted that the Scythians themselves are never named and, therefore, that their role in energizing the prophetic voice of Zephaniah is uncertain.

There are four major divisions in the book of Zephaniah:

> A. Oracles concerning the destruction of Jerusalem: 1:1—2:4.
> B. Oracles concerning the destruction of the nations: 2:5–15.
> C. An oracle on the intransigence of Jerusalem: 3:1–8.
> D. Oracles concerning the remnant which will be restored:
> 3:9–20.

The first section of the book, 1:1—2:4, focuses primarily upon Jerusalem although its concern extends to all humankind, indeed all of creation (1:3). The message is plain and, for the most part, unequivocal. Because of the sinfulness of the people, Yahweh is going to destroy Judah and all of the earth. It is easy to see how such a terrible experience as the Scythian invasion could have inspired this view of a universal holocaust, yet in the prophet's mind the compelling force behind what is about to happen is not some human agency (Scythian or whatever) but the anger of Yahweh over the people's continued evil. Zephaniah 1:2–3 sounds, in its description of the destruction Yahweh is going to bring about, very much like God's decision to destroy the earth by means of the flood (Gen. 6:7).

To some degree the nature of the people's evil is detailed. "Idolatrous priests" (of which there were many in the days of Manasseh, Amon, and young Josiah) are singled out (1:4). They are

"those who bow down on the roofs
to the host of the heavens;
those who bow down and swear to Yahweh
and yet swear by Milcom;
those who have turned back from following Yahweh,
who do not seek Yahweh or inquire of him." (1:5–6)

Punishment is also going to be inflicted upon those members of the royal court who "array themselves in foreign attire" (and perhaps otherwise ape the Assyrians), who leap "over the threshold" (some type of ritual magic), and who perpetrate in the royal palace itself "violence and fraud" (1:8–9).

Like the later Diogenes with his lantern searching for an honest person, so Yahweh is portrayed by Zephaniah as one who, with a lamp, ferrets out the wicked for punishment (1:12, this verse has occasioned the traditional portrait of Zephaniah, found, for example, in medieval stained-glass windows, as a man with a lamp). The "Day of Yahweh" is approaching fast (1:7, 14). It will not be a day of celebration, as many people expect, but it will be a day of wholesale destruction.

A day of wrath is that day,
a day of distress and anguish,
a day of ruin and devastation,
a day of darkness and gloom,
a day of clouds and thick darkness,
a day of trumpet blast and battle cry. (1:15–16)

Amos had struck the same chord (Amos 5:18–20, see pp. 21–22), but the fierce energy with which Zephaniah emphasizes this theme of the Day of Yahweh surpasses even that of the prophet who probably influenced him.

This section is not totally negative, however. Zephaniah 2:1–4 indicates that there is still time for repentance. The destructive wrath of Yahweh will not be turned back, but those who approach Yahweh on the basis of *mishpat* ("commands"), *tsedheq* ("righteousness") and *'anawah* ("humility") may be spared the awful devastation (2:3). In his use of these words Zephaniah demonstrates his knowledge of and indebtedness to the prophetic tradition which had developed before him.

In the second section within the book, 2:5–15, the sphere of the prophet's concern is extended to Judah's neighbors (2:4 seems to be a kind of bridge between this section and the preceding one). In 2:5–7 the Philistines are specified as the object of Yahweh's wrath. Their towns will be leveled to the extent that they will become

meadows for shepherds
and folds for flocks. (2:6)

They will then be occupied by "the remnant of the house of Judah" which Yahweh will restore after the devastation. This concept of the remnant, with which we are already familiar from the oracles of Isaiah, is developed more fully in the final section of the book.

Two Transjordanian peoples, the Moabites and the Ammonites, are targeted next (2:8–11). Their offense is that "they scoffed and boasted against the people of Yahweh of hosts" (2:10). They also will be destroyed and their lands occupied by the remnant of Judah (vs. 9). Some scholars feel that this section is from a time later than Zephaniah.

Assyria, now at the height of its powers, will also be devastated (2:13–15).[30] It would doubtless have been difficult for some in Zephaniah's time to believe it, but the capital city of this proud nation, Nineveh, will be laid low.

> Herds shall lie down in the midst of her,
>   all the beasts of the field;
> the vulture and the hedgehog
>   shall lodge in her capitals;
> the owl shall hoot in the window,
>   the raven croak on the threshold;
>
> . . .
>
> Every one who passes by her
>   hisses and shakes his fist. (2:14–15)

The third section, 3:1–8, returns our attention to the Jerusalem community once more. Every level of the nation's leadership is corrupt, including the officials of the royal administration, the judges, the priests, and the prophets (3:4). The *mishpat* of Yahweh is contrasted with the "unjust" character of the nation (vs. 5). Not even the example of the devastation of the surrounding nations has been sufficient to call Judah back from its sinful ways (vss. 6–7). Therefore, destruction, which is terrible in its universal application to all the earth, will come (vs. 8).

The final section, 3:9–20, sings in a lyrical manner of the salvation of the remnant, and the contrast in tone between this section and those which have preceded is obvious. The section begins with a brief statement about the universal nature of Yahweh's salvation (vss. 9–10), but the thought quickly turns to the salvation of the remnant of Judah, namely, those within the nation who are "humble and lowly" (vs. 12).

> "they shall do no wrong
>   and utter no lies,
> nor shall there be found in their mouth
>   a deceitful tongue." (3:13)

They will dwell in perfect security under the protection of Yahweh (vs. 13).

The final part of this section, verses 14–20, is very similar in content and

---

[30] Many scholars feel that the brief reference to Ethiopia in 2:12 is a fragment of a longer oracle against that people who were closely allied with the Egyptians.

mood to the literature associated with the Second Isaiah (Isa. 40—55), and some scholars have suggested that it, or perhaps all of 3:9–20, therefore comes from the time near the Jerusalem restoration (c. 538). That may indeed be true, especially when we consider that the book of Zephaniah, like other prophetic literature in the Old Testament, was surely subjected to the editorial influences of later writers and scribes who kept the prophetic tradition alive.

The Theology of Zephaniah

The task of distinguishing between the prophet's own words and those of later editors is much more difficult with regard to this material than with some other prophetic materials. Therefore, we will discuss the theology of the book of Zephaniah as a canonical unity, realizing at the same time that other persons than the prophet himself have helped to shape that theology.

A. *A righteous God is offended by human sin.* Zephaniah does not go to pains to portray the character of Israel's God, but it is clear that his faith is grounded in a God who is morally responsible and who demands moral integrity and spiritual purity from the people. The heterodox syncretism which Manasseh had imposed upon Judah and which was still a feature of life during Josiah's youth comes in, as we have seen, for special censure. Yet it is wrong to think that Zephaniah's concern is limited to cultic matters. *Mishpat* ("commands"), *tsedheq* ("righeousness"), and *'anawah* ("humility") are identified as the ideals by which the saved remnant are to be identified (2:3). This is in accord with the character of Yahweh who is righteous (*tsadiq*) and who each morning "shows forth his *mishpat*" ("justice," 3:5). In his description of the ideal society which Yahweh will create beyond the judgment, there will be a universal acknowledgement of Yahweh's rule (3:9) and life will be characterized by humility, integrity, and truthfulness (3:12–13). It is the current absence of these qualities which angers and offends Yahweh.

B. *Yahweh will destroy all creation.* As we have observed, Zephaniah's primary concern is with Judah, but in his eyes Yahweh's judgment will extend to all creation. Foreign nations will be destroyed because of their godlessness (2:5–15), and all living creatures will cease to exist.

> "I will utterly sweep away everything
>   from the face of the earth," says Yahweh.
> I will sweep away man and beast;
>   I will sweep away the birds of the air
>   and the fish of the sea.
> I will overthrow the wicked;

> I will cut off mankind
> from the face of the earth," says Yahweh. (1:2–3)

This occurrence is the Day of Yahweh, and to that day reference is made time and again (1:7, 10, 12, 14; 2:2; 3:8, 9, 11,16). In some places it seems, as with Amos, that the Day of Yahweh is near at hand (1:14), whereas at other times it seems to be somewhere in the distance (3:8). It is this latter characteristic of the Day of Yahweh which has caused the book of Zephaniah to be considered by some as forming part of the transition in the Old Testament from prophecy to apocalyptic.

The portrait here of the total destruction of life upon earth has spoken forcefully to the people of God in times of great disaster, such as during the Middle Ages when war, famine, and disease frequently wiped out entire populations. The thirteenth century (A.D.) poem, *Dies Irae*, attributed (probably erroneously) to Thomas of Celano but doubtless inspired by Zephaniah's description of the Day of Yahweh, was enormously popular in medieval Europe and was incorporated into the Mass for the Dead.

> Day of wrath! O day of mourning!
> See fulfilled the prophets' warning,
> Heaven and earth in ashes burning!
>
> Death is struck and nature quaking,
> All creation is awaking,
> To its judge an answer making.[31]

C. *A remnant of the Jerusalem community will be restored to its land and will preside over a renewed humankind.* How this concept is to be reconciled to that of the destruction of all living creatures is not clear and is one of the problems which cause scholars to detect more than one hand at work in the book of Zephaniah. The idea of the remnant who may be saved is suggested in 2:3 where those who are righteous and humble may perhaps be hidden from Yahweh's wrath on the awful day. It is referred to again in 2:7, 9 where the remnant is depicted as inheriting the lands of Judah's evil neighbors after the judgment has taken place. It is most fully discussed, however, in 3:9–20 where the remnant will preside over a humankind which acknowledges Yahweh (vss. 9–10). This remnant will dwell in safety and in a golden age will be admired by all the peoples of the earth (3:20).

---

[31] Translated by W. J. Irons and quoted from Charles L. Taylor, Jr. *The Interpreters' Bible.* New York: Abingdon, 1966, vol. 6, p. 1012.

7
NAHUM

Date of Nahum's Work: c. 712 B.C.
Location: Unknown, but probably Jerusalem.
Central Theological Concept: Yahweh will destroy Nineveh
    because of its sin.
An Outline of the Book of Nahum will be found on p. 89.

The Historical Context of Nahum's Work

In our discussion of the historical context of Zephaniah's work we noticed how the maximum extent of Assyrian power was achieved during the final years of Esarhaddon and the early years of his son Ashurbanipal (668–627). This latter king's conquest of Egypt and his destruction of Thebes in 663 meant that Assyrian power extended from the high Iranian plateau northeast of the Tigris River to Upper Egypt, an expanse of a thousand miles. In spite of this outward appearance of power, however, the Assyrian Empire suffered a serious weakness in the form of the extreme hatred with which many of Assyria's vassal states viewed their master. To some extent such an emotion could be expected, but the intensity of the hatred which many peoples in Syria-Palestine and elsewhere felt for their Assyrian overlords seems unusually strong, perhaps occasioned by what appears to be the Assyrians' well-earned reputation for cruelty. The Assyrians themselves made no secret of their custom of inflicting unnecessary pain upon their subjects, indeed they may have gone out of their way to promote such a reputation for cruelty in order to foster terror, and thus submission, among those populations whom they wished to rule. Assyrian reliefs carved into rock portray prisoners impaled upon stakes outside the walls of the besieged Judean city of Lachish. Another relief depicts a prisoner, pinioned face down in a spread-eagle position, being skinned alive by Assyrian torturers. In fairness to the Assyrians it should be remembered that they had no monopoly on cruelty, as the Old

Testament attests,[32] but they apparently went to great lengths to use terror as an instrument of policy, both domestic and foreign.

The hatred which this cruelty inspired was apparently a threat to the Assyrians even during the period of their greatest military strength. The Medes who lived on the Iranian plateau were a constant source of trouble along Assyria's northeastern frontier. On one occasion Esarhaddon made a treaty with the Scythians to help keep the Medes at bay, an alliance sealed by the gift of his daughter in marriage to the Scythian ruler. To the south, not even the destruction of Thebes quenched the Egyptian thirst for freedom, while nearer home the Babylonians chafed under the domination of the Assyrians.

Because the Assyrian historical records are sketchy, no one knows the precise details of Ashurbanipal's reign of more than forty years, but this administration which began with such strength ended with the virtual collapse of the Assyrian Empire. Undoubtedly the pent-up anger of Assyria's subjects played a major role in the kindgom's decline, and internal feuding among Assyrian officials may have played another. What we do know is that in 626 a Babylonian prince, Nabopolassar, raised an army and evicted the Assyrians from his home. Ashurbanipal had died the previous year, and his death may have been a silent signal to the subject peoples of the empire that the time for rebellion had come. In 612 the Babylonians were joined by the Medes and the Scythians, and a combined force of these allies fell upon Assyria's capital, Nineveh, routed the Assyrian forces there, and sacked the city. The Greek historian Xenophon says that the destruction of Nineveh coincided with a flooding of the Tigris River, on whose banks the city lay, a natural calamity which added to the human carnage all around. What remained of the Assyrian army fled westward to the city of Haran, an Assyrian provincial capital, and the midpoint of the journey of Abraham many years before (Gen. 11:31).

The Prophet and the Book

Absolutely nothing is known about Nahum the man other than the fact that he was a native of Elkosh (1:1). Even the location of that village is uncertain, although the most likely identification is somewhere in the Judean countryside. There is nothing in the material associated with Nahum which gives the slightest clue to the setting in which the prophet worked, but Jerusalem is generally considered to be the most likely locale for his activity. Unlike other prophetic figures, neither Nahum's ancestry nor his occupation

---

[32]See Amos 1.

is disclosed. It does seem likely, however, that his words were spoken just before the fall of Nineveh in 612.

The book of Nahum is composed of two major divisions:

A. An acrostic poem: 1:1–9.
B. A longer poem: 1:10—3:19.

Into the second section have been inserted a number of editorial notes which, in some cases, interrupt the literary and conceptual "flow" of the poem (1:12–13, 15 [see Isa. 52:7], 2:2).

The first section, 1:1–10, is a fragment of what appears to have once been a longer literary unit. The reason for this conclusion is that, whereas the poem is an alphabetic acrostic, only the first twelve (out of a possible twenty-two) letters of the Hebrew alphabet are represented. What is more, the alphabetical sequence is disturbed at several points in such a manner as to cause it to appear that the poem has suffered some structural damage in the process of transmission. Because this poetic fragment makes no direct reference to Nineveh (as does the longer poem) some scholars are of the opinion that it is from another source than the longer poem and was placed before it in the form of an introduction.

The theme of the acrostic poem is that a righteous God will destroy the wicked. Yahweh is "jealous," "avenging," and "wrathful" (1:2). This anger is by no means capricious (1:3), and for those who love Yahweh, there is still "a stronghold in the day of trouble" (1:7). But this Yahweh of unlimited power will crush those who offer resistance.

> But with an overflowing flood
>> he will make a full end of his adversaries,
>> and will pursue his enemies into darkness. (1:8)

The longer poem, 1:10—3:19, utilizes the general description of the avenging wrath of Yahweh and applies it in a specific way to the Assyrian Empire, or more precisely, to the Assyrian capital city of Nineveh. In the first part (2:1–9) there is an account of the assault upon Nineveh by the combined forces of Babylonians, Medes, and Scythians (although these attackers are not mentioned by name). The prophet mocks the orders which the Assyrian commanders bark out to their men:

> Man the ramparts;
> watch the road;
>> gird your loins;
>> collect all your strength. (2:1)

But it is of no use, for Yahweh has determined the fall of the city (the statement, "Behold, I am against you, says Yahweh of hosts" occurs twice: 2:13; 3:5).

> The river gates are opened,
>   the palace is in dismay;
> its mistress is stripped, she is carried off,
>   her maidens lamenting,
> moaning like doves,
>   and beating their breasts.
> Nineveh is like a pool
>   whose waters run away.
> "Halt! halt!" they cry;
>   but none turns back.
> Plunder the silver,
>   plunder the gold!
> There is no end of treasure,
>   or wealth of every precious thing. (2:6–9)

The references to "pool" and "waters" may reflect the flooding of the Tigris which Xenophon reports.

Yahweh has now turned the tables on Nineveh and the one who had caused so much suffering and terror has become the laughingstock of former victims.

> . . . [I] will lift up your skirts over your face;
> and I will let nations look on your nakedness
>   and kingdoms on your shame. (3:5)

Nineveh has no friends among the human family, and those who have suffered at its hand now rejoice that their tormentor has fallen.

> There is no assuaging your hurt,
>   your wound is grievous.
> All who hear the news of you
>   clap their hands over you.
> For upon whom has not come
>   your unceasing evil? (3:19)

The Theology of Nahum

There is only one basic theological postulate in the prophecy of Nahum and that is that *a righteous God stands in judgment upon and will destroy human evil*. The Old Testament, unlike much modern thought, does not make a significant distinction between the reality of evil and those who commit that evil, a fact which is the occasion for such Old Testament literature as the book of Nahum. God will destroy humans who commit evil (in spite of the fact that anger is not God's basic attitude toward humanity: 1:3, 7) because that is the most visible evidence of God's hatred of evil. The prophet's personal hatred of Assyria, when joined to this fundamental theological conviction, results in his proclamation of the downfall of that city by the hand of God.

Many who have read the book of Nahum have wondered why there is no strong word of grace here to balance the strong word of judgment. The answer is that the prophet, speaking under the influence of the events of his time (cf. modern anger at the Nazis over the horrors of the concentration camps), is not immediately concerned with grace. From a Christian perspective we know that Nahum has not spoken the last word, for we remember Jesus' command that we love our enemies (Matt. 5:44). The Jewish tradition also knew that there was an important statement about God's compassion which must be placed alongside such a statement as this about God's wrath (cf. the book of Jonah, which will be discussed later). Nevertheless, Nahum has declared an important, if partial, truth about the God of Israel and the Father of Jesus Christ. Yahweh's anger will not stand idle while evil runs roughshod over the humanity which Yahweh has created and loves. In order to realize the importance of Nahum's single theological affirmation, one need only consider how distressing and hopeless the human condition would be if that affirmation were not true.

8
HABAKKUK

Date of Habakkuk's Work: c. 610–600 B.C.
Location: unknown, but probably Jerusalem.
Central Theological Concept: God is still in control of this
   world in spite of the apparent triumph of evil.
An Outline of the Book of Habakkuk will be found on pp. 94–
   95.

The Historical Context of Habakkuk's Work

The Assyrian Empire, whose destruction had been celebrated by Nahum, had inflicted such cruelty and suffering upon its conquered subjects that almost any change in the political fortunes of the ancient Near East would have been welcomed by its inhabitants, including the Judeans. At the time of the fall of Nineveh in 612 the Davidic king who ruled in Jerusalem was Josiah (640–609), grandson of the infamous Manasseh, who had been placed upon the throne as a tender boy of eight. Josiah was to prove to be as good a king as Manasseh had been evil, and he had already seized the opportunity offered by the death of the Assyrian king Asshurbanipal (627) and by the rebellion of the Babylonian prince Nabopolassar (626) to begin to reassert his nation's independence. According to 2 Chronicles 34:6–7 Josiah reclaimed important cities in the Northern Kingdom, a move doubtless made possible by the withdrawal of Assyrian forces for duty nearer home. The statement is also made (2 Chron. 34:3–5) that at this same time Josiah began to reform the practices of worship in the Jerusalem Temple and elsewhere in the land, practices which were still tainted with the idolatry his grandfather and father had promoted.

In 621 Josiah had inaugurated even more sweeping reforms in public worship, a reformation inspired by the discovery in the Temple of the book of Deuteronomy, as described in 2 Kings 22—23. At this time Josiah attempted to confine the worship of God to the Jerusalem Temple by suppressing the activities of the lesser shrines throughout the land, shrines where idolatrous practices were especially well-entrenched. The Temple itself was purified and rededicated, and the people were encouraged to worship God joyfully and with singleness of heart. It was under the impetus of this reformation that the Deuteronomistic History was written, or at least begun, a history of Israel in the Land of Promise which is contained in our present biblical books of Joshua, Judges, Samuel, and Kings.

According to the spiritual ideals of the book of Deuteronomy and of the Josianic Reformation, the king and people who obeyed and worshiped God in pure ways would prosper (read the deuteronomistic assessment of good King Hezekiah in 2 Kings 18:1–7), while the king and people who disobeyed God would suffer (cf. the assessment of evil Manasseh in 2 Kings 21:1–16). The fall of Nineveh in 612 and the further opportunity this provided godly Josiah to strengthen the independence of his nation seemed an important confirmation of this set of beliefs.

Imagine the shock when in 609 King Josiah was killed in battle with the Egyptians at Megiddo and his nation forced once more to recognize the supremacy of an invader. The Egyptians under Pharaoh Necho were on their way to assist the last Assyrian remnant which had fled from Nineveh and taken refuge in the Assyrian provincial center of Haran. The Egyptians were not motivated by any special love for the Assyrians, who had treated Egypt harshly during the reigns of Kings Esarhaddon and Ashurbanipal, but by the hope that they might seize the lands of Syria-Palestine which they had ruled many centuries before and which now appeared ripe for the plucking. Josiah correctly interpreted the Egyptian intentions and set out to frustrate their advance, but the results of his effort were fatal.

Necho installed his own puppet upon Judah's throne, a son of Josiah named Jehoiakim, and then proceeded northward to stake his claim to the lands at least as far as the Euphrates River. The Babylonians, however, had other ideas. Nabopolassar had apparently grown ill, for the Babylonian army was now commanded by his son, the vigorous prince Nebuchadrezzar (also spelled Nebuchadnezzar in the Old Testament). In a decisive battle in 605 at Carchemish on the banks of the Euphrates, the Babylonians so thoroughly defeated the Egyptians that Necho's forces seem to have retreated back to Egypt without offering further resistance to the Babylonians.

> And the king of Egypt did not come again out of his land, for the king of Babylon had taken all that belonged to the king of Egypt from the Brook of Egypt to the river Euphrates. (2 Kings 24:7)

At some undetermined time shortly after the Battle of Carchemish (there is no record, biblical or otherwise, of the event) the Babylonian army claimed Jerusalem and all Judah. Jehoiakim, the Egyptian vassal, was forced to acknowledge a new master and costly Judean tribute was now sent off to Babylon.

The spiritual cost of this terrible reversal was even greater, however, and men and women began to probe their hearts to find answers to their searching questions. How could God allow such a terrible thing to happen? If the reformation ideals of good King Josiah had been correct, God should have allowed the king and the nation to prosper. Instead, the king had been killed and the nation subjected to new foreign masters. Why should this be so? Why should the wicked Babylonians, whose evils were only slightly less than those of the Assyrians, be allowed to triumph while good Judah had been trampled in the dust?

The problem of the apparent victory of evil in a world presided over by a good and righteous God is one with which men and women of faith have wrestled from the earliest times. In late sixth-century Judah, however, this problem surfaced with a new urgency, and it is the problem which the book of Habakkuk addresses.

The Prophet and the Book

The Old Testament has provided its readers with no direct information about the prophet Habakkuk other than his name. Even this name has a quality of mystery about it, for it is related to no known Hebrew word and appears to derive from an Akkadian plant name. A much later piece of Jewish literature found in the Septuagint, Bel and the Dragon, identifies Habakkuk as a Levitical priest, and modern scholars who have noted a certain liturgical quality in the book of Habakkuk are inclined to feel that this priestly identification is correct. We have no way of knowing the circumstances under which the oracles of Habakkuk were delivered, but if he was indeed a cultic prophet attached to the Jerusalem Temple, then the oracles may have been uttered initially in connection with the Temple services of worship. The only direct evidence for dating the work of Habakkuk is the reference to "the Chaldeans" in 1:6,[33] thus placing his activity in the context of those years near the close of the seventh century.

The book of Habakkuk displays the following outline:

    A. The prophet's questions and Yahweh's replies: 1:1—2:5.
       1. First question: 1:1–4.
       2. First reply: 1:5–11.
       3. Second question: 1:12–17.
       4. Second reply: 2:1–5.

---

[33] The Neo-Babylonians of Nebuchadrezzar, unlike the earlier Babylonians in the time of Hammurabi (eighteenth century B.C.), were referred to as Chaldeans after the name of the area in southern Mesopotamia from which the ruling classes had come.

B. A series of five woes: 2:6–20.

C. A psalm of praise: 3:1–19.

The first section, 1:1—2:5, is composed of two passages in which the prophet questions Yahweh's ways in dealing with the people, and each of these passages is followed by a response from Yahweh.

> O Yahweh, how long shall I cry for help,
> and thou wilt not hear? (1:2)

This complaint is also found upon the lips of the psalmist (13:1) and comprises one of the several reasons for concluding that this material was used in the public worship of God. The first question asks, in essence, why does a righteous God tolerate the powerful and the unrighteous heathens and allow them to oppress God's own righteous people? Habakkuk's concern here embraces what is now a traditional indictment: *tsedheq* ("righteousness") and *mishpat* ("justice") are being suppressed, yet the culpable party is not Israel (as with Amos and others), but *Yahweh*:

> So the law is slacked
> and *mishpat* never goes forth.
> For the wicked surround the righteous,
> so *mishpat* goes forth perverted. (1:4)

The reply to the first question, 1:5–11, takes the form of a simple affirmation by Yahweh that, in spite of appearances, human events are not out of control but are being shaped and determined by the God of Israel. Interestingly, there is no "thus says Yahweh" or other familiar prophetic formula which announces this passage as an oracle from God. Rather, there is the use of the first person pronoun in verses 5 and 6 which signifies that the words are those of Yahweh: "I am doing a work," "I am rousing the Chaldeans." In other words, that which is taking place in Israel's world is according to the design of God who has chosen to use the Babylonians as a powerful instrument of destruction. What follows is a description of the Babylonians which not only portrays their cruelty (vs. 7) and their military might (vss. 8–10), but even acknowledges their godlessness (vs. 11).

The second question by the prophet, 1:12–17, seems designed to probe the preceding answer which, in the mind of the prophet, has raised as many problems as it has solved. Yahweh is a God of uncompromising justice, a Rock (vs. 12) who is

> . . . of purer eyes than to behold evil
> and canst not look on wrong. (1:13)

How can such a God acquiesce in the murderous activities of such a terrible people, much less call them as designated agents? It is interesting that the reference to the nets of the evil Babylonians (vs. 15) has been confirmed by archaeology which has discovered carvings and paintings from both Mesopotamia and Egypt in which prisoners of war are shown gathered up into large nets.

The second reply by Yahweh, 2:1–5, begins with a statement by the prophet that he will station himself in a familiar retreat (the "tower" of 2:1) and will not budge until Yahweh has provided him with an answer to his complaint. That answer comes in the form of a vision (vs. 2) in which the prophet is commanded to write Yahweh's answer in such large characters that even a speeding runner (perhaps one fleeing from the approaching Babylonians) may read it. It is not an easy and superficial answer, for so profound a question requires an answer whose truth may not be obvious for some time. Yet the answer is here, and those who love Yahweh must exercise patience in coming to an understanding of it (vs. 3). The answer is:

> "Behold, he whose soul is not upright in him shall fail,
>   but the righteous shall live by his faith." (2:4)

Yahweh's ways are true, in spite of the terrible nature of present circumstances. And those men and women who wish to find justice and who wish to apprehend Yahweh will do so in their own hearts.

The second major section, 2:6–20, is a series of five woes directed against the Babylonians. The first woe (vss. 6–8) denounces the Chaldeans for their policy of robbing the nations which they conquer. Ultimately the tables will be turned and they themselves will be robbed and plundered (vs. 8).

The second woe (vss. 9–11) is aimed at the policy of using the plunder to strengthen the conqueror's own nation ("his house," vs. 9). Even the stone and the wood with which the fortifications are built will convict the conqueror (vs. 11).

The third woe (vss. 12–14) indicts Nebuchadrezzar's nation for its cruelty and bloodshed and lifts up a higher vision of a world of peace and godliness. Verse 14 is a quotation from Isaiah 11:9.

The fourth woe (vss. 15–17) uses the image of a drunken and crazed individual to portray the foolishness and irresponsibility of Babylon. In the end Babylon will drink from another cup, that of Yahweh's anger (vs. 16).

The fifth woe (vs. 19)[34] denounces Babylon's idolatrous worship of Marduk, a denunciation which comes to full flower in the Second Isaiah (Isa. 44:9–20). The woes are concluded by a statement (vs. 20) concerning the holiness of Yahweh, doubtless intended to contrast the authenticity of the worship of Yahweh with the folly of idolatry.

The third major section is the psalm of chapter 3. Many years ago some

---

[34] Verse 18 seems to be an editorial addition to the fifth woe.

scholars suggested that this psalm might be a later addition to the text of the book of Habakkuk, a hypothesis which has been confirmed by the discovery of the Habakkuk Commentary among the Dead Sea Scrolls from which this entire psalm is missing. It is a celebration of the power of Yahweh and a rededication on the part of the worshiper. Yahweh is portrayed as a mighty and destructive presence coming out of the desert (vss. 2–7). The imagery of Yahweh's victory over the forces of chaos at the time of creation is recalled (vss. 8–15; cf. Isa. 51:9–10). No matter how blighted human life may become, the psalmist will keep faith with Yahweh, rejoicing and celebrating Yahweh's presence in human life (vss. 16–19). It may have been this latter emphasis, as well as the anticipation of vengeance upon Israel's invaders (vss. 13–14) which caused this psalm to be attached to the book of Habakkuk.

The Theology of the Book of Habakkuk

As we have already observed, the problem of (apparently) triumphant evil in a world presided over by a just God is the central theological focus of the book of Habakkuk. The book of Job is perhaps that part of the Old Testament which we most often associate with the question of theodicy (see esp. Job 21), but other parts of the Bible struggle with the same issue (e.g., John 9:1–3). There is even a sense in which Jesus' question from the cross, "My God, my God, why hast thou forsaken me?" (Matt. 27:46, a quotation of Ps. 22:1), addresses this same problem of faith. The long history of concern over this matter should suggest to us that there is no facile answer, for if there were, it would have been forthcoming at a very early time. Habakkuk's courage in raising the question in the first place and the answers which his oracles provide should be seen as a part of the overarching effort of writers in both Testaments to shed light in what is frequently a dark corner of the human spirit. The answers which Habakkuk provides, therefore, may be considered as partial. Nevertheless, they make an important contribution to the biblical discussion of the problem. For Christians, the ultimate answer to the question of theodicy is found in the cross of Christ where the Father allowed his Son to become vulnerable to the evil in this world, but raised him from the tomb as a promise that sin and death will finally be crushed by the power of God's love (John 5:18; 13:3).

A. *God is in control of the events of this world.* This message is not unique to Habakkuk, and we have already discussed important statements by Habakkuk's prophetic predecessors which make the same basic point. But in the context of the question which Habakkuk raises it is particularly significant. Yahweh's first reply (1:5–11) is a proclamation of this principle, which also finds expression in the concluding psalm. Human events may *seem* to be random and meaningless, or in times when great evil is perpetrated, they may actually seem to be the working out of some malevolent design, as if an evil force had somehow gained control of human destiny. But appearances to the contrary, God is still the Lord of history and is capable of claiming even evil persons and evil events to bring about eventual loving purposes.

> . . . I am doing a work in your days
> that you would not believe if told. (1:5)

God's activity in human life may not be logical or, in some instances, even credible. But it is *God's* activity, and therefore God's people must not lose heart or believe that they have been abandoned.

B. *The answer to such a vexing problem as that raised by Habakkuk does not come easily, even to those who are earnest in their search for it.* Because the pain which evil inflicts upon godly men and women is often very intense, it is only natural that God's people would want quick and satisfying answers. But that is simply not the reality of this dilemma. The answer to the question of theodicy is not like the solution to a crossword puzzle, certain, definite, and easily located in the next morning's newspaper. It is all bound up in the mystery of God's ways. And so following his second question, Habakkuk stations himself (either figuratively or literally) so as to wait patiently for the word of God (2:1). When that word comes, one of the things which it affirms is the necessity of spiritual patience.

> "If it seem slow, wait for it;
> it will surely come, it will not delay." (2:3)

Most men and women of faith feel that they never fully comprehend the reason behind certain evil events in a world claimed by a sovereign, loving God. And even those who claim some insight into this dilemma affirm that this insight is the result of years of reflection and of living the life of faith day by day.

C. *Those who find joy in life and meaning in this evil-filled world will do so by means of an inner commitment, not by means of logical explanations nor by having the events of life transpire only in joyful and happy ways.* The key to this theological principle and the central text of the entire book of Habakkuk is 2:4. The verse is composed of two lines, the first of which may be translated: "When a person is puffed up, his/her soul is not right." In other words, false pride, greed, self-centeredness, and other destructive qualities are of no help at all when men and women are confronted with the basic issues of life. That is especially true when these persons find that they must suddenly deal with suffering or evil for which there is no ready explanation.

The second line of 2:4 is positive: "the righteous (*tsadiq*) person will live by his/her faithfulness (*'emunah*)." One may wish to refer to the chart on p. 41 and the accompanying discussion to be reminded of the important place of these two words in the preaching of Hosea.[35] *'emunah* means "faith" (so RSV) not in a conceptual sense (as in "I believe that God exists"), but rather in a sense of absolute trust and dependence. In other words, insight into the problem of evil comes to men and women not by logical means or even less by ignoring the problem until its presence is inescapable. Rather it comes to men and women of spiritual awareness who are confident that God has certain purposes and knows, even if humans do not, that these purposes in human life are loving and full of grace.

Habakkuk 2:4 has played an interesting role in Christian history, a role which has caused it to be one of the more important texts in the whole body of Old Testament prophetic literature. St. Paul, in writing to the Christians of Rome, quotes Habakkuk 2:4 as a means of illustrating his comment on the centrality of faith in the life of the Christian.

> For I am not ashamed of the gospel: it is the power of God for salvation to every one who has faith, to the Jew first and also to the Greek. For in it the righteousness of God is revealed through faith for faith; as it is written, "He who through faith is righteous shall live." (Rom. 1:16–17)

There is a significant difference in the manner in which this text appears here and in Habakkuk 2:4 in that Paul's quotation appears to mean that the quality of righteousness is attained *by means of* one's trust in God. Habakkuk 2:4, on the other hand, seems to mean that trust in God is the natural expression of the righteous man or woman. This is not to say that Paul does violence to Habakkuk 2:4, but he does interpret it in a manner which relates to his larger discussion of the nature of faith in his letter to the Romans.

Martin Luther, at a critical time in his own life, was profoundly influenced by Habakkuk 2:4 when he read Paul's quotation of the verse in Romans 1:17. Luther is reported to have written the Latin word *sola* ("only") in the margin of his Bible beside Romans 1:17, a significant early expression of what became for him the important Reformation doctrine of justification by faith alone.

D. *Yahweh is a majestic God whose holiness must be acknowledged by all worshipers.* The whole of the psalm in chapter 3 resonates to the nature of God as a transcendent and awe-inspiring Deity. But there is a special sense in which Habakkuk 2:20 has communicated to generations of Jews and Christians the reverence and respect due to God, especially in moments of worship.

---

[35] *tsadiq* is the adjectival form of *tsedheq/tsedhaqah*.

> But Yahweh is in his holy temple;
> > let all the earth keep silence before him. (2:20)

E. *When men and women respond to the presence of God in human life, theirs is a sensation of joy and gladness.* It is perhaps appropriate that the book of Habakkuk, which is otherwise so filled with sober questions of imponderable significance, with "woes," and with a concern over the presence of evil in God's world, should end on a note of joy and celebration:

> yet I will rejoice in Yahweh,
> > I will joy in the God of my salvation.
> Yahweh, the Lord, is my strength;
> > he makes my feet like hinds' feet,
> > he makes me tread upon my high places. (3:18–19)

9
JEREMIAH

Date of Jeremiah's Work: from 627 to some time after 587.
Location: Jerusalem.
Central Theological Concepts: Because of Judah's sin Yahweh
will destroy the land through the agency of the Babylonian
king Nebuchadrezzar. However, God still has a future with
Judah which involves a return to the land.
An Outline of the Book of Jeremiah will be found on p. 118.

Jeremiah is one of the towering figures in all of the Old Testament and,
some would maintain, the greatest of all of the Hebrew prophets. There are
several reasons for this judgment. First, Jeremiah's ministry was of unusual
duration, lasting over four of the most turbulent and decisive decades in the
history of the Jerusalem community. Jeremiah not only foretold the destruction of the city as had others (e.g., Micah) but also lived to see the dreadful
series of events he predicted, and because of his continuing work, he provided a prophetic commentary upon God's judgment even as it was happen-
ing. Second, the personality of the prophet stands forth from the pages of the
book which bears his name as does no other Old Testament prophet, and we
see him as a man of deep human emotions, one who actually suffered with
his people and who, although he objected to God over his call to be a prophet,
fulfilled the commission laid upon him with painful faithfulness. The suffer-
ings of Jeremiah are more real to the modern reader perhaps than those of
any other Old Testament personality, and in this way he anticipates the passion of Christ. Yet Jeremiah was not without hope for the future, and a third
reason for his importance is that he spoke important words by which men
and women of his time comprehended their own tragic experiences and by
which Christians have understood the dynamics of God's ways of judgment
and love.

The Historical Context of Jeremiah's Work

Jeremiah was a contemporary of the prophets Nahum and Habakkuk and
the lives of all three were impacted by the military and political maelstrom

into which Judah was drawn during their lifetimes.[36] As we have previously discussed, the Assyrian monarch Ashurbanipal died in 627 after a reign of four decades, an event which signaled to some that the demise of the vast Assyrian empire was near. In the next year the Babylonian Nabopolassar expelled the Assyrians from his city, and not long after that King Josiah of Judah took steps to reestablish the old kingdom of David by claiming important cities of the now-vanished Northern Kingdom. In 612 the Assyrian capital of Nineveh itself fell to the Babylonians, the Medes, and the Scythians, and it must have seemed to everyone in Jerusalem that God was at last beginning to smile upon Judah and that the spiritual ideals proclaimed with such energy by Josiah in 622 were surely correct.

Then came the calamity of 609 when good King Josiah was killed in the effort to turn back the invading Egyptian army, and his place was taken upon Judah's throne by his son Jehoiakim.[37] Shortly after the Battle of Carchemish in 605, in which the Egyptians were soundly defeated by the Babylonians under Nebuchadrezzar, Jerusalem was subjected to Babylonian rule and Jehoiakim, although he retained his crown, was forced to swear allegiance to his new overlord at this time.

The character of this new king was not at all pleasing to those who had known and loved his father. In spite of his vassalage to the Egyptians at first, then to the Babylonians, Jehoiakim somehow found the resources to appease his self-indulgent appetite. He rebuilt the royal palace to more luxurious dimensions than it had known during the days of his father, and he impressed Judean citizens to work upon the project under conditions of virtual servitude (Jer. 22:13–17). In addition, he showed none of his father's concern for purity in worship, an attitude which earned him the censure of the deuteronomistic historians (2 Kings 23:37).

If Jehoiakim favored close ties between his nation and Egypt, he must have been encouraged by the results of a military encounter between the Babylonians and the Egyptians which took place somewhere in Syria-Palestine in the year 601. We know of the battle only from a brief Babylonian record, but Nebuchadrezzar, who had succeeded his father Nabopolassar as king following the Battle of Carchemish in 605, suffered a setback. The extent to which Babylonian control over Judah was damaged by this battle is un-

---

[36]The student may wish to reread the sections describing the historical contexts of Nahum's (pp. 87–88) and Habakkah's (pp. 92–94) works.

[37]Josiah was succeeded immediately by a son named Jehoahaz. This prince, who was younger than Jehoiakim, was then removed by Pharaoh Necho, who placed Jehoiakim on the throne as his puppet (2 Kings 23:30–34). Some scholars feel that the reason Jehoiakim was at first passed over in favor of his younger brother was that the older prince was a known Egyptian sympathizer. This is certainly consistent with his later actions and could have made him unacceptable to the freedom-loving Judeans.

known, but it may have helped to inspire thoughts of rebellion in Jehoiakim's mind, for the Judean king renounced his vassalage to the Babylonians about this time probably in the hope (vain, as it turned out) that the Egyptians would come to his aid.

Nebuchadrezzar did not respond immediately, perhaps because of the weakened condition of his army,[38] and before the Babylonian king could attack Jerusalem, Jehoiakim died (some have suggested, without foundation, that he was murdered) and was succeeded by his eighteen-year-old son, Jehoiachin (2 Kings 24:8). Reading between the lines of the account of Jehoiachin's brief reign in 2 Kings, we gain the impression that the lad wanted no part of the insurrection which his father had begun. When the Babylonian army finally moved against Jerusalem, the city fell with ease (597) and certain of the leading men and women, including the young king, were transported to captivity in Babylon. Zedekiah, a son of Josiah (and therefore Jehoiachin's uncle), was placed upon Judah's throne by the nation's Babylonian masters.

A Babylonian account of the first fall of Jerusalem has survived, and it reads as follows:

> Year 7, month Kislimu: The king of Akkad [Babylon] moved his army into Hatti land, laid siege to the city of Judah and the king took the city on the second day of the month Addaru. He appointed in it a (new) king of his liking, took heavy booty from it and brought it to Babylon.[39]

Zedekiah was to rule Judah for a decade, and those who were close to him must have sensed soon that he was no more comfortable in the role of Babylonian puppet than his brother Jehoiakim had been. At one point during his reign,[40] he participated in a conference with several representatives from nations who were subservient to the Babylonians, an act which earned him a sharp denunciation by Jeremiah as we will see (Jer. 27:1–11). When Zedekiah finally decided to defy Babylonian authority, there were doubtless many in Judah who not only expected such a move but also supported it. This time, however, events turned out even worse for Jerusalem than they did following Jehoiakim's revolt of a decade earlier. Nebuchadrezzar laid siege to the city and, after a war of attrition which lasted for a year and a half, Jerusalem fell.

---

[38] 2 Kings 24:2 records how bands of Chaldeans, Syrians, Moabites, and Ammonites harrassed Jerusalem at the time of Jehoiakim's revolt. These were probably mercenary forces of Nebuchadrezzar, or at least his allies, whom the Babylonian king unleashed until his own army could arrive to suppress the Judean insurrection.

[39] ANET, p. 564.

[40] Many scholars feel that Jeremiah 27:1, which places this conference in the year of Zedekiah's accession, is incorrect and prefer to see it in the context of the death of Pharaoh Necho and the coming to power of an energetic new Egyptian ruler, Psammetichus II, in 594.

Zedekiah was blinded and carried off into exile after having been forced to watch the execution of his sons (2 Kings 25:1–7). As for Jerusalem, it was extensively damaged. The Temple, the royal palace, and the city walls were destroyed, and most of the citizens were carried off with their king into captivity in Babylon.

This time Nebuchadrezzar had no intention of placing another Davidic king on the throne, so he appointed a Jewish governor over a Judah which was now tightly bound to the empire. The new governor was Gedaliah whose father, Ahikam, had served in the court of King Jehoiakim and had been instrumental in saving Jeremiah's life on one occasion (26:24). But Gedaliah was seen as too pro-Babylonian by some fanatical Jewish patriots, and he was murdered. The assassins fled to Egypt forcing Jeremiah, who was known to be regarded favorably by the Babylonians, to accompany them as a hostage. The last words we have from Jeremiah are uttered in the land of his captivity.

The Prophet

The book of Jeremiah is the most autobiographical of all of the prophetic literature with the result that the personality of the prophet is in some ways quite well-defined. However, because the passages within this book are not always arranged in systematic order, it is not entirely possible to fit together in strict chronological sequence the pieces of information we have about Jeremiah's ministry.

Jeremiah was born into a priestly family of the village of Anathoth just north of Jerusalem (1:1). We know nothing of Jeremiah's father Hilkiah except that he served as a priest, as Jeremiah himself may have at least during his young adulthood. The first of the four periods in Jeremiah's public ministry, the *Early Ministry* (626–609), began when Jeremiah received a call from Yahweh to become a prophet (1:2). Some of the details of the call, including Jeremiah's initial negative reaction, are related in 1:4–10. It will be remembered that this was approximately the same time as the death of the Assyrian emperor Ashurbanipal and the uprising of the Babylonian prince Nabopolassar, and some scholars have suggested that there may have been some connection between these decisive events and Jeremiah's call. If Jeremiah sensed that the present world political order was about to undergo convulsive changes, that fact may have sharpened his sensitivity to the need for a fresh word from Yahweh to the people of Judah.

The young Jeremiah had been deeply impressed by his predecessors in the prophetic tradition, many of whose oracles echo within Jeremiah's own. Jeremiah, as did Hosea, compares the relationship between God and Judah to that between a husband and wife, and recalls an earlier golden age when that love flourished.

> "I remember the devotion of your youth,
>   your love as a bride,
> how you followed me in the wilderness,
>   in a land not sown." (2:2; cf. Hosea 2:15; 9:10; 11:1–2)

But Israel had shattered that relationship by spurning Yahweh's love and serving other gods, an apostasy which Jeremiah, following Hosea, describes as harlotry.

> "How well you direct your course
>   to seek lovers!
> So that even to wicked women
>   you have taught your ways." (2:33; cf. 5:7–9)

False worship, however, was not Jeremiah's only concern. Justice and truth are absent from the land, and like Zephaniah who portrayed Yahweh as searching for the wicked with a lamp (Zeph. 1:12), young Jeremiah portrays God's vain search for those who practice morality.

> Run to and fro through the streets of Jerusalem,
>   look and take note!
> Search her squares to see
>   if you can find a man,
> one who does justice (*mishpat*)
>   and seeks truth (*ᵉmunah*)
> that I may pardon her. (5:1)

Jeremiah also reveals the influence of Amos, Hosea, and Micah in his skillful use of verbal imagery to portray the greed of some which leads them to oppress and rob others.

> "For wicked men are found among my people;
>   they lurk like fowlers lying in wait.
> They set a trap;
>   they catch men.
> Like a basket full of birds,
>   their houses are full of treachery;
> therefore they have become great and rich,
>   they have grown fat and sleek.
> They know no bounds in deeds of wickedness;
>   they judge not with justice (*mishpat*)
> the cause of the fatherless, to make it prosper,
>   and they do not defend the rights of the needy." (5:26–28)

To make bad matters worse, prophets are false and priests are devious (5:31), and there seems to be little reason to hope for the nation's repentance.

Jeremiah is so depressed over the moral and spiritual state of the nation that he identifies with the anguish that God must feel (4:19), and he can foresee no future without disaster for the people. More than once during his Early Ministry he speaks of an avenging nation which Yahweh will cause to descend upon Judah from the north. On one occasion he employs a clever pun to make this point, perhaps inspired by a moment when he sat at home, watching the preparations for the evening meal and brooding over the evil which he knew would come.

> The word of Yahweh came to me a second time, saying, "What do you see?" And I said, "I see a boiling (*naphuach*) pot, facing away from the north." Then Yahweh said to me, "Out of the north evil shall break forth (*tippathach*) upon all the inhabitants of the land." (1:13–14; cf. 4:5–8; 5:15–17; 6:1–5)

It is difficult to know precisely what foreign power Jeremiah had in mind in such passages. Some have suggested that these oracles may have been inspired by the Scythian invasion, but it is not clear that the Scythian threat presented itself during the period of Jeremiah's Early Ministry. What is more, the once dreaded Assyrians were in retreat and the Babylonians had not gained enough strength to present themselves as a threat to Syria-Palestine, as they would in the next decade. In any event, Jeremiah's attitude toward this "foe from the north" becomes the foundation for his later identification of Nebuchadrezzar as the avenging agent of Yahweh.

There is little evidence that the young Jeremiah gained a very wide audience. When the "book of the law" (some form of our book of Deuteronomy) was discovered in the Temple by the priest Hilkiah and presented to King Josiah, the act which became the catalyst for the great reformation of 622, Josiah sent the scroll to be verified as an authentic word from God. He did not send it to Jeremiah, however, but to an otherwise unknown prophetess, Huldah (2 Kings 22:14–20). At a later time, especially during the reign of King Zedekiah, there is no question that the supreme spiritual authority in the land is the prophet from Anathoth (although everyone did not hear his words gladly, by any means), but this is a reputation which the young Jeremiah had not yet gained.

A word is in order concerning the literary skills which Jeremiah demonstrates during this early period of his ministry. We have already noticed his use of the pun in 1:13–14, a literary device which resembles that used by Amos (Amos 8:1–3). A vision which precedes that of the boiling pot also employs a pun.

> And the word of Yahweh came to me, saying, "Jeremiah, what do you see?" And I said, "I see a rod (*shaqedh*) of almond." Then Yahweh said to me, "You have seen well, for I am watching (*shoqedh*) over my word to perform it." (1:11–12)

Jeremiah also relies upon strong verbal images, many of them evocative of rural life, to strengthen the force of his oracles, again a style which reminds us of his predecessors. Judah's spiritual harlotry is compared to wild animals in heat (2:23–24), while the avenging agent of God is "a lion," "a wolf," "a leopard" (5:6; cf. Amos 5:18–20; Hos. 5:14; 13:7–8), and the nation is a vine (6:9; cf. Isa. 5:1–7).

The second major period in Jeremiah's ministry is his *Withdrawal from Public Life* (622–609), a period which begins with the proclamation of Josiah's reformation and ends with that monarch's death at the hands of the Egyptian army. The reasons for Jeremiah's withdrawal are not entirely clear and two contradictory explanations have been offered. The first is that Jeremiah saw in the discovery of the book of Deuteronomy and in the principles of the reform which that discovery inspired a response to his own call for the pure worship of Yahweh and for moral responsibility on the part of the people. Those scholars who put forward this hypothesis call attention to the fact that Josiah was concerned, as was Jeremiah, to purify worship and, in Josiah's case, to see that it remained pure by confining formal acts of worship to the Jerusalem Temple. They also point to the moral demands of the book of Deuteronomy (see, for example, Deut. 10:12–22; 16:20) as evidence that the reformation which Deuteronomy inspired would have caused Jeremiah to believe that the nation would embrace a new morality, a morality in which greed and oppression would be replaced by compassion and justice.

Other scholars, however, feel that the reasons behind Jeremiah's withdrawal from public life at this time were just the opposite, namely, that he viewed Josiah's reformation as superficial, cosmetic, and contributing further to the deterioration of the spiritual and moral fiber of the nation's life. This view draws heavily upon a number of passages in which Jeremiah expresses his scorn of the priests and their handling of the sacred traditions of Israel (e.g., 2:8; 8:8–13), and this view concludes that because Josiah's reformation was also a priestly reformation (in its emphasis upon the cult), Jeremiah could not have supported it. Therefore, he withdrew from public activity in protest over a course of action which he knew would fail in the end. If this is so, his actions would not have been unlike those of Isaiah who withdrew from public life over his opposition to the policies of King Ahaz at the time of the Syro-Ephraimitic War (Isa. 8:16–22). Some scholars have even suggested that Jeremiah actively opposed Josiah's efforts at reform, although direct evidence for such opposition is lacking.

The death of Josiah at Megiddo in 609 resulted in a spiritual crisis of enormous proportions in Judah and caused Jeremiah to resume his public ministry. This marks the beginning of the third period in the prophet's ministry, his *Ministry under Jehoiakim* (609–597). Josiah's death not only created the political confusion one would expect from the sudden and violent death of a reigning monarch but also seems to have caused deep spiritual searching among men and women in Judah. Adopting the principles of the book of Deuteronomy which had inspired it (see especially Deut. 7:12–16), Josiah's reformation had insisted that when God's people do what is right they will prosper and that when they do not they will be punished. Therefore, how was one to explain the death of this good king and the subsequent submission of Judah to another foreign power in the light of these teachings?

We have already discussed the manner in which these questions are reflected in the book of Habakkuk and that prophet's response to them. Jeremiah, after his own fashion, was to respond to them as well, but for the moment the people as a whole apparently decided that the ideals of the reformation had been wrong all along. They were noble ideals, perhaps, and well-intentioned, but they could hardly have been true or events would not have turned out as they did. The only vestige of Josiah's reforming principles which remained alive had to do with Jerusalem as the city of God and the Temple as the place where people met God in worship. Reflecting Isaiah's statement about Yahweh's concern to protect this city (Isa. 37:33–35) and Josiah's command that all worship be centralized there, a twisted parody of these teachings emerged about the time of Jehoiakim's coronation. It was the false belief that, because Jerusalem was the special city of Yahweh, no harm could ever befall it.

It is difficult to be entirely sure, but it seems that it was this twisted understanding of the nature of Yahweh's relationship to this city and Temple and the false confidence that the misunderstanding inspired which motivated Jeremiah to resume his public role. Early in Jehoiakim's reign (perhaps in 605) Jeremiah preached his famous "Temple sermon," recorded in Jeremiah 7 (in some detail) and 26 (in outline, accompanied by a description of the popular reaction).[41] In this important declaration Jeremiah denounced the false confidence of the people by mocking the words of those who preach that confidence.

> "Do not trust in these deceptive words: 'This is the temple of Yahweh, the temple of Yahweh, the temple of Yahweh.'" (7:4)

Jeremiah viewed with alarm the same social and personal evils which he had denounced during his Early Ministry. There is theft, murder, adultery, and false worship (7:9). Even the sacrifice of children is practiced in the Valley of Hinnom just outside Jerusalem (7:31). And yet there is still time for the people to repent and to receive the gracious mercy of Yahweh.

---

[41] The fact that this oracle is reported in two very different ways and in two different places in the book of Jeremiah gives important evidence of the "non-systematic" manner in which this book was edited.

"For if you truly amend your ways and your doings, if you truly execute justice one with another, if you do not oppress the alien, the fatherless or the widow, or shed innocent blood in this place, and if you do not go after other gods to your own hurt, then I will let you dwell in this place, in the land that I gave of old to your fathers for ever." (7:5–7)

Jeremiah even exhorted his hearers to place the principle of obedience to Yahweh before that of offering burnt sacrifices as an act of public worship (7:21–26), an appeal which must have infuriated the Temple priests.[42] On the other hand, if the people persist in their evil, God will destroy Jerusalem and turn it into a heap of rubble, as happened in the case of Shiloh, the old cultic center of Samuel's days which had been destroyed by (presumably) the Philistines and never rebuilt (7:12).

The reaction of Jeremiah's hearers to these strong words was immediate and violent. The Temple priests attempted to have Jeremiah killed and probably would have succeeded had it not been that some members of the tribunal before which Jeremiah was taken remembered Micah's similar words. And the fact that Micah was allowed to live was cited as a legal precedent for allowing Jeremiah to live also (26:7–19). Nevertheless, an atmosphere of confrontation had been set between Jeremiah and the religious and political establishment, an atmosphere which would continue to the end of Jeremiah's ministry and would, on more than one occasion, place his life in jeopardy.

Contrary to Jeremiah's strong words the nation slipped further into a kind of spiritual malaise which Jeremiah knew would ultimately prove to be destructive. It was about this time that King Jehoiakim engaged in the extensive renovation of the royal palace and did so in such a manner as to cause severe hardship to certain of the poorer people of the land, an act for which he was roundly denounced by Jeremiah, as we have already noted (22:13–19). Another prophet, whose name was Uriah and about whom we know nothing apart from the brief notice in 26:20–23, was pursued and executed because he offended the palace officials. And the false prophets, undoubtedly cult prophets attached as priests to the Jerusalem Temple, continued to proclaim their counterfeit good news: "You shall not see the sword, nor shall you have famine, but I will give you assured peace in this place" (14:13).

Jeremiah's reaction to these things was to intensify his preaching of Yahweh's judgment upon this sinful people. It was perhaps during this time that he told his famous parable of the potter and the clay. In it he compared sinful Judah to a vessel which had become spoiled on the potter's wheel as the

---

[42] 7:22 is a fascinating statement by Jeremiah, for it implies that sacrifice has no place in worship, and some scholars point to this text as evidence that Jeremiah could not have supported the theological ideals of Josiah's reformation which laid great value on public worship presided over by the priests.

artisan attempted to form it into an object of perfection. As the potter would destroy the vessel in order to begin again, so Yahweh would destroy sinful Judah in order to set the stage for a new beginning with the people (18:1–11).

During this time Jeremiah's earlier references to a "foe from the north" which would bring Yahweh's wrath upon Judah are revised. Now the identification becomes specific, and the Babylonian army of Nebuchadrezzar is portrayed as that agent by which Yahweh will chasten Judah. The Battle of Carchemish in 605 in which Nebuchadrezzar defeated Pharaoh Necho seems to have served as a catalyst for Jeremiah's views on this subject. Reviving the language of Amos concerning the "Day of Yahweh" (Amos 5:18), Jeremiah described how that awful day will be consummated through the agency of Nebuchadrezzar.

> "That day is the day of Yahweh God of hosts,
>> a day of vengeance,
>> to avenge himself on his foes.
> The sword shall devour and be sated,
>> and drink its fill of their blood.
> For Yahweh God of hosts holds a sacrifice
>> in the north country by the river Euphrates." (46:10)

Not surprisingly, King Jehoiakim and the priests and advisers around him were indignant over Jeremiah's stern preaching. On one occasion during this period a priest named Pashur had Jeremiah arrested and beaten. The prophet was then confined overnight in the stocks which stood by one of the entrances to the Temple courtyard to be ridiculed there by any passerby. When Jeremiah was set free the next morning, he denounced Pashur and promised that he and others like him would fall prey to Nebuchadrezzar (20:1–6).

Ultimately the king himself banned Jeremiah from coming near the royal compound, which included the Temple grounds. It may be that it was under these circumstances that Jeremiah returned to his home in Anathoth, only to discover that his kinfolk and neighbors had also turned against him and would not allow him to remain in his home (11:21), an incident which reminds one of Jesus' later rejection at Nazareth (Luke 4:28–29).

Quite possibly, therefore, it was out in the countryside somewhere that Jeremiah was joined by his companion, the scribe Baruch. Jeremiah dictated to his friend a message which, since the prophet himself could not go to the Temple, was to be read aloud by Baruch in the Temple courtyard. The scroll was a summary of the preaching of Jeremiah and, on the basis of the king's reaction to it, the prophet minced no words concerning the nation's conduct and its fate. When Baruch publicly read the words of the prophet, he was detained and carried into the palace of Jehoiakim where the scroll was taken from him and read to the king. As the reading proceeded, Jehoiakim cut sections away from the scroll with a knife and, over the protests of some of his advisers, burned them one by one in a fire which had been kindled nearby for warmth on a cold day. Baruch then returned to Jeremiah, and in their place of hiding Jeremiah dictated another summary of his teaching (36:1–32). Many scholars believe that this second scroll was the beginning of the formation of our present book of Jeremiah.

When Jehoiakim revolted against Babylonian rule in 601 Jeremiah held no doubts about the outcome of this insurrection. In a bold statement the prophet portrays Nebuchadrezzar as Yahweh's servant who will be the instrument of judgment upon Judah.[43]

> "Therefore thus says Yahweh of hosts: Because you have not obeyed my words, behold I will send for all the tribes of the north, says Yahweh, and for Nebuchadrezzar the king of Babylon, my servant, and I will bring them against this land and its inhabitants, and against all these nations round about; and I will utterly destroy them, and make them a horror, a hissing, and an everlasting reproach." (25:8–9)

As we have previously noticed, Jehoiakim did not live to see the promise of Jeremiah come true but died during the course of his rebellion. His young son, Jehoiachin, and other members of the royal household as well as citizens representing a broad spectrum of Judean life were carried into captivity in Babylon. We have no information on Jeremiah's activities during this terrible time in Jerusalem's life, but the placing of a new puppet king upon the throne, Zedekiah, brother to Jehoiakim, signaled the beginning of the fourth and final period in Jeremiah's public life, his *Ministry Under Zedekiah and Beyond* (597–585?).

The new administration seems to have lost little time in assuming control of the nation's life, with Babylonian help, of course. Perhaps because the human and material devastation had been relatively light, the momentum of life resumed with a minimum of disruption. In fact, the new ruling classes in Jerusalem apparently congratulated themselves that they had escaped the deportation experienced by Jehoiachin and others now in Babylon. They may even have recalled the words of prophets such as Micah and Isaiah concerning Jerusalem's judgment and may have concluded that the judgment had now fallen on the guilty party while they, the favored ones, had been left in Jerusalem to preside over the nation's affairs. If that was their train of thought, Jeremiah was angrily opposed to it and in an important statement (24:1–10) he reported a vision in which two baskets of figs appear, one basket full of edible fruit, the other filled with rotten fruit. The good figs represent the

---

[43] The editorial introduction to this passage (25:1) indicates that it was spoken first shortly after the Battle of Carchemish in 605, but it must surely also represent Jeremiah's attitude toward Jehoiakim's repudiation of Babylonian rule.

exiles, Jeremiah said in so many words, while the bad figs represent people still in the land. As for this latter group,

> ". . . I [Yahweh] will send sword, famine, and pestilence upon them, until they shall be utterly destroyed from the land which I gave to them and their fathers." (24:10)

It was clear that Jeremiah intended to be as uncompromising a critic of Zedekiah's administration as he had been of Jehoiakim's.

On the occasion of the conference apparently initiated by Zedekiah and attended by representatives of several nations which, like Judah, were subject to the Babylonians, Jeremiah again reacted sharply. The purpose of this meeting was probably that of discussing strategies for revolt and may have taken place about the year 594.[44] Jeremiah viewed this event with alarm and he placed upon his neck a yoke like that worn by oxen as they plow in order to call attention to the period of servitude Judah must endure. Also at this time Jeremiah stated in unequivocal terms his conviction that Nebuchadrezzar was acting as an agent of Yahweh, the Creator (27:5–8). It is little wonder that by this time many people considered Jeremiah a traitor to his nation.

At approximately this same time Jeremiah wrote a letter to the community of Jews who were living in Babylon and who were, quite naturally, hoping for some event which would lead to their speedy release and to their return to their land and homes (29:1–32). In this letter Jeremiah rebuked those false prophets who promised freedom, and he counseled patience on the part of the exiles. "Your exile will be long; build houses and live in them, and plant gardens and eat their produce" (29:28). Once more Jeremiah's words, although they were to prove true, angered many who heard and read them.

When Zedekiah revolted against the Babylonians he set in motion a military confrontation which, as we have seen, was to cause great misery and bloodshed among Jerusalem's people and in the end was to result in the destruction of the city, including the Temple. With great courage and with a disregard for his own safety Jeremiah confronted Zedekiah and denounced this foolish policy.

> "Thus says Yahweh: Behold, I am giving this city into the hand of the king of Babylon, and he shall burn it with fire. You shall not escape from his hand, but shall surely be captured and delivered into his hand; you shall see the king of Babylon eye to eye and speak with him face to face; and you shall go to Babylon." (34:2–3)

Yet Jeremiah also seems to have had compassion for the king, for he must have understood the political pressures under which the king worked and he

---

[44] See footnote 40, p. 103.

must have also understood Zedekiah's thirst for freedom. And so he adds: "Thus says Yahweh concerning you: 'You shall not die by the sword. You shall die in peace'" (34:4–5).

Nebuchadrezzar's siege of Jerusalem lasted for a year and a half, as we have noted, but at some point during that time there was a brief respite. Perhaps an Egyptian army appeared somewhere in the south causing the Babylonian forces in Judah to be withdrawn temporarily. The Babylonians were soon to return, but the incident provides us with another insight into Jeremiah's prophetic activity at this period in his life. It seems that before the temporary lifting of the siege, many Hebrew masters had freed their slaves, workers who, like their masters, were Jews, but who had found themselves in a status of indentured servitude either because of their inability to pay their debts or for some other reason. These slaves had become a liability to their masters now that the surrounding lands, occupied by the Babylonian army, could no longer be worked. Also, with food and other supplies inside the besieged city growing short, the masters were finding it more and more difficult to feed their workers. And so the slaves were freed, and the manumission seems to have been done in a manner which publicly affirmed Israel's ancient traditions of human freedom (34:8–10).

Yet no sooner had the siege of Jerusalem been lifted (temporarily, as it turned out), than the masters reclaimed their former slaves, an act which caused Jeremiah to speak out in fury (34:13–22). It may have been about this time that Jeremiah confronted the king with these words:

> "Behold, Pharaoh's army which came to help you is about to return to Egypt, to its own land. And the Chaldeans [i.e., the Babylonians] shall come back and fight against this city; they shall take it and burn it with fire." (37:7–8)

It was during the time of the Babylonian withdrawal that Jeremiah attempted to leave the city to look into the status of his family in Anathoth, presumably because their property had been overrun by the invading Babylonians. But the sentry who was stationed at the gate through which the prophet intended to pass suspected that Jeremiah was trying to defect to the withdrawing Babylonians, and so he arrested him. Jeremiah was then beaten and cast into prison (37:11–15).

When the king heard what had happened, he had Jeremiah brought to him secretly in order not to incur the wrath of his courtiers who despised and feared the prophet. In the privacy of his chambers Zedekiah asked if there were some word from Yahweh. Jeremiah told the king that he would be delivered into the hands of the Babylonians and then, displaying his own humanity, the prophet protested his innocence of any wrongdoing and begged the king for mercy. Zedekiah, who apparently sensed the prophet's authority and spiritual integrity but who feared his own lieutenants, dared not release Jeremiah, but he did provide him with better quarters (37:16–21).

During his imprisonment Jeremiah was visited by a cousin whose name was Hanamel (32:7–8). The man came requesting that Jeremiah assume the obligations of a "redeemer," that is, one who acts according to ancient Hebrew law (Lev. 25:25) to prevent endangered property from passing out of the family. Hanamel was presumably in bad financial straits because the Babylonian army (which had perhaps returned by now) had overrun his property near Anathoth, thus preventing him from raising his usual crop with which to pay his debts. Unless Jeremiah were to redeem the property, it would have to be sold to someone outside the family. Jeremiah responded positively to Hanamel's request and did so in a manner which allowed him to speak a word of hope for the future. The prophet caused the bill of sale and the deed to be witnessed properly and signed, and he then had them stored in an earthenware pot

> ". . . that they may last for a long time. For thus says Yahweh of hosts, the God of Israel: Houses and fields and vineyards shall again be bought in this land." (32:14–15)

This is an important statement for it indicates that Jeremiah believed that, beyond Yahweh's judgment upon the nation, there would be restoration and a return to the land. It may also have been about this time that Jeremiah spoke the words recorded in 31:31–34, an important passage to which we will give some detailed attention at the end of this chapter.

In the meantime Jeremiah's enemies in the royal court had heard of the favorable treatment the prophet had received from the king, so they demanded of Zedekiah that Jeremiah be put to death. The king was not prepared to let that happen, but neither was he prepared to stand up to his subordinates, so he allowed them to cast Jeremiah into a cistern where he certainly would have died if it had not been for the kindly intercession of an Ethiopian eunuch. The man, whose name was Ebed-melech (or perhaps this was his title, since the term means "servant of the king"), made ropes out of rags and old clothes and drew the prophet up out of the muck. Then, probably with the secret connivance of the king, he placed Jeremiah in more comfortable quarters (38:1–13).

Once more Zedekiah had Jeremiah brought to him, again taking pains to maintain secrecy. The king asked the prophet for guidance, and Jeremiah counseled submission to the Babylonians. Zedekiah, however, expressed his fears of his own people and had the prophet returned to his place of confinement (38:14–28). It was the last recorded meeting between the two men.

When Jerusalem fell to the Babylonians, Jeremiah was released from prison. The Babylonians had learned of Jeremiah and, like the Judeans, they seem to have regarded him as a Babylonian sympathizer, for they treated him with kindness, entrusting him to Gedaliah, their newly appointed governor. After Gedaliah was murdered by Jewish nationalists, Jeremiah was forced to accompany them to Egypt from which the prophet spoke his last recorded words (43:8—44:30).

The "Confessions" of Jeremiah

We have already referred to the fact that the book of Jeremiah is the most autobiographical of the prophetic books of the Old Testament. This is true not only in the sense that we have frequent references which relate Jeremiah's oracles to the events of his world but also in that there are a number of passages in which the prophet speaks of his own feelings and moods. These latter passages are often referred to in a collective sense as Jeremiah's "Confessions," although that name is somewhat misleading in that only a few of them deal with the prophet's concern over his own sinfulness. The commonly accepted texts which fall into this category are 10:23–24; 11:18—12:6; 15:10–21; 17:9–10, 14–18; 18:19–23; and 20:7–12. Of a somewhat different nature, but expressive of the prophet's personality nonetheless, are such passages as 1:4–10 (the account of the prophet's call); 8:18—9:1 (a portrait of the prophet's sorrow over the people's sin); and 16:1–4 (a statement concerning Jeremiah's domestic life).

Several themes emerge from these texts. One is that Jeremiah's message causes within the prophet a profound sorrow. Jeremiah has often been called the "weeping prophet," a reputation which derives as much from his (erroneous) association with the book of Lamentations as from his own utterances. Yet there exist within Jeremiah's more introspective statements comments on the fact that his heart is broken over the people's sin and over Yahweh's reaction to that sin.

> My grief is beyond healing,
> my heart is sick within me.
> For the wound of the daughter of my people is my heart wounded,
> I mourn, and dismay has taken hold on me. (8:18, 21)

> My anguish, my anguish! I writhe in pain!
> Oh, the walls of my heart!
> My heart is beating wildly;
> I cannot keep silent;
> For I hear the sound of the trumpet,
> the alarm of war. (4:19)

Another theme which emerges from the "Confessions" and similar passages is that of the loneliness of the prophet. This should not be surprising in light of the extent to which Jeremiah was persecuted by his enemies. What emerges here is the picture of a man who felt called by God to deny to himself the consolation of a wife and children (16:1–4) and whose sensitive spirit was often crushed by the hostility and alienation he felt from his enemies.

> I did not sit in the company of the merrymakers,
>   nor did I rejoice;
> I sat alone, because thy hand was upon me,
>   for thou hast filled me with indignation. (15:17)

Jeremiah curses the day he was born (15:10; 20:14–18), and he shakes his fist in the face of God for calling him to a task for which his strength is not sufficient.

> O Yahweh, thou hast deceived me,
>   and I was deceived;
> thou art stronger than I,
>   and thou hast prevailed.
> I have become a laughingstock all the day;
>   every one mocks me. (20:7)

A third theme emerges logically from the second. In the face of his own persecution and heartbreak Jeremiah wonders aloud why it is that Yahweh allows evil men and women to prosper at the same time that the godly suffer so greatly (12:1). In his anger he calls upon Yahweh to punish his enemies.

> Is evil a recompense for good?
>   Yet they have dug a pit for my life.
> Remember how I stood before thee
>   to speak good for them,
>   to turn away thy wrath from them.
> Therefore deliver up their children to famine;
>   give them over to the power of the sword,
> let their wives become childless and widowed.
>   May their men meet death by pestilence,
>   their youths be slain by the sword in battle. (18:20–21)

These are shocking words to hear from a great man of God, and there is no way to ignore their presence in Jeremiah's utterances. At the same time it must be remembered that ancient Hebrew thought did not distinguish, as does much modern thought, between evil and those men and women who commit evil deeds. Therefore, we would not expect to hear Jeremiah say something like, "Destroy the evil in my enemies, but spare them as persons." Jeremiah was convinced that his enemies were God's enemies, and he therefore calls for their destruction as a means of destroying that evil that is within them. This is a far cry from Jesus' words on the cross (Luke 23:34).

Jeremiah's awareness of the bitterness and evil within his own soul, however, leads to a fourth theme, namely, Jeremiah confesses his own sinfulness and experiences the restoring grace of God.

> Heal me, O Yahweh, and I shall be healed;
>   save me, and I shall be saved;
>   for thou art my praise. (17:14)

> Therefore thus says Yahweh:
> "If you return, I will restore you,
>   and you shall stand before me.
> If you utter what is precious, and not what is worthless,
>   you shall be as my mouth." (15:19)

Finally, after all of his struggles Jeremiah returns time and again to an awareness that God *is* present in his life and that he must prophesy. For to fail to do so would be to deny something which was profoundly a part of his nature.

> Thy words were found, and I ate them,
>   and thy words became to me a joy
>   and the delight of my heart;
> for I am called by thy name,
>   O Yahweh, God of hosts. (15:16)

> If I say, "I will not mention him,
>   or speak any more in his name,"
> there is in my heart as it were a burning fire
>   shut up in my bones,
> and I am weary with holding it in,
>   and I cannot. (20:9)

These texts and the emotions which they express are very important in providing us with an insight into the soul of the prophet, for they remind us that Jeremiah and others in the prophetic tradition were not plaster saints. They were flesh and blood persons who spoke their words both out of a deep commitment to the living God and as a result of great courage. At the same time, Jeremiah's "Confessions" are a reminder to his modern readers that the life of faith is never easy, that the Christian often experiences loneliness, frustration, and despair. Only the grace of God which sustains us and, in the end, renews us makes it possible for us to follow (even imperfectly) the command of Christ.

The Book of Jeremiah

The book which bears Jeremiah's name does not, as we have observed earlier, lend itself to easy analysis. The history of its formation seems to have been quite complex, and the various passages have been arranged, for the most part, according to no easily discernible pattern. The following outline, however, may be considered as representing the major divisions within the book.

> A. Visions and oracles from Jeremiah's Early Ministry: 1—6.
> B. Other declarations by the prophet from 605 and after: 7—25.
> C. Baruch's memoirs: 26—29.
> D. Additional oracles and biographical notices: 30—45.
> E. Oracles against foreign nations: 46—51.
> F. A historical appendix: 52.

The nature of the oracles in the first major section, 1—6, has been discussed in connection with Jeremiah's Early Ministry, during which period the prophet's indebtedness to his predecessors in the prophetic tradition surfaced. In addition to his early sermons, this section also contains a brief editorial introduction (1:1–3) and a brief account of Jeremiah's call (1:4–10).

The second section, 7—25, is made up of materials relating to widely separated points in the prophet's life. The earliest passage is probably 7:1–15, the so-called "Temple sermon" delivered in 605, but other passages describe events in Jeremiah's ministry and words he spoke as late as the time of King Zedekiah. Oracles, parables, prayers, and poems are all represented here.

The third section, 26—29, consists of biographical notes presumably made by Jeremiah's friend and scribe, Baruch. The main focus of attention here is the conflict between the prophet and the religious establishment of his day.

The fourth section, 30—45, is characterized by further biographical notices (again, from Baruch) in which are contained brief summaries of Jeremiah's actions and his sermons. These follow no strict chronological order and describe events from the reigns of both Jehoiakim and Zedekiah as well as from the period following the fall of Jerusalem in 587.

Many of the oracles against foreign nations, 46—51, date from a time later than Jeremiah, although some seem to be from the prophet himself. The historical appendix, chapter 52, is copied with very little change from 2 Kings 24:18—25:30.

The history of the composition of the book of Jeremiah has been a subject of fascination to scholars, not only because of the structural complexity of the book but also because in the passage 36:1–32 we seem to have an account of the circumstances under which the nucleus of the book was composed. Most scholars consider that this second scroll (the first having been burned by Jehoiakim) formed a kind of "first edition" of the book. It is impossible for us to say with precision just what the contents of that "first edition" were, but it was doubtlessly composed of a number of Jeremiah's oracles dating from the time of his call up to his dictation of the scroll.

To this "first edition" were added later other sermons, prayers, poems, and the like composed by the prophet after the incidents recorded in chapter 36 and contained in the second and fourth sections of our book. Once more, the person responsible for putting together this anthology was likely Baruch. It may have been about this time that Baruch also added the biographical material contained in his "memoirs" as well as the material in the fourth major section of our book.

Subsequent to this, the book of Jeremiah came into the hands of a group of editors who were, in some unknown fashion, closely associated with the authors of the Deuteronomistic History. These persons may have contributed to the present arrangement of the material (we cannot be sure), but they certainly introduced material of their own which contained their particular theological understanding. The most obvious instance of this is chapter 52 which is a very lengthy passage lifted with almost no alteration from the Deuteronomistic History. But other, less extensive examples of the activity of the deuteronomists may be identified. One may read, for example, 9:12–16 and find there a theological outlook which, in its emphasis on the law, is more akin to the deuteronomists than to Jeremiah.

The Theology of Jeremiah

Our discussion has drawn attention to the fact that Jeremiah, especially during his Early Ministry, was deeply influenced by his prophetic predecessors. We should therefore not be surprised to discover that the theology of Jeremiah has many points of contact with the earlier Hebrew prophets. Yet it is important to notice the distinctive contributions of Jeremiah himself.

A. *Yahweh, Israel's God, is the righteous creator of the world and of the nations.* There is in Jeremiah a faith in the creator God which occasionally receives direct expression.

> "It is I [Yahweh] who by my great power and my outstretched arm have made the earth, with the men and animals that are on the earth, and I give it to whomever it seems right to me." (27:5; cf. 5:22)

But more often the creative activity of God is more subtly described and in a manner which acts as the foundation for some additional message the prophet wishes to convey. This is to be seen, for example, in Jeremiah's images of God as the potter at the wheel (18:1–11) and as the "fountain of living waters" (2:13).

Yahweh, who, as the creator of all people, can summon the Babylonian ruler Nebuchadrezzar at will (27:6–7; cf. 25:8–14), has a special relationship with Israel as its father (3:19) and husband (2:2). To Israel more than to any other people Yahweh has been revealed as a God of love and justice, power and righteousness, and in this regard Jeremiah's indebtedness to the prophetic tradition again becomes clear:

> ". . . let him who glories glory in this, that he understands and knows me, that I am Yahweh who practice steadfast love (*chesedh*), justice (*mishpat*), and righteousness (*ts^edhaqah*) in the earth; for in these things I delight, says Yahweh." (9:24)

There is no doubting of Yahweh's love for Israel on Jeremiah's part. The nation is "the first fruits of his [Yahweh's] harvest" (2:3), Yahweh's "beloved" (11:15; 12:7), and Yahweh's "flock" (13:17). Yet Yahweh's righteousness is such as not to tolerate the nation's sin, which Jeremiah describes in terms of faithlessness to Yahweh (2:13) and the abandonment of justice and truth (5:1). Therefore, Yahweh, who is "a lion," "a wolf," and "a leopard" (5:6), will destroy the nation.

B. *The source of the nation's sinfulness is to be found in the heart of the individual, a heart which Yahweh yearns to redeem.* Jeremiah, more than any other Hebrew prophet, is concerned over the spiritual condition of the individual man and woman. He also emphasizes, to a greater degree than any other Hebrew prophet, the moral and spiritual deviousness of humankind, an insight which apparently comes to him as a result of his own spiritual struggles.

> The heart is deceitful above all things,
>   and desperately corrupt;
>   who can understand it? (17:9)

The "stubbornness of their evil hearts" is a phrase which Jeremiah uses to describe this deceitfulness (7:24; see also 13:10; 23:17).

Yet men and women, although they are fundamentally corrupted, are not so totally lost as to be beyond the redemptive power of Yahweh's love. It is still possible for them to put their evil ways aside and, with a change of heart, to enter into a new relationship with Yahweh. This declaration is at the center of 31:31–34, but it is also an important aspect of the prophet's "Temple sermon" (chaps. 7; 26). Here we have an important insight not only into the nature of human sinfulness but also into the nature of Yahweh's mercy.

> "For if you truly amend your ways and your doings, if you truly execute justice (*mishpat*) one with another, if you do not oppress the alien, the fatherless or the widow, or shed innocent blood in this place, and if you do not go after other gods to your own hurt, then I will let you dwell in this place, in the land that I gave of old to your fathers for ever." (7:5–7; cf. 4:14)

Jeremiah, in fact, says more about the need for repentance than any other Hebrew prophet, his favorite word for repentance being the verb "to return," *shuv*.

> Return, O faithless children, says Yahweh;
>   for I am your master; (3:14; cf. 4:1; 18:11)

If the heart is the seat of evil, then it is the heart itself which must be changed. In one passage Jeremiah refers to the ritual of circumcision which every male child received as a sign of his identification with Israel, and he pleads:

> "Circumcise yourselves to Yahweh,
>   remove the foreskin of your hearts,
>   O men of Judah and inhabitants of Jerusalem;
> lest my wrath go forth like fire,
>   and burn with none to quench it,
>   because of the evil of your doings." (4:4; cf. Deut. 10:16; 30:6)

It appears, however, that as Jeremiah grew older and no fundamental repentance on the part of the people came about, he became more and more pessimistic that the destruction of the nation could be averted. In those oracles dating from the reigns of Jehoiakim and Zedekiah there is great gloom (see, for example, 38:17–23).

C. *Beyond the destruction which Yahweh's righteousness will bring about there is to be a future for the people in the land.* As Jeremiah's hope was dimmed that the people would respond immediately to his words, his realization seems to have grown that the future would be the arena of Yahweh's saving activity. Although Jeremiah is not specific about the time when this restoration will take place,[45] it is apparent that he anticipates it will take the form of the people's return to the land. There is little in Jeremiah of grand visions of a restored Jerusalem reigning in splendor over the other nations with a Davidic king at its head, as we will find in some of the later prophets. Rather, Jeremiah's hope is for a restoration based upon the people's new relationship to Yahweh, as evidenced from this passage from Jeremiah's letter to the exiles.

> "For thus says Yahweh: When seventy years are completed for Babylon, I will visit you, and I will fulfil to you my promise and bring you back to this place. For I know the plans I have for you, says Yahweh, plans for welfare and not for evil, to give you a future and a hope. Then you will call upon me and come and pray to me, and I will hear you. You will seek me and find me; when you seek me with all your heart, I will be found by

---

[45] The "seventy years" of 29:10 (that is, ten times a sabbath of years; compare our phrase "a month of Sundays") should be thought of as a symbolic way of saying "a long time." The Exile, in fact, lasted just under sixty years.

> you, says Yahweh, and I will restore your fortunes and gather you from
> all the nations and all the places where I have driven you, says Yahweh,
> and I will bring you back to the place from which I sent you into exile."
> (29:10–14)

Another important text having to do with the restoration of the people to the land is that which describes Jeremiah's purchase of Hanamel's field in chapter 32 (see especially vss. 14–15).

A Key Text: Jeremiah 31:31–34

Jeremiah is responsible, in this text, for expressing one of the most profound insights of the Old Testament faith. The author of the New Testament letter to the Hebrews refers to this passage twice, 8:8–12 (where the passage is quoted in its entirety) and 10:16–17. The passage is also referred to in the words used at the Last Supper, "the new covenant in my blood" (Luke 22:20; 1 Cor. 11:25). Furthermore, it inspired the distinction made in 2 Corinthians 3:5–6 which ultimately leads the early church to distinguish the two parts of the Christian Bible as the Old and New Testaments. Some nineteenth-century scholars doubted that the passage was the work of Jeremiah himself, but the modern scholarly consensus is that it expresses the thought of the prophet, although someone, most likely Baruch, has rephrased and expanded Jeremiah's original statement.

Verse 31: The phrase, "Behold, the days are coming," is used three times in chapter 31 (vss. 27, 38) to refer to God's future saving activity. Jeremiah appears to have in mind some specific time in the ordinary course of history when Yahweh will make a new covenant with the nation. The Hebrew word translated "make" literally means "to cut" and is the verb ordinarily associated with the concept of covenant-making in the Old Testament.

Verse 32: The old covenant, from which the new is to be distinguished, is here identified with Israel's encounter with God at the time of the Exodus. In Old Testament thought the covenant which Yahweh made with Israel at that time is associated in a particular way with the receiving of the law by Moses on Mt. Sinai (Exod. 19—20). Even in the period of his Early Ministry, Jeremiah was acutely aware that God's people had not kept the law (5:4–5), and that conviction is repeated here in the phrase "my covenant which they broke." Also repeated here is the image of Yahweh as Israel's "husband," an echo of early oracles, as in 2:2 and in 3:14 (where RSV has "master" for "husband").

Verse 33: In a very important declaration Jeremiah describes the new law as being fundamentally different from the old. This difference is to be found in the fact that, whereas the old law was written upon tablets of stone, the new law is to be written upon the human heart, that is, it is to be internalized. Jeremiah has previously expressed this same idea by different means (4:4), and his teaching ultimately led to the New Testament promise of the regeneration of the human heart in Jesus Christ. The statement, "I will be their God, and they shall be my people," is a description of the relationship which will exist under the new covenant, and parallels Exodus 20:2 (the prologue to the Ten Commandments) which describes the relationship under the old covenant. Notice that the fundamental nature of the relationship has not changed, only its means of expression. Whereas under the old covenant men and women responded to God by obeying a written law, under the new they respond in love and commitment out of a basic reorientation of their hearts.

Verse 34: The "knowledge of God" was emphasized by Hosea who used the concept as a play upon words to repudiate the people's carnal knowledge of Baal, of which cultic prostitution was a reprehensible expression (Hos. 2:20; 4:1, 6; 5:4; 6:6). The concept is one of Jeremiah's borrowings from his predecessor (Jer. 2:8; 4:22; 9:3, 6, 24; 22:16), and the later prophet understands this knowledge to mean both a confession that the qualities of Yahweh are steadfast love (*chesedh*), justice (*mishpat*), and righteousness (*ts^edhaqah*) (see 9:24) and the incorporation of these qualities into one's own life (22:16). Jeremiah portrays a time when all of the people will "know God" in the above ways, to which Yahweh's response will be that of the forgiveness of sin.

As stated above, the early Christian community pointed to Jesus Christ as the fulfillment of this promise of a new covenant, and it understood that the "hearts" of verse 33 are the lives of those men and women who have responded to God's love in Christ and who have been transformed as a result of that love (John 3:3).

10
EZEKIEL

Date of Ezekiel's Work: from 592 to approximately 571.
Location: Either Jerusalem or Babylon, probably the latter.
Central Theological Concepts: God has not forgotten the
   Jews exiled to Babylon, but will judge those Jews still
   living in Judah and will ultimately restore the people.
An Outline of the Book of Ezekiel will be found on p. 113.

The Historical Context of Ezekiel's Work

Ezekiel was a younger contemporary of Jeremiah who lived through the terrible national crises which so profoundly impacted Jeremiah's life and work. The student will wish to be familiar with the main outline of Judah's history between the years 621 and 587, as discussed in the chapter on Habakkuk (pp. 92–94) and in that on Jeremiah (pp. 101–104).

The Prophet and the Book

Very little direct information is given about the individual Ezekiel in the book which bears his name. Yet it is possible to infer some facts about this man from the literature associated with him and thus to reconstruct something approaching a personal portrait. We do know that Ezekiel was a priest, the son of a certain Buzi (1:3). If the reference to the "thirtieth year" in 1:1 is an indication of Ezekiel's age at the time of his call in 592, he would have been born in 622 or at about the time of the finding of the "book of the law" (Deut.) which sparked the reformation of Josiah (2 Kings 22). Young Ezekiel probably grew up in Jerusalem and was trained for the priesthood in a school attached to the Temple. The first thirteen years of his life would have coincided with the religious and patriotic enthusiasm which characterized the life of the Temple community, and it was perhaps during those early years that his love for the true and distinctive worship of Yahweh would have been nurtured. He would also have been a contemporary of the spiritual and political reaction which set in following the death of Josiah at Megiddo in 609. As we know from the preaching of Jeremiah (Jer. 7:1–20; 26:1–6), this was a period in which the forms of worship were maintained, but were deprived of much of their deeper spiritual and moral content. Some members of the priestly community were doubtless accomplices in this trivialization of the Yahweh faith, but Ezekiel is probably to be identified with a group, perhaps a minority, who, like Jeremiah, saw the disastrous consequences of this hollow religion.

Ezekiel was among the group of Jews who were forced to make the long trek from Jerusalem to Babylon after the first fall of the city following the revolt of Jehoiakim. Jehoiakim's son and successor, the eighteen-year-old Jehoiachin, together with other persons of wealth and rank, were a part of this first deportation, individuals who were compelled to begin a new life far from the homeland which they loved. Ezekiel lived in the Jewish settlement of Tel-abib (3:15, from which the modern Israeli city received its name), probably an agricultural village on the banks of the River Chebar (1:1). This stream may have been one of the many new irrigation canals which the Babylonian king Nebuchadrezzar had built near Babylon and which were intended to draw from the waters of the Euphrates River. Their purpose was to create newly arable lands in order to help support Babylon's growing population.

We do not know how Ezekiel spent the first five years of his captivity, but he probably joined his exiled compatriots in longing for an imminent end to their captivity and a speedy return to their homes. In 592, however, Ezekiel experienced a vision of God which gave to his life a new direction and which inspired a ministry which was to bear much spiritual fruit for his people. The account of Ezekiel's call to be a prophet is contained in the first three chapters of the book of Ezekiel and it marks the beginning of the first of two important periods in Ezekiel's ministry: the *Early Ministry*: (592–587). As we will see, this early period is characterized primarily by words of judgment upon the Jerusalem community.

One is struck by a number of things in reading the narrative of Ezekiel s call (chaps. 1–3). To begin with, the language which the prophet uses to describe his experience is highly pictorial and symbolic: a flashing storm cloud, strange creatures, wheels within wheels, and the like. Bizarre visions and equally bizarre behavior are to become a characteristic of Ezekiel, a subject to which we will return. Beyond the unusual symbolism, however, two other elements stand out in this passage. One is Ezekiel's realization that Yahweh, the God of Israel, is not confined to the land of Judah nor is the worship of Yahweh confined to the Jerusalem Temple, as many of Ezekiel's fellow exiles undoubtedly had been led to believe. The presence of Yahweh was here, in Babylon, with the people. This is the significance of the refer-

ence to the "glory of Yahweh" in 1:28, a phrase by which the priests of
ancient Israel made reference to the saving presence of Yahweh among the
people.

Another important element within this narrative is the affirmation that
Yahweh has designated Ezekiel to be a prophet. Ezekiel eats the scroll offered
by God and the prophet declares that "it was in my mouth as sweet as honey"
(3:3). In other words, the presence of Yahweh has been internalized within
the prophet in such a manner that his words become the Word of Yahweh.
(Cf. similar metaphors in Isa. 6:7 and Jer. 1:9.)

In the visions and oracles which follow Ezekiel's call, the prophet portrays life in Jerusalem in terms of degradation and sin. In doing so, Ezekiel
expresses a judgment which was certainly consistent with that of Jeremiah,
who was active in Jerusalem at this same time, but Ezekiel describes the
nation's sin in much more lurid detail than does Jeremiah. In Ezekiel 8:1—
11:25 there is an extended account of the prophet's denunciation of Jerusalem. It is in the year following Ezekiel's call (8:1) and the prophet is in the
Jerusalem Temple (whether his presence there was literal or imaginative we
will discuss in a moment). There he sees the evidences of the nation's idolatrous customs.

> So I went in and saw; and there, portrayed upon the wall round about,
> were all kinds of creeping things, and loathsome beasts, and all the idols
> of the house of Israel. (8:10)

Ezekiel also finds evidence of the worship of the Babylonian deity Tammuz
(8:14) and of the sun god (8:16). Because of these and other impure practices, Ezekiel declares that Yahweh will destroy the city. His words are so
powerful that one of the Judean idolaters, a man named Pelatiah, falls down
dead (11:13).

This lengthy passage brings into sharp focus a debate which has raged for
many years over the location of Ezekiel's prophetic ministry. It seems certain, as we have said, that Babylon was Ezekiel's home after the time of the
first deportation in 597. But because of the detailed nature of the references
to events in Jerusalem, some scholars have offered the hypothesis that he
traveled back to the Judean capital on one or more occasions. They suggest
that a reference such as that to Pelatiah's death is not likely if Ezekiel had
not actually been in the Jerusalem Temple. In support of this view there is
the efficiency with which the Babylonians tied together the various parts of
their empire, making communications and transporation between Jerusalem
and Babylon by no means out of the question (compare Jeremiah's letter to
the exiles, Jer. 29). Other scholars, however, cite the manner in which the
text itself describes Ezekiel's going back and forth between Babylon and
Jerusalem to be in supernatural fashion (see 11:24), and they propose the

view that, while Ezekiel remained physically present in Babylon for the duration of his active ministry, his inspired imagination was such that he felt himself to be psychologically and spiritually in Jerusalem at times. The present discussion of Ezekiel embraces the latter view.[46]

In a lengthy oracle (or perhaps series of oracles, 22:1–31) the prophet extends his catalog of Jerusalem's sins. There is murder, idolatry, economic oppression, irreverence toward holy things, sexual immorality, and the like. In response to this unfaithfulness on the part of the people, Yahweh will bring judgment to bear upon Jerusalem in such a manner that the city's fate reminds the prophet of metal which has been melted in the heat of a great furnace (vss. 17–22). So great is the wickedness of the city that not even the presence of the three holy individuals, Noah, Daniel, and Job, would be sufficient to save it (14:14).[47]

Characteristic of Ezekiel's prophetic style are the unusual actions with which he accompanies some of his words and the allegories which he composes. During Ezekiel's Early Ministry these have the effect, as do his oracles, of declaring the sinfulness and coming destruction of the city. Typical of the kind of symbolic action which Ezekiel performed during his Early Ministry is the material in chapter 5. Here the prophet shaves his hair and beard, then divides the shorn mass into three piles with the help of a sword. One pile of hair is burned, a second is hacked with the sword, and the third is tossed up so that it is scattered by the winds. This strange behavior is an object lesson in God's judgment upon Jerusalem (5:5).

> "A third part of you shall die of pestilence and be consumed with famine in the midst of you; a third part shall fall by the sword round about you; and a third part I will scatter to all the winds and will unsheath the sword after them." (5:12)

On another occasion Ezekiel is bound with ropes (or perhaps binds himself) and lies on his left side for three hundred and ninety days, a period equal to the siege of Jerusalem in 588–587, and on his right side for forty days, the number of years of exile (actually fifty-nine) which are in store for Jerusalem (4:4–8). The prophet also eats cheap and repugnant food to symbolize the conditions of life in Jerusalem under siege (4:9–17). Later, he acts out the departure of Jerusalem's people for exile by making a hole in a wall, crawling through it, and, with his belongings on his back, walking away

---

[46] A third alternative is put forward by some scholars who believe that Ezekiel's ministry was confined to Jerusalem, but that his oracles and visions are described in such a manner as to make it appear that he was in Babylon. This view has attracted few supporters.

[47] This is the first mention in the Old Testament (see also Ezek. 28:3) of a person named Daniel, a name which also occurs in the Ugaritic literature. This verse may have helped to provide the name of the chief protagonist of the later book of Daniel. See p. 223.

(12:1–7). When the siege of Jerusalem actually begins, Ezekiel experiences the loss of his wife, an event which under normal circumstances would be an occasion for a public expression of grief. However, the prophet refuses to weep as a sign of the manner in which the people should react to Jerusalem's destruction (24:15–27).

The allegories which the prophet composes are no less vivid than his symbolic actions. An allegory is a narrative story whose components (or characters) represent realities external to the story itself. The story makes important statements about those realities by means of the interaction among the story's components. (A good biblical example of an allegory is found in the Parable of the Sower and the parable's interpretation in Mark 4:1–20.) Ezekiel employs this literary device to great effect on several occasions.

Jerusalem is like a vine which has no practical usefulness in that it cannot be used as building material or even as a peg from which to hang a pot. As men and women thus burn vines in the fire, so Yahweh will destroy Jerusalem (15:1–8). Jerusalem is also like a waif, a little girl, whom Yahweh rescued when she had been deserted as a child. Yahweh loved, cared for, and provided her with jewels and fine clothing. But the child grew up, became a harlot, and gave herself to others (16:1–22).

The image of sin as harlotry, which Ezekiel had probably learned from Hosea (Hos. 1; 3), is the theme of another extended allegory. Here Samaria and Jerusalem are portrayed as twin sisters whom Yahweh has married and who have born Yahweh's children. But the sisters are unfaithful. The one, Samaria (named Oholah in the allegory), has been destroyed by her lovers, the Assyrians. And the other, Jerusalem (Oholibah), who has foolishly refused to learn from the lesson of Samaria, will in turn be destroyed by her lovers, the Babylonians (23:1–49).

Another allegory, in which the Davidic family is portrayed as a family of lions, describes the sad fate of Kings Jehoahaz and Jehoiachin (19:1–9). The image of Jerusalem as a destroyed vine recurs in 17:1–24 and 19:10–14. The first of these two allegories contains a passage which the early Christian community came to interpret as a statement concerning Christ (vss. 22–24).

As we have stated, the early oracles, actions, and allegories of Ezekiel contain the same basic declaration: Yahweh will destroy Jerusalem because of its sinfulness. If Ezekiel lived and worked in Babylon, there is some question concerning the extent to which the Jerusalem Jews responded to or even knew about his message. Their effect upon the Jewish exiles in Babylon, however, would seem more certain, and it is possible (or even probable) that it was this group which constituted the primary audience for Ezekiel's ministry. Ezekiel's messages of God's judgment upon Jerusalem are likely to have inspired a certain hope among the exiles. There is reason to believe that many of the Jerusalem Jews ridiculed their exiled kinfolk and, in addition to offering little to them by way of solace and comfort, actually went so far as to make the claim that Jerusalem was now a better place because of the absence of the exiles, a repudiation which the exiles would have keenly felt. (This is the attitude which Jeremiah harshly criticized in his vision of the baskets of figs, Jer. 24:1–10.) Thus Ezekiel's words and actions, in spite of their mood of tragedy over the coming destruction of the city, would have reminded the exiles of the basic unity of the two Jewish communities and of God's promise to extend concern for justice and righteousness to them both.

In addition, Ezekiel's affirmation of the presence of Yahweh in Babylon would have offered another, more positive cause for hope among the exiles. Ancient Israelite tradition had placed great emphasis on the relationship between Yahweh and the land, an association which was especially strong in the minds of many in the Jerusalem community since that city was the location of Yahweh's Temple and was the city from which Yahweh's anointed Davidic king ruled. Although Jeremiah had attacked such a view as superficial and dangerous (Jer. 7:4), there were still many Jews now in Babylon who must have felt that, because they had been forced to leave their beloved land, they must also have left their God behind as well.

> Then he said to me, "Son of man, these bones are the whole house of Israel. Behold, they say, 'Our bones are dried up, and our hope is lost; we are clean cut off.'" (Ezek. 37:11)

Ezekiel's affirmation that "the glory of Yahweh" is present in Babylon and his insistence that he, a fellow exile, spoke the words of Yahweh must have caused many of his hearers to take new heart.

The event which marks the watershed in Ezekiel's public life and which therefore inaugurates the beginning of his *Late Ministry* (587–571) is the collapse of Zedekiah's revolt and the destruction of Jerusalem by the Babylonians. We have no record in the Old Testament or elsewhere of the manner in which the community of Jews already in exile greeted their compatriots who joined them in 587, but the impact upon the already existing community of exiles must have been profound. It certainly was in the case of Ezekiel, for the nature of his prophetic message changes abruptly with the fall of Jerusalem. Whereas his Early Ministry had been characterized by words and deeds pointing to Yahweh's judgment upon Jerusalem, his Late Ministry emphasizes Yahweh's intention to save and to restore this people.

Perhaps the most celebrated passage in this connection is 37:1–14, the prophet's vision of the valley of dry bones. Whether this vision was prompted by Ezekiel's experience of an actual event, such as his surveying the scene of a great battle, or was entirely an "interior" experience, one cannot say. At Yahweh's direction the prophet speaks to the bones, and they come together, first to form cadavers then living persons. The spiritual purpose of the vision is made clear in the verses (11–14) which follow the narrative portion of the passage: the seemingly dead bones represent the seemingly dead people of Yahweh who will be brought to life again by Yahweh's power. There are at least two interesting features of this passage, in addition to its central theological affirmation. One is that it takes the form of a vision-and-allegory combination, two charateristics of Ezekiel's work which, as we have seen, are also prominent during his Early Ministry. The other feature of this passage worthy of note is the play upon the Hebrew word *ruach*, which may be translated (as does RSV) by the English "breath," "wind," or "spirit." The winds which blow (vs. 9) and the breath which enters the corpses (vss. 5, 6, 9) are, in reality, the Spirit of God (vs. 14). Many students of Ezekiel have pointed to the Yahwist's description of the creation of the first human being (Gen. 2:7) as perhaps the source from which Ezekiel drew the material for his word play (see also Eccles. 12:7 which describes death as a reversal of the "process" described in Gen. 2:7). In any event, the point of Ezekiel's vision-allegory is plain: Yahweh has not forgotten the people but will restore them to life in their own land.

Another vision follows immediately after that of the dry bones in chapter 37, that of the two sticks (vss. 15–28). Here the elements of vision and allegory are joined to that of symbolic action in order to proclaim the prophet's message of hope and restoration. The two sticks which become one stick (tied together?) represent the two parts of the divided kingdom, Israel (the Northern Kingdom, in the text "Joseph") and Judah. These will be reunited into one nation and will be ruled over by a Davidic king. At that time the reunited nation will cease to sin and will experience a restoration of its relationship to God. (Cf. the theological similarities between this passage and Jer. 31:31–34.) In fairness it must be pointed out that this promise was not fulfilled in any literal sense, because the Northern Kingdom was not restored as was Judah. What is more, the descendants of the citizens of the North, that is, the Samaritans, never experienced reconciliation with the Jews of the South, as the New Testament makes very clear (see John 4:9). Some Christian commentators have therefore considered the king to be Jesus and the fulfillment of the promise to be something which takes place either within history in the hearts of individual Christians or at the end of human history. The manner in which prophecies of this nature are to be understood and interpreted is a subject discussed in the final (before the Appendix) chapter of this book (see pp. 206–13).

The messianic figure is unquestionably present in the extended oracle of chapter 34. This passage contains a lovely portrait of Yahweh as the good shepherd who gathers the scattered sheep and gently restores them to their place (vss. 11–16, notice the series of first person singular pronouns in this passage which emphasize the compassionate action of Yahweh). A number of scholars have drawn attention to the similarity between the images here and those in Psalm 23. This text may also have provided Jesus with the literary inspiration for such images as those concerning the lost sheep (Matt. 18:10–14; Luke 15:3–7) and the good shepherd (John 10:1–30).[48] The Davidic king motif (Ezek. 34:23–24) portrays the restoration of the human monarchy as the means by which contact is made between the compassionate rule of Yahweh and the flock. The Davidic king is here portrayed as the under-shepherd who embodies and carries out the gentle love of Yahweh. Again, the connections between this imagery and the New Testament portrayal of the ministry of Christ are obvious (see below).

Another passage which dwells upon the theme of restoration is 36:22–32. Here the salvation of the nation is described in terms of the restoration of the people to the land, a land which will produce the necessities of life in abundance as a sign of the benevolent protection of Yahweh. One interesting feature of this passage is the description of Yahweh's motivation for saving the nation. It is not simply for the sake of the people that they will be redeemed (vs. 32), but primarily because it is an act consistent with Yahweh's own nature. The nation's behavior which has led to its judgment has communicated a false message to humankind concerning the character of Yahweh. This act of restoration will set the matter straight.

> "And I will vindicate the holiness of my great name, which has been profaned among the nations, and which you have profaned among them; and the nations will know that I am Yahweh, says the Lord Yahweh, when through you I vindicate my holiness before their eyes." (36:23)

As a part of his message of restoration Ezekiel emphasizes the moral and spiritual responsibility of the individual man and woman before God. This is by no means a new theological concept for the prophetic tradition. Isaiah called upon King Ahaz to heed God's will for his life (Isa. 7:1–9), and Jeremiah directed attention to the need for every person to make his/her own moral and spiritual commitments (Jer. 31:29–30). But so heavily has the prophetic tradition emphasized the corporate nature of Israel's sin and the corporate manner of God's response, that Ezekiel's message concerning the individual comes as a fresh breeze. The old Hebrew proverb (also quoted in Jer. 31:29) is referred to in a negative way by Ezekiel. It was perhaps a proverb which the exiles often repeated as a means of explaining their present predicament, but Yahweh wants to hear it no more.

> The word of Yahweh came to me again: "What do you mean by repeating this proverb concerning the land of Israel, 'The fathers have eaten sour

---

[48]Note also 34:17–22 which may lie behind the "final judgment" passage in Matthew 25:31–46.

> grapes, and the children's teeth are set on edge'? As I live, says the Lord
> Yahweh, this proverb shall no more be used by you in Israel." (18:1–3)

Then Ezekiel summarizes his theology of individual responsibility in these
words:

> "When the son has done what is lawful and right, and has been careful to
> observe all my statutes, he shall surely live. . . . The son shall not suffer
> for the iniquity of the father, nor the father suffer for the iniquity of the
> son; the righteousness of the righteous shall be upon himself, and the
> wickedness of the wicked shall be upon himself." (18:19–20)

This principle of individual responsibility proclaimed a new freedom before God. No longer did the individual Jewish man or woman stand condemned for the sins of his/her ancestors. A great weight had been lifted off
their shoulders, for now each person could achieve a relationship with Yahweh based upon his/her own response to Yahweh's presence in human life.
Ezekiel's message gave the exiles new reason for hope, and it also prepared
the way for the Christian understanding of the need of each individual to
respond to the love of Christ and to incorporate that love into his/her own
life.

A final manner in which Ezekiel declared God's intention to restore the
nation is contained in his extended description of the New Temple in chapters
40—48. With Yahweh as his guide the prophet inspects this new sanctuary
and reports what he sees in meticulous detail. The new building is similar to
the old edifice of Solomon (which, it will be remembered, had been destroyed by the Babylonians in 587), but it is different in several important
respects. Unlike the old, the New Temple is not adjacent to the royal palace
but is entirely separate, standing in the midst of a holy tract of land especially
set aside for it. The dimensions are larger and the elevation is higher, symbolizing God's holiness and expanded presence in the life of the restored
community. The glory of Yahweh, which the prophet had encountered in the
vision of his call (1:28) and which had departed from the Jerusalem Temple
(11:22–23), is seen entering the New Temple from the east (43:2), a symbol
of the return of Yahweh with the people from exile.

Perhaps the most graphic image of the divine renewal of the nation's life
in this long passage is that of the image of the river of life (47:1–12). Ezekiel
is shown the river flowing from the New Temple and, as it flows toward the
east, it becomes progressively deeper until the prophet can no longer wade
through it. The river ultimately makes its way to the Dead Sea, and all along
its path new life springs forth. When it finally enters the brackish waters of
the Dead Sea, they lose their salinity (vs. 8).

> "And wherever the river goes every living creature which swarms will
> live, and there will be very many fish; for this water goes there, that the

waters of the sea may become fresh; so everything will live where the river goes. . . . And on the banks, on both sides of the river, there will grow all kinds of trees for food. Their leaves will not wither nor their fruit fail, but they will bear fresh fruit every mouth, because the water for them flows from the sanctuary. Their fruit will be for food, and their leaves for healing." (47:9–12)

The book of Ezekiel is characterized by three well-defined parts each of which exhibits its own theological focus. In this regard, the book may be said to have the most logical and orderly arrangement of any of the books of the Hebrew prophets.

A. Prophecies from Ezekiel's Early Ministry: 1—24.
B. Oracles concerning foreign nations: 25—32.
C. Prophecies from Ezekiel's Late Ministry: 33—48.

The first part of the book (1—24) contains those oracles, visions, allegories, and narratives whose primary message is that of the coming judgment upon Jerusalem and Judah, while the final section is primarily concerned with the restoration of the people of God. The second section is a collection of oracles in which the foreign states, Ammon, Moab, Edom, Philistia, Tyre, Sidon, and Egypt, are called to account for their sins before Yahweh.

Although the book displays evidence of having been edited by other persons, perhaps the prophet's disciples, the prophet himself seems to stand behind most of the material contained in it. The peculiarities of Ezekiel's prophetic style are generally consistent throughout the entire book, and this fact leads to the conclusion that it is basically the work of a single individual.

Some scholars have called attention to an unusual symmetry which the book of Ezekiel exhibits. The first section begins with a record of the prophet's call (1:1—3:27), while the third section opens with a reaffirmation of that call (33:1–22). In the latter instance, the prophet's mouth is reopened by Yahweh when the fugitive from the fall of Jerusalem, who had been promised at the conclusion of the first section (24:27), presents himself to the prophet (33:21–22). His message is that the doom of the city, which had been promised by Ezekiel, has come to pass.

The mountains of Israel are prominent in section one (where they receive words of judgment, 6:1–14) and in section three (where they receive words of salvation, 36:1–15). The terrible sins practiced in the old Temple and God's intended response to those sins is the subject of a lengthy passage in the first section (chaps. 8—11), whereas the New Temple and the promise of new life for God's people which it symbolizes are described in an even longer passage in the second section (40—48). As noted above, both of these passages mention the glory of Yahweh (see 1:28) which first leaves the old Temple (11:22–23), but then returns to the New (43:2). The recital of Israel's history in the first section emphasizes the nation's sin (20:1–49), while a similar recital in the third section emphasizes God's grace in the new age to come (36:16–38).

The Theology of Ezekiel

At least four theological postulates characterize the message of Ezekiel. Although these principles have their roots in the prophetic tradition as received by Ezekiel, they are, in certain ways, distinctive in his treatment of them.

A. *Yahweh stands in judgment over human sin.* We have found this to be an important theme in each of the prophets, and it is not surprising that it should be emphasized by Ezekiel. What is unusual, however, is that in the teaching of Ezekiel only one part of the community of God's people is singled out as the object of future judgment. That is, of course, Jerusalem and Judah, while another part, the Babylonian Jews, is described as already having suffered the consequences of the nation's sin.

When Ezekiel describes sin, it is most often in cultic terms, a view which harmonizes well with Ezekiel's vocation as a priest. The nation is guilty of idolatry (8:7–18), which the prophet compares, as had Hosea before him, to sexual prostitution (23:1–21). Child sacrifice is expressly condemned (16:20; 20:31), and this practice is repulsive to the prophet not only because it is inhumane but also because it is a distortion of the true worship of God. This is not to say that Ezekiel was unconcerned with personal immorality (see 22:6–12), but his emphasis in describing sin is upon the legal and cultic aspects of righteousness before God: "I Yahweh am your God; walk in my statutes, and be careful to observe my ordinances" (20:19).

Because of this record of sinfulness, one part of the nation has already suffered judgment, and the Jerusalem community will suffer as well. In a manner similar to Jeremiah, Ezekiel describes the Babylonians as the instrument who will bring God's judgment to pass.

> "the Babylonians and all the Chaldeans, . . . shall come against you from the north with chariots and wagons and a host of peoples; they shall set themselves against you on every side with buckler, shield, and helmet, and I will commit the judgment to them, and they shall judge you according to their judgments." (23:23–24; cf. 5:11–12; 8:18; 20:38)

It is undoubtedly because the prophet understood the Babylonians to be acting as the agent of Yahweh that they are not included among the foreign nations which, in the second section of the book (chaps. 25—32), are named to receive, along with Judah, the judgment of God.

B. *Beyond judgment, Yahweh is with the people, wherever they may be, bringing them life.* One of the important characteristics of the account of Ezekiel's call to be a prophet was, as we saw, his conviction concerning the presence of Yahweh. This was an especially important message for a people who considered themselves to be cut off from their land and, therefore, from their God. Ezekiel's awareness of the presence of "the glory of Yahweh" (1:28) by the banks of the River Chebar in Babylonia and his sensation of having been chosen to speak the words of Yahweh in this alien land were both indications that Yahweh had not abandoned this people, but was with them in their exile.

After the fall of Jerusalem in 587 and the exile of virtually the entire Jerusalem community, the emphasis in Ezekiel's message becomes that of restoration. Here it is interesting to notice how often the symbols concerning God's salvation have to do with the restoring to life of this seemingly dead people. In the vision of the valley of dry bones, the Yahwist's account of the creation of the first human is recalled (Gen. 2:7, as noted above) and, as there, the lifeless human body (in this case, bodies) receives the *ruach* of Yahweh, which fills it (them) with breath and life.

In a similar way, the vision of the river of life which flows from the New Temple portrays the salvation of God in terms of the restoration of life out of death. The Dead Sea, rather than dead bones, is prominent here and, as the fresh waters flow into this salty, arid region, fish begin to populate the waters once more and vegetation crowds the banks (47:3–12).

In other metaphors of salvation the theme of Yahweh as the restorer of life is replaced by other images which have the same effect. Yahweh is the good shepherd who protects the life of the sheep and brings them together after they have strayed (34:11–16). It is Yahweh who sprinkles the people with clean water, thus washing away their sin (36:25).

C. *Individuals, as well as the nation, have an obligation to respond to the presence of Yahweh, a response which centers upon the commitment of the heart.* We have already discussed important texts from chapter 18 which express Ezekiel's views on the place of the individual before Yahweh. To these may be added such a statement as this:

> "When the righteous [individual] turns from his righteousness, and commits iniquity, he shall die for it. And when the wicked [individual] turns from his wickedness, and does what is lawful and right, he shall live by it. Yet you say, 'The way of Yahweh is not just.' O house of Israel, I will judge each of you according to his ways." (33:18–20; cf. 3:16–21; 14:12-23)

The effect of this emphasis upon the individual was to create a sense of freedom, an awareness that the individual need not be damned by the sins of the past but could enter into a wholesome and saving relationship with God on the basis of his/her own commitment.

The nature of this commitment is also sketched by the prophet. It is not only a commitment to the keeping of the law (as in 20:19 quoted above) but also one which involves a reorientation of the heart. Perhaps Ezekiel had been influenced at this point by Jeremiah (Jer. 31:31–34) or possibly even by the book of Deuteronomy (10:16) which had played so important a role in the life of the nation when the prophet was a youth. In any event, his words describe faith in Yahweh in terms of inner spiritual renewal.

> "A new heart I will give you, and a new spirit I will put within you; and I will take out of your flesh the heart of stone and give you a heart of flesh. And I will put my spirit (*ruach*) within you, and cause you to walk in my statutes and be careful to observe my ordinances." (36:26–27; cf. 11:19; 18:31)

D. *Yahweh's rule over the people will be embodied in a king of the line of David.* Texts which express a messianic expectation play a prominent part in the message of Isaiah, as we have seen. While that emphasis is not as great in the record of Ezekiel's prophetic ministry, there are nevertheless two significant passages which must be considered in any discussion of Ezekiel's theology. The first of these comes within the context of the portrait in chapter 34 of Yahweh as the good shepherd who sustains (vss. 11–16) and judges (vss. 17–22) the flock. The human shepherd, "my servant David," presides over the peace which results from Yahweh's restoration of the people. A second text amplifies the same theme.

> "My servant David shall be king over them; and they shall all have one shepherd. They shall follow my ordinances and be careful to observe my statutes. They shall dwell in the land where your fathers dwelt that I gave to my servant Jacob; they and their children and their children's children shall dwell there for ever; and David my servant shall be their prince for ever." (37:24–25)

As has been true of the messianic texts of Isaiah, those of Ezekiel have often been identified by Christians as looking forward to the role of the ultimate Davidic king, Jesus Christ.

The Influence of Ezekiel on the New Testament

We have already called attention to the fact that a number of passages in the book of Ezekiel reappear in the New Testament. Upon close examination the student of Ezekiel discovers that the thought and language of the prophet recur most often in the New Testament books of John and Revelation. The most obvious point of contact between Ezekiel and John is, as previously observed, the image of Yahweh, the Good Shepherd (Ezek. 34) which becomes the material for Jesus' discourse in which he identifies that Good Shepherd as himself (John 10:1–39). The analogy is even more tightly drawn by Jesus' identification of himself with the Davidic personality who will carry out God's intention to be a shepherd to the people.

> "And I will set up over them one shepherd, my servant David, and he shall feed them: he shall feed them and be their shepherd." (Ezek. 34:23)

> "I am the good shepherd.". . . "My sheep hear my voice, and I know them, and they follow me; and I give them eternal life, . . . My father, who has given them to me, is greater than all, . . . " (John 10:11, 27–29)

In a similar manner the parable of the kindly shepherd (who seeks the one lost sheep and having found it returns it to the fold with great rejoicing), which is told in both Matthew (18:10–14) and Luke (15:3–7), seems to draw heavily upon Ezekiel 34, especially verse 12.

Another set of images from Ezekiel which reappears in the Gospel of John has to do with the allegory of Judah as a useless vine which will be destroyed by fire (Ezek. 15). In John this becomes the allegory in which Jesus himself is the vine and God is the vinedresser. Jesus' followers are the branches of the vine, and those who are useless and withered are gathered and burned (John 15:1–11).

The phrase "son of man," which occurs frequently in Ezekiel as a designation for the prophet, also occurs in all four gospels as a reference to Jesus. In Ezekiel the phrase is simply a poetic way of saying "man," whereas in the gospels it has the added importance of emphasizing the humanity of Christ.

The primary theological connection between the books of Ezekiel and Revelation is that they both contain apocalyptic elements. Indeed, Revelation is by definition an apocalypse, a Greek word which means "revelation" and which appears in the Greek text of Revelation 1:1. Apocalyptic literature developed in the late Old Testament period and continued for some centuries thereafter in both Jewish and Christian use. The book of Revelation is the most extensive example of this genre in the New Testament, although there are other, shorter examples (e.g., Mark 13). Apocalyptic literature is characterized by a number of distinctive elements among which are a tendency toward highly developed symbolism and an expectation that God will overthrow some present and powerful evil by a series of mighty acts, thus bringing an end to the present age and ushering in God's righteous kingdom. As one would imagine, apocalyptic tended to flourish (as has subsequent interest in apocalyptic) during times which were uncertain and dangerous. The period of the Exile and the period of the church's persecution by Rome thus provided fertile ground for the flowering of apocalyptic. Although the book of Ezekiel is not apocalyptic literature, as such, it certainly contains apocalyptic elements which provided rich material for the later book of Revelation.

To begin with, the manner in which the author of Revelation describes the vision of God is conceptually very near the language of Ezekiel, especially chapters 1—3. In both instances the imagery is bizarre and graphic, and the effect is to convey an impression of a God who is mighty, just, and a very present reality in human life. What is more, the image of the New Jerusalem (Rev. 21:1—22:5) is anticipated by Ezekiel's vision of the New Temple (40—48). Especially striking is the fact that, in both cases, the human recipient of God's revelation is led by God around the new edifice and the entire structure is carefully measured (Ezek. 40:5–16; Rev. 21:15–21). Just as a river of life flowed from beneath the New Temple and gave new life everywhere it flowed (Ezek. 47:3–12), so a strikingly similar phenomenon is described in the New Jerusalem (Rev. 22:1–5) down to the detail of monthly bearing fruit trees.

A final point of contact between Ezekiel and Revelation which should be mentioned here is the reference in both books to the evil figures of Gog and Magog (Ezek. 38—39; Rev. 20:8). In the Ezekiel passage Gog is the ruler of a land called Magog. When this king and his forces come against Israel, Yahweh's wrath will be aroused and will destroy this wicked invader to the accompaniment of terrible natural disasters. It is not certain if the prophet had in mind a specific ruler and nation to which he applied the names Gog and Magog. If so, we have no way of knowing who that ruler and nation were. The theological point of the passage in Ezekiel is, however, less obscure: Yahweh will provide for the people and will protect them against their evil enemies. On the other hand, in Revelation both of these names appear as designations for evil persons who are conspirators with Satan and who will, like Satan, be overthrown in the last times by the power of God.

11
THE SECOND ISAIAH

Date of the Second Isaiah's Work: sometime shortly before 539
B.C.

Location: Babylon.

Central Theological Concepts: Yahweh has forgiven the people's
iniquity and will restore them to their land. Through the
ministry of the "Servant of Yahweh," the knowledge of
Yahweh will be extended to the nations.

An Outline of Isaiah 40—55 will be found on p. 146.

For many years it has been recognized that the book of Isaiah presents a
different mood in chapters 40—55 than is exhibited by most of the material
in 1—39, a spirit of unbounded joy and celebration which is generally not
present in the earlier portion of the book. In the centuries before scholars
applied the tools of literary research to biblical materials it was assumed that
chapters 40—55 were, like 1—39, the work of Isaiah of Jerusalem. It was
believed that the prophet, because he looked forward to a distant day when
God's power would be displayed in remarkable new ways, changed the tone
of his prophecy to one of expansive rejoicing. However, with the rise of
critical scholarship in the eighteenth and nineteenth centuries, it became evident to a large number of scholars that 40—55 represented not a different
mood in the same prophet who is responsible for 1—39 but the work of a
different individual altogether, one who actually lived through the tumultuous
events he celebrated. This writer, who was steeped in the prophecies of Isaiah
of Jerusalem (and who was thus a kind of distant disciple), relied upon many
of the theological concepts of the earlier prophet and used many of his same
words and phrases. And his writings were, perhaps from the very beginning,
considered by devout Jews worthy to be placed alongside those of the great
prophetic contemporary of Kings Ahaz and Hezekiah. Yet this anonymous
prophet of the Exile, whom we call the Second Isaiah for lack of a better
name, also had distinctive literary characteristics of his own. What is more,
he placed the magnificent principles of faith which Isaiah of Jerusalem had
proclaimed into a new service.

In brief, there are at least three primary differences between 1—39 and

40—55 which lead scholars to the belief that the latter block of material is
the work of the anonymous prophet of the Exile:

(1) A difference of mood, as mentioned above. In 1—39 there is a concern for the nation's present sin, and judgment is often spoken of as a future
act of God. In 40—55 judgment is a thing of the past, and the immediate
future will be the setting for a great act of God's salvation. The language of
40—55 is correspondingly different from that of 1—39 in that it expresses
this difference of mood (e.g., the often repeated phrase in 40—55, "fear
not").

(2) A difference of setting. Isaiah 1—39 clearly reflects the work of Isaiah
of Jerusalem who was active from 741—701. The setting in 40—55 is equally
clearly the community of Jewish exiles in Babylon.

(3) A difference in time. The names of Isaiah's contemporaries appear a
number of times in 1—39: Ahaz, Hezekiah, and Sennacherib, for example.
The only proper name of a historical personality to appear in 40—55 is that
of the Persian king, Cyrus (550–530), who is accurately described in his
historical role as the one who releases the Jews from their exile.[49]

The Historical Context of the Second Isaiah's Work

The dynamic Babylonian king Nebuchadrezzar died in 562 and the vast
empire which he had erected began to decline. The decades following his
death were characterized by the brief reigns of several kings, none of whom
seems to have possessed Nebuchadrezzar's skills. The final Babylonian monarch, Nabonidus, ascended the throne in 555 and soon thereafter mysteri-
ously deserted the imperial city for life in the Arabian desert, leaving Babylon
in the charge of his son Bel-shar-usar (the biblical Belshazzar, Dan. 5:1,2).
If the Persian records (our best source of information) are accurate, there
were many in Babylon who not only expected the collapse of their kingdom,
but who actually welcomed it in the hope that something better would come
out of the ashes. In October of 539 Babylon fell without a fight to the advancing army of Cyrus, King of Persia.

Cyrus was an individual of uncommon ability. The son of a Persian king
and a Median princess, Cyrus had merged the two nations of his parents
when he overthrew his grandfather, King Astyges of Media, about 550.[50] He

---

[49] For a discussion of Isaiah 56—66, see the chapter on the Third Isaiah, pp. 170–79.

[50] The Medes, it will be remembered, were a fierce people who had cooperated with the Babylonians to help overthrow Assyria almost a century before. The merger of the two nations
which Cyrus accomplished was to stamp the phrase "the Medes and the Persians" so deeply
upon the memory of the Near Eastern peoples that it appears in the book of Daniel (6:8, 12)
some four centuries later.

thereupon embarked upon a decade of conquest which was to extend his borders from the area of modern Pakistan to the Aegean Sea, a distance of some two thousand miles, an empire which was the largest yet in human history. Cyrus' conquests in Ionia (modern western Turkey) brought him into contact with the rich Greek city-states of that region. The conflict between Persians and Greeks was to last for two centuries and was to be the occasion for the first authentic writing of history by Europeans, as Herodotus, Xenophon, and other Greeks developed striking new ways of recording human events in their chronicles of the Persian wars.

During all of this time Cyrus had ignored Babylon, his nearest important neighbor to the South. But in 539 his armies marched into middle Mesopotamia and within days Babylon fell. A Persian document, the so-called Cyrus Cylinder, records the event in these words.

> Marduk [the most important Babylonian god] . . . beheld with pleasure his [i.e., Cyrus'] good deeds and his upright mind (and therefore) ordered him to march against his city Babylon. . . . going at his side like a real friend. His widespread troops . . . strolled along, their weapons packed away. Without any battle, he made him enter his town Babylon, sparing Babylon any calamity.[51]

The fall of Babylon marked the first time since the Sumerians first united the city-states of Lower Mesopotamia about 3000 B.C. that the rich Mesopotamian valley was ruled from outside.

Cyrus' domestic policy was very different from that of his predecessors, the Assyrians and the Babylonians, both of whom had used enforced exile as a means of subduing their conquered peoples. Cyrus seems to have believed that the various national groups within his empire would be more cooperative if they were allowed a large measure of autonomy, including the exercise of their own religious customs upon their native soil. Accordingly, one of his first acts after entering Babylon, where many other foreign peoples in addition to the Jews had been brought, was to demonstrate his new policy of tolerance. The Cyrus Cylinder describes how he allowed many of the former captives of the Babylonians to return home, carrying with them the idols of their deities which the Babylonians had seized. It was within this context that the restoration of the Jerusalem community, promised by Ezekiel and others, took place. The book of Ezra records the imperial edict of 539 in these words:

> "A record. In the first year of Cyrus the king, Cyrus the king issued a decree: Concerning the house of God at Jerusalem, let the house be rebuilt, the place where sacrifices are offered and burnt offerings are brought; . . . let the cost be paid from the royal treasury. And also let the gold and silver vessels of the house of God, which Nebuchadnezzar took out of the

[51] ANET, p. 315.

> temple that is in Jerusalem and brought to Babylon, be restored and brought
> back to the temple which is in Jerusalem, each to its place; you shall put
> them in the house of God." (Ezra 6:2–5; cf. 1:2–4)

Many of the Jews had become so acclimated to life in Babylon that they did
not want to leave and return to a rubble-filled city which most of them had
never seen. But others, who remembered the traditions of Jerusalem and who
longed to resume the Jewish presence there, celebrated that the long ordeal
of Exile was over. It was in expectation of these events that the Second Isaiah
carried on his public ministry.

The Prophet and the Book

There is not a shred of biographical information given in the Old Testament about the Second Isaiah, who remains a personality unknown to us. It
may be assumed that he was himself a Jew of the Exile who, as stated above,
was deeply committed to the prophetic traditions associated with Isaiah of
Jerusalem, but beyond that not much may be said. We cannot even be absolutely sure that this person was a man in light of the fact that female prophets
were by no means unknown in ancient Israel (2 Kings 22:14). The only
personal reference to the prophet is the use of the first person in 40:6 (part of
a brief record of the prophet's call, 40:6–8), but this tells us nothing about
the individual behind the words.

The words, therefore, must be the focus of attention in any study of the
Second Isaiah, and the richness of imagery and style which one finds here
more than compensates the reader for whatever frustrations may be felt in
not being able to discover the personality of the prophet. Scholars have identified a number of literary forms in chapters 40—55 which are not only
interesting in their own right, but which throw important light on the theological content of the Second Isaiah's message.

One of these is the so-called trial speech, whose imagery we are familiar
with from the oracles of Hosea (see p. 34). Here the setting is the court of
law (perhaps, as in Hosea, the council of village elders is specifically in the
prophet's mind). Israel (or in some passages Israel's neighbors) is on trial and
Yahweh, through a spokesperson, the prophet, acts the role of judge and
prosecuting attorney.

> Set forth your case, says Yahweh;
>   bring your proofs, says the King of Jacob. (41:21)

In these passages Israel is charged with past sins and is commanded to answer for them. Surprisingly, however, the tribunal, although delivering a ver-

dict on the nation's guilt, declares that the penalty for that guilt has been paid. Furthermore, what is in order now is not some additional expression of Yahweh's justice, but an act of Yahweh's compassion. In some instances the note of salvation is struck in the trial speech itself.

> "I, I am He
>   who blots out your transgressions for my own sake,
>   and I will not remember your sins." (43:25)

In other instances the same effect is achieved when a trial speech in which Israel is condemned is followed by an oracle of salvation (see below) in which the nation's deliverance is declared, as in 42:18—43:13. This particular passage is interesting because in it the prophet recites portions of Israel's long history (see specifically 43:1–5) in a manner somewhat reminiscent of Ezekiel 20. But whereas the emphasis in Ezekiel is on coming judgment, the emphasis here is on the mercy of Yahweh. The following are examples of the Trial Speech in the literature of the Second Isaiah: 41:1–4, 21–29; 42:18–25; and 43:22–28.

Another form of speech is the disputation, a philosophical argument in which a question is first raised, then answered in a forceful, sometimes polemical, manner. This literary form is perhaps to be associated with the schools of wisdom which flourished in Israel from the time of Solomon and which (in Israel and in other ancient Near Eastern societies) assumed that truth could be attained by means of the logic of the human mind. The give and take of rational debate was thus a product of this view of life (cf. the debates between Job and his three "comforters," Job 3—31), an argumentation which was engaged in for the purpose of uncovering truth. In the literature of the Second Isaiah the disputation typically addresses the question of Yahweh's nature and ability to do what the prophet claims that Yahweh is about to do, namely save the people.

> Why do you say, O Jacob,
>   and speak, O Israel,
> "My way is hid from Yahweh,
>   and my right is disregarded by my God?"
> Have you not known? Have you not heard?
> Yahweh is the everlasting God,
>   the Creator of the ends of the earth.
> He does not faint or grow weary,
>   his understanding is unsearchable.
> He gives power to the faint,
>   and to him who has no might he increases strength. (40:27–29)

Chapter 40 provides good examples of disputation speeches of the Second Isaiah and, although there is some debate about the best manner in which to identify the individual speeches, one way is to view the following as units: 40:12–17, 18–26, 27–31.

A third form of speech in Isaiah 40—55 is that of the oracle of salvation. Some Old Testament scholars have connected this literary form to the words of the priest when absolving some worshiper of sin or when declaring some individual to be just in the eyes of the law or medically clean (say, from leprosy) in the eyes of the community. Examples of this priestly function may be found in the book of Psalms.

> Blessed is he whose trangression is forgiven,
>   whose sin is covered.
> Blessed is the man to whom Yahweh imputes no iniquity,
>   and in whose spirit there is no deceit.
>
> . . .
>
> Be glad in Yahweh, and rejoice, O righteous,
>   and shout for joy, all you upright in heart! (Ps. 32:1–2, 11)[52]

Here the emphasis is upon the saving activity of Yahweh and upon the spirit of joy which this kindles in the heart of the one who is saved.

In this form of speech as employed by the Second Isaiah, God is not urging the people to account for their sinful ways (as in the trial speeches), and there is no dialogue among the various parties in the attempt to attain truth (as in the disputation speeches). The emphasis here is on simple declaration, the affirmation that Yahweh is about to deliver the people and that they, therefore, should rejoice.

> fear not, for I am with you,
>   be not dismayed, for I am your God;
> I will strengthen you, I will help you,
>   I will uphold you with my victorious right hand. (41:10)

The imperative "fear not" is a prominent feature of the various examples of the oracle of salvation in this literature, and the phrase often occurs in close association with two of the Second Isaiah's favorite titles for Yahweh, "Redeemer" and "the Holy One of Israel." (The frequent use of the latter phrase represents one of the closest points of contact between the thought of the Second Isaiah and that of Isaiah of Jerusalem, as in Isa. 6:1–8.) A reading of the following oracles of salvation will demonstrate the manner in which these three expressions tend to be clustered together by the Second Isaiah: 40:1–11; 41:8–20; 43:1–21. Also prominent here is the declaration that what is about to happen is the result of Yahweh's own loving initiative.

---

[52] A number of scholars have drawn attention to numerous parallels between the language of the Second Isaiah and that of the Psalms. This is probably related to the prominent place which the Psalms may have occupied in the worship of the exiled Jews (note, for example, Ps. 137).

A fourth literary form in Isaiah 40—55, and undoubtedly the one which has been the subject of the most discussion, is that of the Servant Songs: 42:1–4; 49:1–6; 50:4–9; and 52:13—53:12. These four poems have received this designation because they borrow the language of the royal court to describe an individual and/or a group who is to do the work of Yahweh, the King. The intense discussion which has raged around these passages has centered upon two basic questions. (1) What is the relationship of these passages to the rest of the material in 40—55 and to each other? (2) Who is the servant?

With respect to the first of these questions, many Old Testament scholars feel the poems to be the work of the Second Isaiah himself, a judgment based upon close similarities of language and thought between the poems and the literature in which they are imbedded. Other scholars, however, perhaps a minority, feel that they come from a different hand than the surrounding material, some scholars going so far as to say that the four Servant Songs do not display a unity of authorship among themselves.

The question concerning the identity of the servant is complicated by the fact that the role is not described in a consistent manner in each of the four poems. At some points, for example, the servant appears passive (42:3) and resigned to suffering (53:7), while at other points he appears militant and triumphant (49:2). Nor is the role of the servant always described in the same manner among the Servant Songs (where he usually appears to be an individual [but see 49:3]) as it is in the surrounding literature (where "my servant . . . whom I have chosen" [41:8] is clearly identified with the nation). In light of these considerations, the question asked by the Ethiopian eunuch, when he was first introduced to this literature by the Apostle Philip, becomes understandable: "About whom, pray, does the prophet say this, about himself or about someone else?" (Acts 8:34). The tools of Old Testament scholarship have never succeeded in providing a satisfactory answer to this question, which has caused the answer supplied by the faith of the Christian church to assume all the more significance, as we will discuss below. There can be little doubt that in these Servant Songs Jesus found much conceptual framework for his own ministry, so that he is led to make the astonishing proclamation that the Messiah must suffer and die in order to fulfill the will of God (Matt. 16:21–23). On these grounds Christians have understood that whatever contemporary figure(s), if any, the author of the Servant Songs may have had in mind at the time of their writing, the Servant of these poems is none other than Jesus Christ.

Briefly summarized, the contents of the four Servant Songs are as follows:

42:1–4: A gentle servant is commissioned by Yahweh to implement justice (*mishpat*, the word occurs three times in this short passage) among the nations. (See below for a detailed discussion of this passage.)

49:1–6: Here the servant explains his commission as one of bringing the salvation of Yahweh not just to Israel but also to the nations of the earth. (The identification of the servant with Israel in vs. 3 is probably a scribal gloss.)

50:4–9: The servant declares that he will be faithful to his task in spite of persecution, because Yahweh sustains and protects him.

52:13—53:12: The passage is, in large part, a report of those who have benefited from the work of the servant, whom they initially found unattractive, even repulsive. Yet they have come to understand that his suffering and death was for them, and they confess that he will be vindicated and exalted by Yahweh.

The structure of Isaiah 40—55 is complex in the sense that the material does not seem to have been arranged according to clear chronological or thematic formulas. It has been observed, however, that this body of literature is composed of two different types of poetry and that these tend to be gathered into the first and second parts of the whole. On the one hand, there are the shorter oracles, each of which represents a distinctive literary form (as above) and which may have been delivered orally before being reduced to writing. Most of these are found in chapters 40—45. On the other hand, there is a collection of longer poems, many of which exhibit more than one literary form and which appear to have been composed as written documents from the beginning. Most of these are collected in chapters 45—55. There is no significant difference in the theological outlook between these two types of poetry, since the longer poems, for the most part, reflect upon and repeat the themes of the shorter oracles.

Thus something like the following outline of Isaiah 40—55 may be seen:

A. Prologue: The coming of Yahweh: 40:1–11.
B. The spoken oracles of the Second Isaiah: 40:12—44:23.
C. A central proclamation concerning Cyrus: 44:24—45:13.
D. The written poems of the Second Isaiah: 45:14—55:5.
E. Epilogue: The grace of Yahweh: 55:6–13.

At various points the literature is punctuated by material which comes either from the Second Isaiah himself writing in a different frame of mind (possibly the Servant Songs, for example) or from later editors (some scholars have suggested, for example, that 42:5–9 is a later commentary upon or expansion of the first Servant Song in 42:1–4).

No one can be sure, of course, of the process by which the various components of chapters 40—55 were brought together into their present form or how they were added to Isaiah 1—39. Many scholars feel, however, that most of the material is the work of the Second Isaiah himself and that this prophet may also be responsible for the basic shape of his "book." It may also be assumed, they argue, that a group of his followers preserved the prophet's words, possibly using them in services of public worship and certainly transporting them to Jerusalem at the time of the Restoration. This same person or persons may also be responsible for the later editorial additions which may be detected in 40—55. Some scholars identify the person who was primarily responsible for this activity as the Third Isaiah, or that individual(s) whose presence may also be detected in Isaiah 56—66.

The circumstances under which chapters 40—55 were appended to chapters 1—39 is a mystery, but the assumption is that this was done at a very early time, perhaps during a period contemporary to that of the basic editorial activity outlined above. It is clear that well before the Christian era the book of Isaiah had received the form in which we know it, since it is found in this form in both the Septuagint translation and in the scrolls from the Qumran community.

The Theology of the Second Isaiah

The theological themes in chapters 40—55 draw extensively from the traditions of Hebrew prophecy which the Second Isaiah inherited, and in this literature are to be found important affirmations, such as (1) Israel has a special relationship to Yahweh and (2) Yahweh, being a righteous judge, cannot remain indifferent to human sin. Yet these familiar themes, which go back to the time of Amos and beyond, appear in startlingly new form in Isaiah 40—55 and, in some cases, are superseded by new insights which transform these traditional prophetic understandings. Perhaps, therefore, the theology of the Second Isaiah may best be viewed under three headings.

A. *Yahweh, the Holy One of Israel, is the Creator God who has no rivals.* It is remarkable how often the theme of creation by Yahweh surfaces in 40—55. This is, of course, not an affirmation which is unique to the Second Isaiah, but no other Old Testament figure makes so prominent a place for creation theology in his thought as does the anonymous prophet of the Exile.

> "I am Yahweh, who made all things,
>   who stretched out the heavens alone,
>   who spread out the earth. . . ." (44:24)

The Second Isaiah was not concerned simply to affirm the creative power of Yahweh, but to do so in such a manner that left no one in doubt concerning the identity of the Creator. It must be remembered that the exiled Jews lived among a people who themselves possessed a well-developed creation theology and who applied that theology in such a manner that it became a part of the foundation upon which the Babylonian political establishment rested. The great Babylonian creation hymn, the *Enuma elish*, recounted how the powerful deity Marduk first created the heavens and earth by slaying the evil chaos dragon and then, in the midst of the chaos waters, established an ordered world.[53] The pinnacle of this creation was Babylon and each year, upon the occasion of the Babylonian New Year's festival, the *Enuma elish* was publicly recited as a part of the ceremony by which the king was empowered by Marduk to rule for another year. There can be little doubt that the Second Isaiah has this Babylonian myth in mind when he speaks about creation, and he goes to some pains to emphasize that it is not Marduk who created the ordered world but Yahweh. The prophet is even so bold as to use the language of the Babylonian myth to make his point.

> Awake, awake, put on strength,
>   O arm of Yahweh;
> awake, as in days of old,
>   the generations of long ago.
> Was it not thou that didst cut Rahab in pieces,
>   that didst pierce the dragon?
> Was it not thou that didst dry up the sea,
>   the waters of the great deep;
> that didst make the depths of the sea a way
>   for the redeemed to pass over? (51:9–10)

Not only does the prophet wish to make sure that his people understand that it is Yahweh, not Marduk, who is responsible for the ordered world, but he views Yahweh's creation of the world as but the first step in a series of deeds which results in the creation of Israel to be Yahweh's special people. This movement from creation-of-the-world to creation-of-Israel is then viewed as leading to the salvation-(or recreation)-of-Israel. For example, notice in the passage above how skillfully the prophet moves from the imagery of the chaos waters to that of the waters of the Red Sea, so that creation is tied closely to Yahweh's activity as Savior. With this passage may be compared another in which the Exodus event is celebrated as an example of Yahweh's saving deeds in the past.

> "I am Yahweh, your Holy One,
>   the Creator of Israel, your King."
> Thus says Yahweh,
>   who makes a way in the sea,
>   a path in the mighty waters,

---

[53] ANET, pp. 60–72.

> who brings forth chariot and horse,
>> army and warrior;
> they lie down, they cannot rise,
>> they are extinguished, quenched like a wick. (43:15–17; cf.
>> 44:24–28)

Another aspect of the creation theology of the Second Isaiah is his understanding that, other than Yahweh, there are no gods. This goes beyond his concern to identify Yahweh as the true Creator and makes of the Second Isaiah the first explicit monotheist among the Hebrew prophets. Again, the religious and cultural context in which the exiles lived must be remembered, so that the prophet's sharp attacks against the kind of idolatry practiced by the Babylonians, to which many of the Jews must have been attracted, is seen as all the more pertinent. There is no more savage attack upon idolatry anywhere in the Old Testament than the biting irony employed in 44:9–20. This long prose section is introduced by a brief bit of poetry which prepares the reader for what is to come.

> Thus says Yahweh, the King of Israel,
>> and his Redeemer, Yahweh of hosts:
> "I am the first and I am the last;
>> besides me there is no god.
> Who is like me? Let him proclaim it,
>> let him declare and set it forth before me.
> . . .
> Is there a God besides me?
>> There is no Rock; I know not any." (44:6–8)

B. *Yahweh is about to do a new thing, a new act of redemption by which to express love for the people.* We have already noticed how creation and salvation (re-creation) are inextricably tied to one another by the Second Isaiah. The prophet's train of thought is that Israel sinned and was punished. Now, however, that punishment is over and Yahweh, who has filled the role of judge in the past, will now act as redeemer.

> Comfort, comfort my people,
>> says your God.
> Speak tenderly to Jerusalem,
>> and cry to her
> that her time of service is ended,
>> that her iniquity is pardoned,
> that she has received from Yahweh's hand
>> double for all her sins. (40:1–2)

This new act of salvation may be compared, as we have noticed above, to the event of the Exodus. Its true importance, however, lies in the manner in which it expresses the nature of Yahweh. A redeemer was, as we noted in our discussion of Jeremiah 32:6–15 (p. 114), one who took steps to prevent some person or some possession which belonged to the family from being lost. The noun "redeemer" and the verb "to redeem" appear over and again in the literature of the Second Isaiah as a way of describing the saving activity of Yahweh.

> But now thus says Yahweh,
>   he who created you, O Jacob,
>   he who formed you, O Israel:
> "Fear not, for I have redeemed you;
>   I have called you by name, you are mine." (43:1; cf. 41:14; 43:14;
>   44:24)

It is interesting that, in all of the passages which describe the coming salvation, nowhere is God's activity conditioned by any response on the part of the people, a feature which is in sharp contrast to the prophetic teaching generally. Yahweh is going to save Israel not because it has done something by which to have earned salvation but because such a deed is consistent with Yahweh's nature (43:1–7; 43:22—44:5). In the nature of the Deity who saves, and not in that of the people who are saved, is to be found the true quality of this mighty act. This reality is proclaimed in the language which a royal herald might use.

> A voice cries:
> "In the wilderness prepare the way of Yahweh,
>   make straight in the desert a highway for our God.
> Every valley shall be lifted up,
>   and every mountain and hill be made low;
> the uneven ground shall become level,
>   and the rough places a plain.
> And the glory of Yahweh shall be revealed,
>   and all flesh shall see it together,
>   for the mouth of Yahweh has spoken." (40:3–5)

Finally, Cyrus the Persian is identified as the one who is to carry out the will of Yahweh. It may be that Jeremiah's identification of Nebuchadrezzar as the human instrument of Yahweh's judgment inspired the Second Isaiah at this point, for on one occasion he refers to Cyrus as "one from the north" (41:25; cf. Jer. 4:6). The impressive military accomplishments of Cyrus are said to be nothing other than the work of Yahweh (41:1–4), and on two occasions the prophet uses language usually reserved for the royal house of David to describe the work of the Persian king, "my (Yahweh's) shepherd (44:28; cf. Ezek. 34:23) and "his (Yahweh's) anointed" (Hebrew: *mashiach* [messiah] 45:1; cf. Ps. 2:2).

> "who says of Cyrus, 'He is my shepherd,
>   and he shall fulfil all my purpose';

saying of Jerusalem, 'She shall be built,'
    and of the temple, 'Your foundation shall be laid.'" (44:28)

Yahweh, who had in the past used one foreign monarch to judge the nation, will now use another to re-create it.

C. *The beneficiaries of the new salvation are not to be just the people of Judah alone, but all the nations.* Again, in making such a statement, the Second Isaiah drew upon the theological traditions of Israel, for long ago the Yahwist had described the call of Abraham in these terms (Gen. 12:1–3). The anonymous prophet of the Exile, however, gave this ancient insight new life.

"I am Yahweh, I have called you in righteousness,
    I have taken you by the hand and kept you;
I have given you as a covenant to the people,
    a light to the nations,
    to open the eyes that are blind,
to bring out the prisoners from the dungeon,
    from the prison those who sit in darkness." (42:6–7)

It is within the Servant Songs that this declaration of the universal nature of Yahweh's salvation is emphasized most dramatically. The servant is one who will "bring forth justice (*mishpat*) to the nations" (42:1) and "startle many nations" (52:15).

"It is too light a thing that you should be my servant
    to raise up the tribes of Jacob
    and to restore the preserved of Israel;
I will give you as a light to the nations,
    that my salvation may reach to the end of the earth." (49:6)

There can be little doubt that the universalism of the Second Isaiah played an important role in helping to shape the missionary imperative of the Christian church (Matt. 28:19–20).

Two Key Texts

A. 40:1–5

Because the theological message of the Second Isaiah is woven throughout the literature associated with him, there is no single text or group of texts which stands out from the rest. However, it is helpful to examine the language and thought of this important prophet, and two texts have therefore been chosen which represent key elements in his message. The first of these, 40:1–5, represents the words with which the "book" opens and is a part, as noted above, of a longer prologue, 40:1–11. And yet, verses 1–5 also make a small literary unity within the larger one and may be studied for their own sake.

In order to demonstrate the poetic parallelism of the passage, the RSV text may be arranged as follows:

> Comfort, comfort my people, says your God.

> Speak tenderly to Jerusalem,
> And cry to her

> that her time of service is ended,
> that her iniquity is pardoned,
> that she has received from Yahweh's hand double for all her sins.

> A voice cries:

> "In the wilderness prepare the way of Yahweh,
> make straight in the desert a highway for our God.

> Every valley shall be lifted up,
> and every mountain and hill be made low;

> the uneven ground shall become level,
> and the rough places a plain.

> And the glory of Yahweh shall be revealed,
> and all flesh shall see it together,

> for the mouth of Yahweh has spoken."

Verse 1: The passage opens with a word from Yahweh. The twice repeated imperative, "comfort, comfort," is plural in form, meaning that those who are to do the comforting of Yahweh's people are the members of the divine council who, at appointed times, gather to do the bidding of Yahweh (cf. Job 1:6). The repetition of the imperative is a characteristic of the style of the prophet ("awake, awake," 51:9; 52:1; "depart, depart," 52:11) which implies urgency. Some scholars have connected the use of the verb "to comfort" here with its use in Lamentations (poems which express sorrow over the destruction of Jerusalem) where it is associated with the idea of the comforter as one who helps (Lam. 2:13). At the time of the destruction of the city there was no one to comfort/help, but that situation is being reversed by the present action of Yahweh.

Verse 2: "Speak tenderly to Jerusalem" in the first line is literally "speak [again, plural] to the heart of Jerusalem." The message is one of release and redemption. The Hebrew word which RSV translates "warfare" (RSV margin: "time of service") is a reference to the period of a soldier's active duty. The release of the nation is compared to the moment of joy when the soldier is discharged and sent home from the battle. The mention of the nation's iniquity is a point of direct contact with the prophets of the past who denounced Israel for its sin, the difference now being, however, that that sin has been pardoned by God. The "double" punishment referred to in the last phrase of verse 2 is a hyperbolic way of saying that the nation has suffered more than enough. Verse 2 announces in the tersest possible form the "Gospel" of the Second Isaiah and, in a sense, all that follows in 40—55 is a commentary upon this central declaration. Forgiveness and salvation are inseparable in the thought of the Second Isaiah, indeed, in that of the entire Old Testament.

Verses 3–4: The poetic parallelism of these verses, demonstrated above, leaves no doubt that the manner in which the RSV punctuates verse 3 captures the meaning of the original Hebrew. The Septuagint, however, renders verse 3: "A voice [cries] in the wilderness, 'Prepare . . . ,'" a reading which has found its way into the New Testament (Mark 1:3 and parallels; John 1:23) where the voice-in-the-wilderness is understood to be that of John the Baptist. This is another example of the manner in which the Greek translation of the Old Testament helped to shape the New Testament interpretation of some key Old Testament passages (see the discussion of Isa. 7:14, p. 74ff.). The owner of the voice is not identified, but perhaps it is that of the prophet.

The redemption of the nation is described in terms of a victorious march by a conquering monarch and the royal retinue. The "way of Yahweh" and the "highway for our God" are doubtless contrasted to the great Processional Way in the city of Babylon, one of a number of points at which the prophet uses the context of the Babylonian world as a foil for his thought. This central thoroughfare through the heart of the city was the avenue down which Marduk was carried in the annual New Year's celebration, a procession in which the idol was followed by the king. It was also the avenue which saw the parades of Babylon's conquering armies and was perhaps the thoroughfare by which two waves of Hebrew exiles had been marched into the city in disgrace years before. Compared to the "way of Yahweh," the great Processional Way was nothing, for "the highway of our God" will cut straight across the desert (the shortest route from Babylon to Jerusalem), leveling mountains and elevating valleys along the way. It will become the pathway for the returning exiles who, having entered Babylon in sorrow and defeat, will depart in triumphant joy.

Verse 5: As the ultimate act of salvation, Yahweh's own nature will be revealed (literal Hebrew: "the glory of Yahweh will be uncovered"). We have discussed above the reason which the prophet gives for Yahweh's saving grace: not the nation's virtue or even its repentance, but the gracious character of Yahweh. Here that idea is emphasized by means of the reference to the "glory," that term by which the priests, especially, referred to Yahweh's saving presence in Israel's life (see the discussion of Ezek. 1:28, pp. 125–26). By means of this gracious act, all humankind (note the prophet's universal field of concern) will know that Yahweh, the sole God, is active in the life of this people

Israel. The phrase "for the mouth of Yahweh has spoken" ends the brief oracle and, in effect, brackets verses 1–5 as an authentic declaration of Yahweh (the first of the pair of brackets being "says your God" in vs. 1).

Our passage thus introduces the prologue and summarizes in anticipation the essential message of the prophet. Beyond that, however, it points to the climax of the "book" where "comfort, comfort" (40:1) becomes "awake, awake" (52:1) and "depart, depart" (52:11). In addition, the fact that the prologue and the epilogue (55:6–13) were placed in their present positions for purposes of literary and theological balance is demonstrated by the echo of 40:4 in 55:12:

> "For you shall go out in joy,
>   and be led forth in peace;
> the mountains and the hills before you
>   shall break forth into singing,
>   and all the trees of the field shall clap their hands." (55:12)

The "wilderness" and "desert" of 40:3 are also contrasted in the rain, the snow, and the budding life forms of 55:10.

B. 42:1–4

This passage constitutes the first of the four Servant Songs, as discussed above. As such it sets the tone for those which follow and, in certain respects, anticipates features found in them. The reader of these songs is struck at once, on the one hand, by their beauty and theological power, and, on the other, by the veiled manner in which they describe the Servant and his mission. These characteristics of the songs have thus caused them to be a source of great fascination to many students of the Bible, both Jewish and Christian.

Verse 1: The song begins with language very similar to that used by the Second Isaiah generally, a fact which has strengthened the belief of many scholars that the songs (or at least the first three of them) are the work of the prophet. The word "behold" appears seventeen times in 40—55 and only thirteen times in all other prophetic literature combined. The fact that Yahweh would designate a special servant is, of course, consistent with the view of much of the rest of the Old Testament which describes the manner in which such figures as Moses, Gideon, Samuel, David, and even such foreigners as Nebuchadrezzar and Cyrus are appointed by Yahweh for special tasks. However, many scholars feel that the royal ideology is especially prominent here and that, just as a human king possessed servants to carry out royal policies, some of whom were quite powerful and influential, so Israel's King, Yahweh (43:15), has designated a human as an agent of the royal rule.

Having called this servant, Yahweh endows him with "my (Yahweh's) Spirit" in order to equip him to do the divine will. The language of the third line of verse 1 seems closely related to the understanding of the manner in which Yahweh worked through the Judges and the early Kings of Israel (specifically Saul and David). At that time Yahweh's Spirit was the means by which the individual was empowered to do tasks which would otherwise have been beyond his ability ("and the spirit of God came mightily upon Saul," 1 Sam. 11:6 [cf. Judg. 3:10; 6:34]). In the same manner Yahweh will endow this special Servant.

The fourth line of verse 1 is the first of three places within this short poem in which the mission of the Servant is identified:

> he will bring forth *mishpat* to the nations (vs. 1).
> he will faithfully bring forth *misphat* (vs. 3).
> . . . till he has established *mishpat* in the earth (vs. 4).

The striking feature here is, of course, the repetition of *mishpat* (RSV: "justice"). We have earlier discussed the legal and relational nature of this important Hebrew term (see pp. 28–29), but notice should be taken here of the special manner in which the Second Isaiah understands and uses it. A prominent theme in the trial speeches is that *mishpat* involves the acknowledgement that it is Yahweh alone who is God and who is in control of human affairs (see especially 41:1–4 [where RSV translates *mishpat* as "judgment," vs. 1] and 45:20–25). Many commentators have therefore concluded that the *mishpat* which the Servant is to bring is the universal knowledge of Yahweh as God. In this connection, it is striking that 42:6–7 describes this *mishpat* in terms of the giving of sight to the blind and the liberation of the imprisoned. (It will be remembered, as noted above, that 42:5–9 seems to be a reflection or commentary upon 42:1–4.)

Verses 2–3: Here reference is made to the manner in which the Servant will carry out his mission. It is interesting that this is expressed by means of five negatives, a feature more striking in the Hebrew original, where the negative particle *lo'* occurs five times, than in English translation. In other words, the reader is not told precisely how the Servant will do Yahweh's will but is told how the Servant will *not* perform that will. A characteristic of gentleness is certainly expressed here, but the manner of expression only serves to heighten the sense of mystery concerning the Servant and his task (cf. 50:6; 53:7). Another way of translating the final line of verse 3 would be: "He will truthfully bring forth *mishpat*."

Verse 4: Something of the character of the Servant is described here in language which closely parallels verse 3. "He will not fail" (RSV) is literally "he will not burn dimly," while "or be discouraged" (RSV) is literally "he will not be bruised." Both of these phrases repeat the thought and language of the preceding verse (also the string of Hebrew negative particles has now been extended to seven). Again, the reader's sense of mystery and awe is increased by the poet's manner of expression, and the yet-to-be-described suffering of the Servant (see 52:13—53:12) is hinted at.

In this verse *mishpat* occurs for the third time, on this occasion with a different verb than in the two previous instances. There seems, however, to be no essential difference in meaning between "bring forth" and "establish."

The final line of the song is parallel to the final line of verse 1. In both lines the universal nature of the Servant's mission is alluded to (see especially 49:6), but *mishpat* now becomes *torah*, "law" or, more accurately, "teaching." The need for all peoples to receive the *mishpat/torah* of Yahweh is implied in the verb "wait," which also suggests their readiness to receive it.

Close analysis of this first Servant Song does little to help us answer the important questions discussed above concerning the relationship of the songs to the remainder of 40—55 and concerning the identity of the Servant. It does help us to understand, however, that the lofty vision of the role and mission of the Servant found fulfillment in none of the Second Isaiah's contemporaries and that the early church had, therefore, good reasons for identifying the servant as Jesus Christ (see especially Matt. 12:17–21).

12
HAGGAI

Date of Haggai's Work: 520 B.C.
Location: Jerusalem.
Central Theological Concept: Yahweh's will is that the
destroyed Temple should be rebuilt and the Davidic prince
Zerubbabel should be crowned King of Judah.
An Outline of the Book of Haggai will be found on p. 60.

The Historical Context of Haggai's Work

In our discussion of the Second Isaiah we noticed that the imperial policy of the Persians was significantly different from that of the Assyrians and the Babylonians in that Cyrus believed that his subject peoples would be more cooperative if they were allowed to practice their own customs on their ancestral lands. One of his first acts following the fall of Babylon, therefore, was to permit a number of the exiled communities to return to their own homes, carrying with them the idols and other accouterments of worship which the Babylonians had seized and brought to Babylon (2 Kings 24:13). One aspect of the implementation of this policy was the issuing of the decree of 539 which allowed the Jews to return to Jerusalem with

> "the gold and silver vessels of the house of God, which Nebuchadnezzar took out of the temple that is in Jerusalem and brought to Babylon . . . ." (Ezra 6:5)

Both versions of Cyrus' decree contained in the book of Ezra state that permission was also given to the Jews to reconstruct the Temple (1:2; 6:3), and one version adds that the Persians encouraged those Jews who did not wish to return to help in the restoration project by providing funds (1:4).

Our knowledge of events surrounding the actual return to Jerusalem and the nature of life within the postexilic community comes primarily from the historical books of Ezra and Nehemiah and the prophetic literature associated with Haggai and Zechariah. Because the material contained in these books is fragmentary and sometimes contradictory,[54] it is impossible to be precise in our understanding of events during this period. The initial return, however, seems to have been led by the Davidic prince Sheshbazzar, who was appointed to oversee Persian interests in the area and to reconstruct the Jerusalem Temple. The circumstances under which the resettlement of Jerusalem and the Temple reconstruction were begun were adverse to say the least. Although certain resources had been supplied to Sheshbazzar and his party by the Persians and by at least some of the Jews who wished to remain in Babylon, these were undoubtedly meager in comparison to the magnitude of the task. The book of Lamentations portrays the city as little more than piles of rubble (Lam. 5:1–18), and the first task of the returning exiles was probably to build suitable shelters for themselves. (It must be remembered that, apart from the very elderly who may have been present, the "returning" exiles had been born in Babylon and had probably never before seen Jerusalem.)

The task of restoration was also complicated by the attitude of those people who were already living in Jerusalem and the surrounding countryside. Some of these would have been Jews whom the Babylonians left behind. Since they had long ago occupied lands which once belonged to exiled families, the question of property rights must have surfaced very soon and would have been a source of friction between the returning Jews and those Jews (we have no idea how many) who had never gone to Babylon in the first place. The Samaritans living in the land proved another problem for the party of Sheshbazzar. These people were the descendants of those few Israelites of the Northern Kingdom whom the Assyrians had not included in their deportations of 722 and after. The Assyrians had imported non-Israelites into the regions of Samaria and the Northern Kingdom (2 Kings 17:24–28), and the intermarriage among Israelite and non-Israelite groups produced the Samaritans. This was a community of people whom the Jews of Jerusalem thoroughly despised, as we know from the New Testament record (John 4:9), but whose traditions of worship were very similar in certain ways to those of the Jews themselves.

In the second year after their arrival in Jerusalem (Ezra 3:8), or about 536, Sheshbazzar and his group laid the foundations for a new Temple at the same site upon which Solomon's magnificent edifice had once stood. This

---

[54] An example of the contradictory nature of this material may be seen in the fact that, whereas Sheshbazzar is generally identified as being the leader of the first effort to restore the Temple (Ezra 1:8; 5:14), reference is also made to Zerubbabel as having attempted the first Temple reconstruction project (3:2,8). Although this has led a few scholars to conclude that these are two names for the same person, most feel that two separate individuals are involved: Sheshbazzar, the son of Jehoiachin (a conclusion based on 1 Chron. 3:18 and on the belief that the Shenazzar mentioned there is the same person as the Sheshbazzar of the book of Ezra), and Zerubbabel, the nephew of Sheshbazzar and grandson of King Jehoiachin (1 Chron. 3:19).

was an accomplishment which caused great rejoicing among most Jews who were present, although the very elderly, who remembered the greater dimensions of the former building, wept over the slight proportions of Sheshbazzar's foundations (3:10–13). Before the work could proceed very far, however, the Samaritans approached with the suggestion that they be permitted to participate in the rebuilding effort (4:2). Whether this was a sincere offer or simply a ruse by which they hoped to interfere with the work, it is impossible to say, but the reaction of the Jews was negative.

> "You have nothing to do with us in building a house to our God; but we alone will build to Yahweh, the God of Israel, as King Cyrus the king of Persia has commanded us." (Ezra 4:3)

The tension between the two communities became so intense that the Temple reconstruction project was discontinued and no further work done for several years. In the interim Sheshbazzar disappeared from the record. Whether he died, went back to Babylon, or settled into an obscure existence in Jerusalem we have no way of knowing.

About 520 another Davidic prince was sent by the Persian authorities to Jerusalem, Zerubbabel, grandson of King Jehoiachin. His mission was probably the result of internal political pressures within the Persian empire as much as it was the result of the special needs of the inhabitants of Jerusalem. The Persian ruler was now Darius I who had gained the throne after the death in 522 of the childless son of Cyrus, King Cambyses (who had succeeded his father in 530). Darius' struggle for the throne against several rivals was bitter and protracted, and it seems that large sections of the empire were convulsed by the conflict. The time of Zerubbabel's mission to Jerusalem coincided with the period in which Darius was consolidating his hold on the empire, and the Jewish prince's primary commission was undoubtedly to secure Judah, a vital outpost on the road to Egypt (also now a Persian province), for the forces of Darius. Zerubbabel was accompanied by other Jews, including a certain Joshua (or Jeshua), a priest. Among other objectives Zerubbabel and Joshua were to complete the Temple reconstruction and reinstate the worship of Yahweh there.

As in the time of Sheshbazzar the project encountered difficulties. There was interference from others once more, not from the Samaritans this time, but from other Persian officials who, in the political confusion, mistook (or perhaps judged correctly, as we will see) the rebuilding efforts of Zerubbabel as some kind of threat against their authority (Ezra 5:3–5). In addition, according to the book of Haggai, Zerubbabel's arrival in Jerusalem coincided with a prolonged drought which forced severe economic deprivation upon the people (Hag. 1:10–11). However, the first obstacle was cleared away when confirmation was received from the Persian court that Zerubbabel's project had the imperial blessing (Ezra 6:1–12). As for the drought, it was apparently endured.

In the year 515 the Temple was completed amid great rejoicing and fervent prayers. Zerubbabel seems to have become the subject of great political expectations on the part of some Jerusalem Jews who hoped that, now that this Davidic prince had finished work upon the Temple, he would submit to being crowned King of Judah so that the house of God and house of David would endure side by side forever, as the prophet Nathan had promised so long before (2 Sam. 7). But Zerubbabel quietly drops out of the biblical record at this point. Whether he was not interested in being King of Judah and simply settled into a quiet life, or whether the Persians considered this royalist sentiment to be a threat to their rule in the area and removed the prince, we do not know. The only certain thing is that, although Zerubbabel disappeared, his Temple became the focal point of renewed religious fervor on the part of the Jews.

The Prophet and the Book

Very little is known about Haggai, the individual. Since his name is related to the Hebrew word meaning "festival," some have suggested that he may have been born on the occasion of one of the important Hebrew holy days. Nothing is known of his ancestry, nor of his vocation. He was probably a priest, for he was certainly interested in strengthening the cult. There is no direct evidence for this, however, and the fact that he seeks priestly guidance concerning a matter of ritual cleanliness (2:10–13) may indicate that he was not ordained. His reference to the splendor of Solomon's Temple (2:3) suggests that he may have been among the original generation of exiles. If so, he would have been a very old man at the time of his prophetic activity.

The dates of Haggai's prophetic oracles are very precisely given in the text of the book which bears his name and reveal that his ministry was one of the shortest of all the canonical prophets. It took place over a period of only four months during the second year of the reign of Darius I, (520 B.C.). There are four carefully delineated oracles each of which forms a major section within the brief (thirty-eight verses) book.

A. A command to rebuild the Temple: 1:1–15.
B. A promise of future glory and wealth: 2:1–9.
C. A statement concerning ritual holiness and uncleanliness: 2:10–19.
D. A messianic promise: 2:20–23.

Haggai's first oracle, 1:1–15, is directed to Zerubbabel and his priestly associate Joshua, and it consists of a command to proceed with the business of rebuilding the Temple. There is no reference to the previous abortive attempt at Temple reconstruction by Sheshbazzar, but the failure of that enterprise may have been on the prophet's mind. He calls attention to the fact that, whereas the people have provided for their shelter, they are content to let Yahweh's house lie in ruins (vs. 4). In the prophet's view this is the cause of the present state of economic deprivation. Harvests have been meager, food is scarce, and a drought has settled in upon the land. The people must

> "Go up to the hills and bring wood and build the house [Temple], that I [Yahweh] may take pleasure in it and that I may appear in my glory, . . . " (1:8)

In response, Zerubbabel and Joshua begin to direct the reconstruction, so that three weeks later the work actually begins (1:15).

Within a month of the beginning of work on the Temple, Haggai has spoken again, 2:1–9. In reading between the lines of this second oracle one senses that the workers have become discouraged, perhaps because the new Temple will be so poor in comparison to the old (2:3; cf. Ezra 3:10–13). Haggai urges the workers to take heart. Yahweh is at work in human history to bring to pass a glorious future for the Temple and for all Jerusalem. Some scholars view Yahweh's promise that "I will shake the heavens and the earth" (2:6) to be a reference to the unsettled conditions in the Persian empire during the early months of Darius' reign. However that may be, it is clear that the prophet expects some universal upheaval to result in great good for the Jerusalem community.

> ". . . I will shake all nations, so that the treasures of all nations shall come in, and I will fill this house with splendor, says Yahweh of hosts. The silver is mine, and the gold is mine, says Yahweh of hosts. The latter splendor of this house shall be greater than the former, says Yahweh of hosts; and in this place I will give prosperity, says Yahweh of hosts." (2:7-9)

A third oracle, 2:10–19, delivered two months after the second, is very difficult to interpret. The prophet secures the opinion of the priests that ritual holiness is not contagious, whereas ritual uncleanliness is. This insight is then applied to "this people," "this nation" (vs. 14), in a manner which is obscure. Some scholars feel that the prophet is saying that those who were previously unwilling to work on the Temple should now be disqualified from participating in the reconstruction project (although that seems contrary to 1:8), and other scholars feel that it is a reference to the unworthiness of the Samaritans to join the Jewish workers (cf. Ezra 4:2). This third oracle is concluded by the prophet's pointing out that since work on the Temple began, material conditions in the land have improved and will continue to do so (2:15–19).

The final oracle, 2:20–23, is directed at Zerubbabel and he is described in language which is clearly royalist. In Jeremiah 22:24 the Davidic ruler Jehoiachin is referred to as Yahweh's "signet ring." Whether Haggai had this text specifically in his mind is uncertain, but the imagery is the same. The upheavals mentioned in 2:6 are referred to once more (2:21), and the prophet seems to say that, just as the present political chaos will result in renewed wealth and importance for Jerusalem, so it will also result in the reestablishment of the Davidic monarchy.

> "On that day, says Yahweh of hosts, I will take you, O Zerubbabel my servant, the son of Shealtiel, says Yahweh, and make you like a signet ring; for I have chosen you, says Yahweh of hosts." (2:23)

The Theology of Haggai

The theological content of the book of Haggai is notable as much for what is absent as for what is present. Like the prophets of old, Haggai understands himself to be the speaker of Yahweh's word, and the prophetic formula "says Yahweh" appears over and again in this brief book. Also in keeping with his predecessors in the prophetic tradition, Haggai draws a close connection between the people's sin and God's judgment. What is distinctive about Haggai, however, is that his understanding of righteousness and sin is basically cultic in nature (contrast Amos 5:21–24). The people have sinned because they have not erected a new Temple structure, and Yahweh has judged that sin by sending drought and economic deprivation. There is no mention of *mishpat*, *ts*e*dhaqah*, or any other lofty moral principle so important to Amos, Hosea, and others. Nor do we sense a concern that other nations should share in the knowledge of Yahweh's love, as in the Second Isaiah. For Haggai the other nations are important because they will enrich Jerusalem (2:7).

Yet the student of Haggai's prophecies should not go too far in criticizing the prophet for what he did not say. Although Haggai's concern is intensely narrow, it may be (we cannot know for certain) that without his prodding and that of his contemporary Zechariah, the Zerubbabel Temple might never have been built. And without a Temple as the focal point of its spiritual life, late Old Testament Judaism might not have developed as it did, to the possible detriment of all humankind. After all, it was in the Second Temple community that the words of the prophets of old were treasured and reproduced, to say nothing of the law and all the other Hebrew literature then existing which is now a part of the Jewish and Christian scriptures. It was in the Second Temple that the ancient forms of worship were preserved and adapted, forms of worship which are indispensable to modern Judaism, Christianity, and Islam. Haggai is clearly a prophet of "organized religion," and the literature which bears his name reminds us at once of the strengths and weaknesses of that aspect of human life before God.

13
ZECHARIAH

Date of Zechariah's Work: 520–518 B.C.
Location: Jerusalem.
Central Theological Concepts: It is Yahweh's will that
 Zerubbabel and Joshua rebuild the Temple and reinstate
 priestly worship there. With the coronation of Zerubbabel
 as the new Davidic king Yahweh will inaugurate
 a new era of prosperity and glory for Jerusalem.
An Outline of Zechariah 1—8 will be found on p. 165.

The Prophet and the Book

Very little is known about the personal life of the prophet Zechariah whose name means "Yahweh remembers." He was either the son (Ezra 5:1) or grandson (Zech. 1:1) of a certain priest named Iddo, who was among the exiled Jews who "returned" to Jerusalem with Zerubbabel about 520 (Neh. 12:4). He may have been associated with a guild of cultic prophets, and he certainly represents an important element within Hebrew prophecy, going back at least as far as Ezekiel, which placed great importance upon Israel's cult and upon the priestly office. For a number of important reasons which are cited later in this book,[55] the prophet is believed to be responsible only for chapters 1—8 of the book which bears his name, Zechariah 9–14 originating in a later period.

As was the case with Zechariah's contemporary, Haggai, the oracles of this prophet are dated precisely. We are therefore able to know that Zechariah's first oracle (eighth month, second year of Darius [1:1]) was delivered only a month before the last two oracles of Haggai (ninth month, second year of Darius [Hag. 2:10, 20]).[56] The influence of Haggai upon Zechariah is less precisely known, but it is generally believed that Zechariah knew of Haggai's work and, in some respects, built upon it. Nevertheless, Zechariah's prophecy is characterized by certain qualities which make it different from that of Haggai, the most important being the presence of certain apocalyptic elements.

---

[55] See pp. 201–05.

[56] For the historical context of Zechariah's work, one should consult pp. 157–60.

Apocalyptic is a genre of Jewish and (later) Christian literature which shares with classical Hebrew prophecy a strong conviction that a righteous God will destroy human evil (and evil humans) but will save those who show themselves faithful. Apocalyptic differs from Hebrew prophecy, among other things, in that it often conveys its message by means of bizarre images and symbols. Apocalyptic also shows an increasing tendency with the passage of time to identify the moment of God's judgment as occuring at the end of human history instead of within the flow of history, as did classical Hebrew prophecy. We have already studied the oracles of Ezekiel, which are note-worthy for the distinctive nature of their imagery and for the fact that they include an extended vision of a restored Jerusalem and a restored Temple (chaps. 40—48) which seem in some unspecified way to be "extra-historical." Certain of these tendencies toward apocalyptic may also be seen in Zechariah 1—8, among them the presence of unusual (often baffling) imagery, although Zechariah clearly seems to have the immediate future in mind as the arena of the new messianic age.

Perhaps the best manner of viewing the structure of Zechariah 1—8 is in terms of the three dates given for the prophet's activity:

A. Oracle of the eighth month, second year of Darius (520): 1:1–6.
B. Oracles and visions of the eleventh month, second year (520): 1:7—6:15.
C. Oracles and visions of the ninth month, fourth year of Darius (518): 7:1—8:23.

The first section, 1:1–6, is a general call to repentance on the part of the people. The sinful past which resulted in Yahweh's judgment upon the nation is recalled and the people are urged to follow a different example of conduct. There is also an emphasis upon the importance of the prophetic office, but no specific mention (as yet) of Temple, priesthood, or cult. This brief oracle may be considered to serve as an introduction to the book and also as a means by which the work of Zechariah is linked to the prophets of old.

The second section, 1:7—6:15, is composed of a series of oracles and visions, the latter being significant because of their unusual symbolism. Three visions (1:7—2:5) stand at the beginning of this section, the first of which (1:7–17) seems to reflect the period of tranquility which resulted when Darius secured his hold upon the throne of Persia. It contains the message that Hag-gai had not been mistaken in seeing the "shaking of the nations" (Hag. 2:6–7) as a prelude to Jerusalem's greater glory. The new messianic age will be ushered in despite the present conditions of stability within the empire.

An oracle (2:6–13) follows the three visions and is in turn followed by two additional visions (3:1–10 and 4:1–14). The visions of chapters 3 and 4 are significant in that they declare first Joshua (chap. 3), then Zerubbabel and Joshua (chap. 4) to be worthy of the offices to which they have been called by Yahweh.

The sixth (5:1–4) and seventh (5:5–11) visions describe the moral qualities of life in the new Jerusalem. There will be no false swearing (vs. 3) or thievery (vs. 4). Wickedness itself, personified as a woman exiled to Shinar (Mesopotamia), will be banished from the land (vss. 7–11).

An eighth vision (6:1–15) forms the climax to this second section. The whole world is at peace (vss. 1–8), and the rule of Yahweh is going to be established through the agency of the Davidic prince Zerubbabel (vss. 9–14). In this latter connection, many scholars feel that the name "Joshua" in verse 11 originally read "Zerubbabel" (meaning Branch or Sprout from Babylon) since only then does the play on the word "Branch" of verse 12 make sense.[57] Zechariah's expectation of the enthronement of Zerubbabel thus parallels that expressed only two months before by Haggai (Hag. 2:20–23).

The third section of Zechariah 1—8, 7:1—8:23, is a collection of oracles which portray the glories of life in the new Jerusalem presided over by King Zerubbabel. The tragic history of the nation is again rehearsed (7:1–14), and the future is contrasted to the past. The new Jerusalem will bustle with life, old and young living in harmony with each other (8:4–5) and in harmony with Yahweh: "they shall be my people and I will be their God, in faithfulness and righteousness" (8:8; cf. Jer. 31:31–34). The people are to have no fear and to work hard (8:9, 13—perhaps a reference to the Temple reconstruction project), and Yahweh will bless the land with abundant produce (vs. 12) and will cause the Jews to be honored among the nations (vs. 13). The speaking of truth and the implementation of *mishpat* and *shalom* ("peace") are to characterize life in the new Jerusalem (8:16–17), and the fame of the city will be such that

> "In those days ten men from the nations of every tongue shall take hold of the robe of a Jew, saying, 'Let us go with you, for we have heard that God is with you.'" (8:23)

The Theology of Zechariah 1—8

There are several important respects in which the theological outlook of Zechariah is close to that of Haggai, an affinity which has often caused Jews and Christians alike to speak of the two prophets in the same breath (Ezra 5:1; 6:14). Their most important common convictions are the belief that it

---

[57]"Zerubbabel" may have been effaced from the text in favor of "Joshua," if the Persian authorities reacted with hostility toward the idea of Zerubbabel's coronation as king of Judah.

was Yahweh's will that the Jerusalem community rebuild the Temple under the leadership of Zerubbabel and Joshua and, further, that the Davidic throne should be restored with Zerubbabel as its occupant. The first of these emphases results in the fact that Zechariah, like Haggai, must be listed among the founders of Second Temple Judaism with its intense interest in priesthood and cult. The expectations relating to the coronation of Zerubbabel are certainly dependent upon Ezekiel 34:23–24; 37:24–28; and perhaps also upon Isaiah 9:1–7; 11:1–9. However, there are several points at which Zechariah exhibits theological concerns which are distinctively his own, and it is to these that we now turn.

A. *Visions in which angelic and satanic personalities are prominent are an important means by which Yahweh communicates with this prophet.* The vision (probably ecstatic) was, as we have noticed, an important feature of the prophetic activity of Ezekiel, but for Zechariah the vision has become the "normal" means by which Yahweh's will becomes known. The continuity with the classical Hebrew prophetic tradition is demonstrated by the presence of occasional oracles with their "says Yahweh" (1:4; 2:6), but this feature is clearly subordinate to that of the vision. Each vision includes an angel who speaks to the prophet and who interprets what the prophet "sees." While angelology is by no means confined to Zechariah (cf. 2 Sam. 24:16), no other Old Testament literature gives such a prominent place to these servants of Yahweh, with the result that God is a more remote figure in Zechariah 1—8 than in most other prophetic literature. Many scholars have pointed out that the Old Testament literature which comes from the exilic and postexilic periods and which is closely related to the priestly outlook (notably, the Priestly History and Ezekiel) displays a tendency to view Yahweh in terms of majesty and transcendence (contrast the Yahwist's description of God as "walking in the garden in the cool of the day," Gen. 3:8), and the angelic visions of Zechariah would seem to be consistent with this point of view. But Yahweh is, if somewhat remote in the theology of Zechariah, also omnipotent. Yahweh's angels patrol the earth (1:11), and the dawning of the new messianic age is to be the result not of human effort, but of the divine will:

> Then he [the angel] said to me, "This is the word of Yahweh to Zerubbabel: Not by might, nor by power, but by my Spirit, says Yahweh of hosts." (4:6)

Zechariah's work is also distinctive in that he alone among the Hebrew prophets refers to Satan (3:1–2).[58] Here "the Satan" (Hebrew: "the Adversary") appears in order to accuse and discredit Joshua, but his effort is over-

---

[58] The only other explicit references to Satan in the Old Testament are in Job 1—2 and in 1 Chronicles 21:1.

ruled by Yahweh who affirms the worthiness of Joshua to fulfill his priestly office. Later Jewish and Christian apocalyptic gives a prominent place to Satan as the supernatural personification of evil and as the enemy of God, so that Zechariah's reference may be viewed as one more link with the apocalyptic which flowered in the Intertestamental and New Testament periods.

B. *The visions of Zechariah are characterized by symbols and images which may have had obvious meaning for the prophet's immediate hearers, but they are somewhat obscure for us today.* There is a sense in which the symbolism of Zechariah, like his visions, is more a literary (or oratorical) device than a theological postulate, yet the theology of the prophet and the means by which it is conveyed are closely linked. The prophet's symbolism underscores a sense of a God who, on the one hand, is holy and removed from the scene of human life but who, on the other hand, is deeply concerned over the course of human history, both Jewish and gentile. This is a God who is actively shaping history according to certain purposes and who communicates the divine will to the people through the agency of the prophet. Again, Zechariah's use of unusual symbols demonstrates a further kinship with Ezekiel and forms an important bridge between prophecy and apocalyptic.

C. *The messianic age which is about to dawn will be characterized by the prominence of Jerusalem and by the presence of such qualities as justice and faithfulness to Yahweh.* There has been a tendency among some scholars to compare Haggai and Zechariah unfavorably with their great predecessors in the prophetic tradition who demonstrated a deep passion for justice, mercy, and truth. There is a degree to which such criticism may be valid, for in Zechariah 1—8 there are certainly no thundering demands for purity of heart (in preference to liturgical concerns) as in, say, Hosea 6:6. Yet it would be wrong to dismiss Haggai and Zechariah on these grounds, for we see particularly in the latter prophet not only a belief in the dawning of a new day, but a belief that in the age to come human life will possess a certain quality because of the presence of the Spirit of Yahweh within the human community. To be sure, much of Zechariah's picture of the messianic age rings with a certain nationalism. The Davidic king Zerubbabel will preside over this new age with a Levitical priest at his side (6:9–14).[59] The gentiles will participate in the glories of this new age (an influence of the Second Isaiah?), but their position will clearly be subordinate (8:20–23). And yet the total picture is one of peace, justice, and plenty in a world community where the sovereignty of Yahweh is acknowledged. The picture of the joys of the very old and the very young (8:4–5) and the reference to *mishpat* and *shalom*

---

[59]Zechariah's expectation of a messianic kingdom ruled by Zerubbabel did not, of course, materialize.

(8:16) may go back to such conceptions as Isaiah's portrait of the peaceable kingdom (Isa. 11:6–9) and Ezekiel's expectation of the benevolent rule of Yahweh, the Good Shepherd (Ezek. 34:11–24). In any event, this picture speaks of hope for the future of humanity before God, a hope which, in our age of war and frequent injustice, is often tragically absent from the human heart.

14
THE THIRD ISAIAH

Date of the Third Isaiah's Work: sometime after 538 B.C.
Location: Jerusalem.
Central Theological Concept: Yahweh is a God who
vindicates the righteous and destroys the wicked.
An Outline of Isaiah 56—66 will be found on p. 172.

The Relationship Between Isaiah 56—66
and the Remainder of the Book of Isaiah

Those biblical scholars who, in the eighteenth and nineteenth centuries, first drew attention to the work of the Second Isaiah generally believed that all of Isaiah 40—66 reflected the prophetic activity of this anonymous prophet of the Exile. Later, however, considerable scholarly support was gained for a viewpoint which saw the origins of chapters 56—66 as different from 40—55. Naturally, the name Third Isaiah was associated with chapters 56—66 and the arena of the activity of this prophetic figure was understood to be Jerusalem at a time immediately after the return of the exiles. Today there is still a group of scholars who defend the unity of 40—66, but they constitute a minority. On the other hand, those who agree that 56—66 comes from a later time than 40—55 are divided between those who, on the one hand, believe that essentially one person is behind 56—66 and those who, on the other hand, consider 56—66 to contain material from a number of sources. For purposes of convenience we will speak here of the Third Isaiah, although the student should remember that Isaiah 56—66 may reflect the work of several prophetic individuals.

There are several reasons for concluding that 56—66 reflects a difference of time, place, and prophetic personality than 40—55. First, the audience is no longer the Jews of the Babylonian Exile but Jews of a partially restored Jerusalem. There are no references to a state of bondage on the part of the people, or to the names of Babylonian deities or geographical locations, as in 40—55. Rather, the references are to Jerusalem (66:10; 62:6) and to the Palestinian area generally (63:1). Second, the prophet speaks in a different tone to a people who are of a different mood. The Second Isaiah's sweeping promises of salvation, while echoed by the Third Isaiah (60:1–7), are joined by descriptions of a sinful and wayward people (59:1–8), by threats of judgment (59:18–19), and by appeals to a seemingly disinterested Yahweh to act in order to save the people (64:1–7). Third, there is an interest in the rituals of worship not found in the Second Isaiah. The keeping of the Sabbath is urged (56:2), proper fasting is described (58:1–9), sacrifice is identified as an appropriate act of worship (60:6–7), and the Temple is viewed as the focus of the people's life before Yahweh (62:9). Fourth, 56—66 does not display the theological unity which is characteristic of 40—55. The work of the Second Isaiah has a very sharp focus, i.e., the sins of the people have been forgiven and Yahweh is about to bring about their salvation. The theological concerns of the Third Isaiah, however, are more diffuse. As noted above, 56—66 contains not only promises of salvation but also indictments of the people for their present sin and a concern that the promises of Yahweh will really come true.

These differences have caused a large number of scholars to conclude that the Third Isaiah was a prophet whose theological ideals were nurtured within the Isaiah tradition and who lived among the Jerusalem Jews in the years immediately following the return under Sheshbazzar. As we know from the book of Ezra and from the prophecies of Haggai and Zechariah, this was a very difficult time for the people. There was hostility from their neighbors (Ezra 4:4–5), drought stalked the land (Hag. 1:10–11), and conditions were generally very poor. It must have seemed to some that the large promises of the Second Isaiah and of contemporaries like Haggai and Zechariah were false, for instead of a grand new Jerusalem there was only a shell of a city which bore little relation to the splendid capital of Solomon or to the grand designs of Ezekiel or the Second Isaiah. What is more, the lofty visions of the peaceable kingdom (Isa. 11:6–9; compare 65:25) and of a community where men and women lived in harmony with each other and in obedience to Yahweh (Jer. 31:31–34) remained just that: visions. In the real Jerusalem people were people, lying, cheating, stealing, and generally paying little attention to the moral and spiritual demands of Yahweh (59:1–15). At this juncture the Third Isaiah spoke in order to remind the people (1) that the promises of old were still valid and (2) that repentance for sin and devotion to Yahweh were imperatives which the people must follow.

The Prophet and the Book

There is nothing in Isaiah 56—66 which gives us any clue to the personal life of the Third Isaiah (in spite of what seem to be references to a call, 61:1–4; 62:1), so the individuality of this prophet remains as much in the shadows as that of his great master of the Exile. Some scholars have speculated that, because of an expressed interest in matters pertaining to worship and the cult, the Third Isaiah may have been a priest. However, there are no firm grounds on which to make such a claim.

An outline of Isaiah 56—66 is as follows:

A. A collection of statements dealing with the universal love of Yahweh: 56:1–8.
B. Oracles concerning the sinfulness of the people and of Yahweh's grace: 56:9—57:21.
C. Oracles concerning the importance of proper attitudes in worship: 58:1–14.
D. Statements concerning the sinfulness of the people and Yahweh's promise of judgment: 59:1–21.
E. An oracle of salvation: 60:1–22.
F. An announcement of good tidings to the afflicted: 61:1–11.
G. Promises of Yahweh to Jerusalem: 62:1–12.
H. A declaration concerning Yahweh, the conqueror and judge: 63:1–19.
I. A prayer for Yahweh's intervention: 64:1–12.
J. Further oracles of judgment and salvation: 65:1—66:24.

The first section, 56:1–8, specifies that the gentile and the Jewish eunuch (normally considered unclean and, therefore, unworthy to join other Jews in worship) will participate in the worship of the people of Yahweh. This section may show the influence of the universalism of the Second Isaiah, although the prominence given here to activities within the cult (e.g., "the sabbath," vss. 2, 6) is not a feature of Isaiah 40—55.

The second section, 56:9—57:21, is a series of indictments upon the people's sin (56:9—57:13) climaxed by an oracle concerning Yahweh's grace (57:14–21). Many scholars believe the first part of this section to be preexilic (notice the mention of fertility rites and child sacrifice, 57:5), and that may well be the case. The oracle of salvation in the second section seems deliberately placed where it is in order to "answer" the indictment upon the nation's sin: "For I will not contend for ever, nor will I always be angry" (vs. 16). This section also contains one of the finest statements in the Old Testament concerning the nature of true worship, a favorite theme of the Third Isaiah.

> For thus says the high and lofty One
>> who inhabits eternity, whose name is Holy:
> "I dwell in the high and holy place,
>> and also with him who is of a contrite and humble spirit,
> to revive the spirit of the humble,
>> and to revive the heart of the contrite." (57:15)

It is also interesting to compare 57:14 with 40:3.

The third section, chapter 58, also deals with proper attitudes in worship, the right spirit for fasting and for keeping the sabbath being specifically mentioned. The fourth section, chapter 59, again points to the sinfulness of the people and describes Yahweh's reaction to this sin. Many scholars see in verses 9–15 a liturgical confession of sin which may have been used in services of worship, another possible link between the Third Isaiah and the cult of priestly worship. On the other hand, the mention of *mishpat* and *tsedhaqah* together (vs. 9) recalls the tradition of the prophets of old. The portrait of Yahweh as the righteous warrior (especially vs. 17) undoubtedly inspired the similar description of the Christian life in Ephesians 6:14–17. In contrast to the Second Isaiah who saw Yahweh's judgment as an accomplished fact (Isa. 40:2), the Third Isaiah seems to understand it as a future, perhaps "extra-historical"' event (59:18–19).

The fifth section, chapter 60, declares Yahweh's salvation and exaltation of Jerusalem. A number of scholars feel that the nucleus of chapters 56—66, that "core" around which chapters 56—66 were collected, is chapters 60—62. (This position assumes a number of authors for 56—66.) Certainly, the connections between 40—55 and 56—66 are most obvious here. Noteworthy in chapter 60 is the picture of Jerusalem as the envy of the nations (vs. 3). Jews who have not yet returned from Babylon and elsewhere will now make their way to Jerusalem and worship in the Temple (vss. 4–7). Gentiles will participate in Jerusalem's golden age, although in a subservient manner (vs. 10). And in a mood that contains apocalyptic overtones, a future is anticipated in which

> The sun shall be no more
>   your light by day,
> nor for brightness shall the moon
>   give light to you by night;
> but Yahweh will be your everlasting light,
>   and your God will be your glory. (60:19; cf. Rev. 21:23)

The sixth section, chapter 61, begins with a brief reference to the prophet's call which is strikingly reminiscent of the Servant Songs of Second Isaiah (vss. 1–3). In fact, some early scholars who considered all of 40—66 to be the work of the Second Isaiah identified this passage in that manner. It is especially close in thought to the first two Servant Songs (42:1–4 and 49:1–6). Luke's Gospel recounts that Jesus read from this poem (through the first line of vs. 2) in the Nazareth synagogue and then identified himself as its subject (Luke 4:16–21). This section also speaks, as did the preceding, of the participation of the gentiles in the service of Yahweh, but again in a subordinate manner (vs. 5). The identification of Israel as the nation of priests (vs. 6) is also interesting and corresponds with what we know generally of Israel's self-understanding in the postexilic period.

The seventh section, chapter 62, continues the focus of attention upon Jerusalem as the recipient of Yahweh's grace. The city will have new names which befit its new status (vss. 1–5, 12). The reference to the city walls (vs. 6) does not necessarily mean that this passage was written after 444 B.C., the date of Nehemiah's rebuilding of the walls left in ruins since the destruction of 587. The reference is probably in anticipation of the walls yet to be built, in much the same manner as the several references to the Temple in Third Isaiah do not dictate a date after 515.

The eighth section, chapter 63, describes the wrath and judgment of Yahweh, portrayed here as a returning warrior (vss. 1–6). A statement concerning the mercy of Yahweh (vss. 7–9) is followed by a recital of Israel's sinful history which includes the petition that Yahweh's grace will express itself in new ways.

The ninth section, chapter 64, is an emotional plea for Yahweh to restore the nation and closely corresponds to the mood expressed in the last verses of chapter 63. The plaintive cry, "O that thou wouldst rend the heavens and come down . . . " (vs. 1), is followed by a description of the present plight of the people which suggests that Jerusalem and Judah still lie in ruins (vss. 10–11).

A final section, chapters 65—66, contains elements of both judgment and salvation. The coming glory of Jerusalem is prominent (65:17–25; 66:10–14). The language occasionally becomes apocalyptic (65:17 [cf. Rev. 21:1]; 66:22) and at one point reaches back to Isaiah of Jerusalem (65:25; cf. Isa. 11:6–9) for the portrait of the peaceable kingdom. The anti-liturgical sentiment of 66:3 is in contrast with earlier priestly themes we have noted.

The Theology of the Third Isaiah

The diversity of theological thought in Isaiah 56—66, referred to earlier, has not only distinguished this literature from 40—55, but has also generated considerable conversation over the question of the literary unity of 56—66. In spite of this diversity, however, a number of prominent themes may be identified. The majesty and omnipotence of Yahweh, the choice of Israel to be Yahweh's people, divine anger over human sin, and the Deity's determination to work the divine will in the world, all are themes found in the Third Isaiah which connect this prophet of the restoration with the older traditions of prophecy within Israel. There are, in addition, several themes which find a distinctive expression in the thought of the Third Isaiah.

A. *Yahweh's restoration of Jerusalem is still in the future and, when it comes, it will be a day of great glory for the city and its people.* Yahweh's "glory" (*khavodh*, see pp. 125–26) will be present in the life of the city (60:1–2). The city will be a "crown of beauty" and a "royal diadem" to Yahweh (62:3). All people will respond to the magnificence of the new Jerusalem, both gentiles (62:2) and Jews still scattered abroad (60:4). Great wealth will belong to the city, which will be the place of worship for all people (60:5–7; 66:23). It will be a time of peace and concord (65:25) in which Yahweh's presence will provide all needed light (60:19). The fact that the actual Jerusalem of Sheshbazzar and Zerubbabel was so unlike the expansive visions of the Second Isaiah may have provided the impetus for the work of the Third Isaiah and may have added the tendency to place the realization of Yahweh's promises to Jerusalem beyond the reaches of history (as in 60:19).

B. *Although Yahweh's love is universal, two groups are singled out for special treatment: the gentiles and the wicked.* The gentiles are clearly to be participants in the glories of this new age, an understanding consistent with that of the Second Isaiah, but just as clearly they will occupy a subservient position, a viewpoint not shared with the Second Isaiah. "Foreigners" will join themselves to Yahweh (56:6). They and "aliens" will serve Yahweh in the age to come, but their menial labor is contrasted with the work of the Jews who are to be "priests of Yahweh" and "ministers of our God" (61:5–6). As for the wicked, they are responsible for the delay of the coming of the new age (59:1–2). Yahweh, who judged this people of old, will also act in judgment upon any present enemies (59:18). The prophet implores Yahweh not to allow these wicked people to delay any longer the fulfillment of the divine promises, but to institute the judgment in swift and sure ways (chap. 64).

C. *The worship of Yahweh through sacrifice and joyful song characterizes the life of Yahweh's people.* We have already taken note of an emphasis upon priestly worship in chapters 56—66 which, while consistent with the views of such other restoration prophets as Haggai and Zechariah, is foreign to the Second Isaiah. But very much in the spirit of the Second Isaiah is the mood of joy and celebration in the oracles of the Third Isaiah. In this new age Jerusalem will "thrill and rejoice" (60:5). The prophet rejoices over what is to come to pass (61:10) as does Yahweh also (62:5).

> "But be glad and rejoice for ever
>   in that which I create;
> for behold, I create Jerusalem a rejoicing,
>   and her people a joy.
> I will rejoice in Jerusalem,
>   and be glad in my people;

> no more shall be heard in it the sound of weeping
> and the cry of distress." (65:18–19; cf. Rev. 21:4)

The Isaiah Apocalypse (Isaiah 24—27)

In our discussion of Isaiah 1—39 we took note of the fact that chapters 24—27 display features which indicate that this material is postexilic in origin and that it therefore belongs nearer the time of the Third rather than the First Isaiah. It is not known to what extent the author(s) of this so-called Isaiah Apocalypse knew the work of the Third Isaiah, but perhaps a brief statement about this material is in order here.

The material is primarily concerned with a universal judgment which will affect all humankind.

> Behold, Yahweh will lay waste the earth and make it desolate,
> and he will twist its surface and scatter its inhabitants. (24:1)

An unspecified city (25:1–5) and Moab (25:10) are mentioned in this regard, while Jerusalem is seen as the place from which a reigning Yahweh will execute judgment (24:23; 26:21). In this regard, the Song of the Vineyard of First Isaiah is recalled (Isa. 5:1–7) but with the opposite effect: Yahweh will protect the city and give it peace (27:2–5).

The oracles are interspersed with psalm-like poems (25:1–5; 26:1–6), and the extra-historical flavor of the section (see especially 24:21–23) provides a further interesting link between the book of Isaiah and the development of Jewish and Christian apocalyptic.

The Theological Unity of Isaiah 1—66

Modern biblical scholarship has performed an enormous service in distinguishing the three main sections in the book of Isaiah: 1—39; 40—55; 56—66. Contemporary students of the Old Testament are now able to see that these various sections were composed at different times and in different cultural and political contexts.[60] Furthermore, by identifying the varying circumstances in which the different sections of the book were composed, we are now able to interpret certain texts more precisely than was true in a previous era of biblical scholarship. In addition, many scholars feel that a text

---

[60] Some scholars designate these the Assyrian section (1—39), the Babylonian section (40—55), and the Persian section (56—66).

assumes a greater human and, therefore, spiritual dimension when it is understood that the author was speaking of actual, contemporary circumstances rather than speaking of some future event which, even to the prophet, was understood only vaguely (e.g., the references to Cyrus in 44:28 and 45:1).

Very recently, however, certain scholars have reminded us that, in spite of our legitimate efforts to analyze the book of Isaiah, we must not forget that the Jewish community of faith understood that all sixty-six chapters of Isaiah belonged together in a theological sense and that it is in this form that the book came into the canon of Scripture. Therefore, in addition to asking questions about the theological meaning of the various sections of the book of Isaiah, an important question needs to be asked about the theological unity of this book. In other words, what theological principles hold the book together in spite of the fact that its components were written at widely different times and under vastly different circumstances? In attempting to answer this question the student must work from the Isaiah literature itself, since we know nothing about the history of the method by which the present arrangement of the Isaiah text was arrived at, except that it attained its present form at a very early date.

There is one overarching theological postulate which characterizes all of the major sections of the book of Isaiah and which, in a sense, acts as the book's single most unifying factor: *Yahweh is the Holy One of Israel*. We have already noticed how a conviction concerning the holiness of Yahweh played a central part in the call of the First Isaiah to be a prophet (6:1–8). The threefold repetition of the word "holy" (vs. 3), the behavior of the seraphim in hiding behind their wings from the brilliance of Yahweh's majesty (vs. 2), and the manner in which the prophet is overcome by the holiness of Yahweh (vs. 5)—all of these features underscore the First Isaiah's conviction of the total "otherness" of Israel's God. For the First Isaiah, Yahweh is "the Holy God" (5:16), "the Holy One of Israel," and "the Holy One of Jacob" (29:19, 23), while Mt. Zion is referred to as Yahweh's "holy mountain" (11:9). The Second Isaiah uses the same terminology, the divine titles "Holy One of Israel" and "Redeemer" often being linked with the imperative "fear not" (41:14; 43:1–5). Also, for the Third Isaiah, Yahweh is "the Holy One of Israel" (60:9) and "the high and lofty One who inhabits eternity whose name is Holy" (57:15).

This is not to say that a theology oriented toward Yahweh's holiness was unique to the prophets of the Isaiah tradition, for both Amos (4:2) and the Habakkuk tradition (3:3) refer to Yahweh's holiness. Yet this theological concept plays so central a role in the Isaiah tradition that it gives rise to important theological postulates which provide further links among the various sections of the book of Isaiah. One of these theological "spinoffs" is a commitment to the belief that *Yahweh, the Holy One of Israel, is the only God, the Creator of the Heavens and the Earth.* For the First Isaiah, this centrality of Yahweh in the life of humankind is perhaps seen most vividly in his insistence that only by trusting in Yahweh, and not in military might, can Judah be saved.

> For thus says the Lord Yahweh, the Holy One of Israel,
>   "In returning and rest you shall be saved;
>   in quietness and in trust shall be your strength." (30:15)

In the Second Isaiah the centrality of Yahweh takes the form of a thorough monotheism in that other deities are mocked and ridiculed and their worshipers are held to be fools (44:9–20). Moreover, for the Second Isaiah this commitment to the uniqueness of Yahweh leads to a repeated emphasis upon the work of Yahweh the Creator of all things, especially the Creator of Israel.

> Thus says Yahweh, your Redeemer,
>   who formed you from the womb:
> "I am Yahweh, who made all things,
>   who stretched out the heavens alone" (44:24; see also 42:5–9;
>   43:14–15)

In the Third Isaiah, the centrality of Yahweh is expressed by means of a portrait of a Deity whose throne is heaven, whose footstool is the earth, and who cannot be contained in a building for worship built by human hands (66:1). The Isaiah Apocalypse, like the First Isaiah, views the centrality of Yahweh in terms of that trust which produces peace.

> "Thou dost keep him in perfect peace,
>   whose mind is stayed on thee,
>   because he trusts in thee.
> Trust in Yahweh for ever,
>   for the Lord Yahweh
>   is an everlasting Rock." (26:3–4)

A second theological postulate contingent upon that of Yahweh's holiness is that *Yahweh punishes human sin but saves those who trust the Holy One of Israel.* The First Isaiah saw not only his own sinfulness in the light of Yahweh's holiness (6:5), he saw the nation's sin in those terms as well. Injustice and unrighteousness, as well as false worship, were seen by him to be violations of Yahweh's holiness, for which the nation would be purged.

> Ah, sinful nation,
>   a people laden with iniquity,
> offspring of evildoers,
>   sons who deal corruptly!
> They have forsaken Yahweh,
>   they have despised the Holy One of Israel,
>   they are utterly estranged. (1:4; cf. 1:24–26)

The Second Isaiah is concerned primarily with the restoration of the nation, but it is clear that he, too, sees the nation's past primarily as a drama in which great sins have been judged by Yahweh (40:2). For the prophet of the Exile, however, this holiness is to be revealed in the salvation of Yahweh's people. The liberation from bondage is compared to the Exodus event of old, and the signs of Yahweh's presence in this mighty act of redemption will be inescapable in order

> that men may see and know,
>   may consider and understand together,
> that the hand of Yahweh has done this,
>   the Holy One of Israel has created it. (41:20)

For the Third Isaiah a holy Yahweh is again portrayed as an avenging judge (66:15–16), just as in the oracles of the Isaiah Apocalypse (24:1–3). For both the Isaiah Apocalypse (26:19) and the Third Isaiah (65:17), however, the saving power of a holy God is by no means forgotten.

A third theological corollary of the conviction concerning the holiness of Yahweh is that *Yahweh is the Lord of all nations but relates in a special manner to Israel*. It is not incidental that Yahweh is the Holy One *of Israel*, and in the thought of the First Isaiah the relationship between Yahweh and Israel exhibits two features: Yahweh stands in judgment upon the nation's sin (as above), but the love of Yahweh is not extinguished even by the waywardness of the people. Yahweh hears the people's prayers (37:30–38), and although the sinfulness of the people demands the eventual destruction of the nation, Yahweh will not permit the relationship between them to be completely annihilated. This is expressed during the Early Ministry of First Isaiah by the name of his son: A-Remnant-Shall-Return (7:3). At a later time, the same hope assumes messianic dimensions, as we have previously noticed (7:10–17; 9:1–7; 11:1–9).

In the theology of the Second Isaiah, the figure of the messianic king is absent (except for its application to Cyrus, 45:1), but the Holy One of Israel is one who, having judged the people in the past, is now set to restore them. There is a special feature of this restoration, however. Israel is being redeemed not just for its own sake, but for the sake of all nations (42:5–9).

For the Third Isaiah (where the phrase "Holy One of Israel" occurs in 60:9, 14; cf. 57:15; 58:13) attention is divided betweeen, on the one hand, the salvation of both Israel and, in a subordinate way, all humankind and, on the other hand, the punishment of the wicked. The Isaiah Apocalypse is primarily concerned with Yahweh's judgment upon all humankind, although Israel is singled out as the beneficiary of Yahweh's grace (27:6).

15
OBADIAH

Date of Obadiah's Work: c. 400 B.C.
Location: probably Jerusalem.
Central Theological Concept: Yahweh will destroy wicked
 Edom because of its cruelties to the Jews.
An Outline of the Book of Obadiah will be found on p. 181.

The Historical Context of Obadiah's Work

The shortest book in the Old Testament is a collection of oracles against the Edomites, a group of Semitic people who in ancient times lived in the arid region to the southeast of the Dead Sea. That the biblical Hebrews recognized a blood relationship with the Edomites is acknowledged in the stories of the twin brothers Jacob and Esau (Gen. 25:19—27:45), the latter being considered to be the patriarch of the Edomites. (Edom is called "Esau" in Obad. 6, 9, 18, 19.) The further fact of a long history of hostility between Jews and Edomites is preserved in the elements of tension contained in these narratives. According to the book of Numbers (20:14–21) the Edomites had refused Moses' request for the safe passage of Israel during the time of the wandering in the wilderness, a narrative which is interesting in that it indicates not only that the Edomites had achieved a settled existence at a time before the Hebrews did so, but also that some type of monarchial form of government was in effect among them.

During the period of the Hebrew monarchy, Edom came under the control of both Saul (1 Sam. 14:47) and David. David's conquest was particularly bloody for, after his commander Joab had inflicted wholesale slaughter upon Edomite males (1 Kings 11:15–17), David stationed a permanent army of occupation in the country (2 Sam. 8:13–14). During Solomon's time Edom was important to Israel because of the wealth of its copper and iron mines, which were exploited by the Israelites, and because it offered access to Solomon's important gateway to the outside world, namely, the port of Eziongeber through which passed much of the commerce which enriched Solomon and his court. In the period of the divided monarchies Edom's subservience to the dynasty of David continued for a time. A revolt during the reign of the Davidic King Joram (849–842, 2 Kings 8:20–22) and another in the time of the Syro-Ephraimitic War (734 B.C., 2 Kings 16:6) eventually won freedom for the Edomites. However, they fell to the Assyrians in 732, along with many other nations in the area of Syria-Palestine, and in spite of a series of attempted revolts, Edom continued as an Assyrian vassal until the decline of that power in the late seventh century.

When Nebuchadrezzar conquered Assyria's western provinces, Edom was among those whose loyalties were demanded by this new master from Babylon. Edom was nevertheless present at the conference to which King Zedekiah of Judah invited representatives of neighboring countries in order to plot revolt against Nebuchadrezzar (Jer. 27:3). Yet when Zedekiah actually revolted against Babylonian rule in 588, Edomites joined their Babylonian masters in helping to crush Jerusalem, an indignity which Hebrew poets were not soon to forget (Ps. 137:7; Lam. 4:21–22). With many Jews now in exile in Babylon, Edomites were free to move into depopulated Judah, and this they did in large numbers, primarily into the area around Hebron, a region which in postexilic times was known as Idumea. The Edomite homeland was invaded during the fourth century by a group of Arab peoples, the Nabateans, an event which caused a further migration of Edomites into Idumea. At the time of the Maccabean wars for Jewish independence in the second century, Jewish armies overran Idumea and forced its inhabitants to convert to Judaism. By a curious twist of history the members of an Idumean family, that of Antipater, became the last rulers of Judah, then the Roman province of Judea. This family is most widely known due to the kings named Herod whom we meet in the New Testament.

The Prophet and the Book

Nothing is known about the prophet Obadiah apart from his name, which means "servant of Yahweh" (vs. 1). The background of the book, which is clearly exilic and/or postexilic, would make it impossible that this Obadiah is the officer of King Ahab who bore the same name (1 Kings 18:3–16). Some scholars have suggested, in fact, that "Obadiah" may be a reverent designation for an individual rather than a proper name.

There are two major divisions within this brief book:

A. Oracles concerning Edom's judgment: 1–14.
B. Oracles concerning the Day of Yahweh: 15–21.

The first section, verses 1–9, seems to be an independent unit, a conclusion based on the passage's close similarity to Jeremiah 49:7–22. There has been some debate as to which prophetic tradition borrowed from the other, but something approaching a consensus view is that both passages are based on an earlier original which is best preserved in Obadiah 1–9. The theme here is that Edom will be destroyed, a future event in spite of the use of verbs in the past tense (the so-called "prophetic perfect"). The theme is continued in the remainder of the section, verses 10–14, which is noteworthy because it seems to recall the participation of the Edomites in the destruction of Jerusalem in 587. The blood ties between Jacob and Esau (Israel and Edom) are referred to in an especially bitter way, and the violation of this relationship is the reason given for the judgment which is to occur:

> For the violence done to your brother Jacob,
> shame shall cover you,
> and you shall be cut off for ever. (vs. 10)

In the second section there is a change in the focus of interest according to a number of scholars. Although Edom is still the target of Yahweh's wrath (vs. 18), the Day of Yahweh (cf. Amos 5:18) is to affect "all the nations" (vs. 15). The Edomites as well as other traditional enemies of the Jews will be dispossessed (vss. 19–20), and the entire region will be ruled from Mt. Zion (vs. 21). This difference in emphasis between the two sections of the book of Obadiah has caused some scholars to conclude that, although the first section comes from the time of the Babylonian Exile, the second is to be dated in the following century and is to be viewed as an interpretation of the conquest of Edom by the Nabateans. Other scholars, however, maintain the unity of the book and place its composition at a time after the destruction of Jerusalem in 587.

The Theology of Obadiah

There is but one major theological postulate in the book of Obadiah: *Yahweh will destroy Edom because of its treachery toward Jerusalem.* To this is added, as noted above, the view that all nations will feel the effects of the Day of Yahweh. Oracles against foreign nations are a common feature of prophetic literature (Isa. 13—23; Jer. 46—51; Ezek. 25—32), and there is little to distinguish Obadiah from such literature apart from its almost exclusive preoccupation with Edom. This book has often been criticized for its retributive spirit and for a narrow nationalism which sees the devastation of the peoples of Palestine as the occasion for the Jews' exaltation. There is nothing here of the spirit of universalism which glows in the Second Isaiah or even of the less expansive expression of that same spirit in the Third Isaiah. And one could perhaps argue that the thirst for retribution (vs. 15) was precisely the motivation which led the Edomites to participate in the sack of Jerusalem in 587, for they doubtless would have remembered the cruelties inflicted upon them by a series of Hebrew kings, most notably David. It is this same thirst for retribution which has perpetuated wars ancient and modern, and many of the trouble spots in the world today where fighting reflects ancient enmities may be said to be legacies of the retributive spirit. The Reformation theologian John Calvin pointed out that there are certain biblical passages whose value lies chiefly in the fact that they demonstrate the need for a more elevated approach to human relationships and to the relationship between God and humankind. In the light of Jesus' example on the cross ("Father, forgive them; for they know not what they do"—Luke 23:34), Obadiah would seem to be the kind of biblical material Calvin had in mind.

16
JOEL

Date of Joel's Work: c. 400 B.C.
Location: Jerusalem
Central Theological Concepts: Yahweh, the righteous judge,
will punish evil and vindicate Israel. Present symbols of
this judgment point to a time at the end of history when
Yahweh's ultimate judgment will take place.
An Outline of the Book of Joel will be found on p. 185.

The Prophet and the Book

Nothing is known about Joel, the son of Pethuel, mentioned in 1:1. The name, which means "Yahweh is God," was fairly common among the Hebrews of the Old Testament period, but it is not possible to connect the prophet with any of the several other persons of the same name who are mentioned in the Old Testament. Only somewhat more certain is the historical context in which the prophet lived and worked. He seems to have been at home in Jerusalem at a time after the Exile (3:2). The Temple (1:14) and the city walls (2:9) have been rebuilt, and the priests are the most prominent officials within the community (1:13). All of these features suggest a date of about 400 B.C. for the prophetic activity of Joel.

The prophet was a very literate person not only in the sense that he knew and incorporated previous prophetic writings but also in that his poetic and descriptive powers were considerable. With respect to his allusions to other prophetic literature, there are these obvious examples, although a number of more subtle instances have been pointed out by scholars: (1) his concept of the Day of Yahweh (2:1) draws from a prophetic tradition which goes as far back as Amos (Amos 5:18); (2) at one point (2:32) Joel acknowledges that he is quoting from the prophetic tradition (Obad. 17); (3) the statement which is found in both Isaiah 2:4 and Micah 4:3 is reproduced by Joel (3:10), but its meaning is transposed so that what was a cry for peace becomes a promise of war.

Joel's literary skills are also displayed by the graphic manner in which he describes the locust plague (2:3–11) and the drought (1:15–20). The swarms of omnivorous insects darken the sky and strip the countryside bare, while the drought has caused the fields to burn and watering places to dry up so that both human being and beast are in anguish. No less remarkable is the manner in which the prophet uses this natural disaster as a conceptual springboard by which he moves into his various images of the coming Day of Yahweh.

There are two distinct divisions within the book of Joel:[61]

A. Oracles concerning the locust plague and the drought: 1:1—2:27.

B. Oracles concerning the Day of Yahweh: 2:28—3:21.

Although a few scholars have suggested that the locust plague and the drought of the first section may be only symbolic in nature, the vivid manner in which they are described is evidence against that point of view. It is likely that the prophet and his fellow citizens of Judah experienced genuine natural disasters of this type and that the prophet, like others in the Old Testament tradition (cf. Hag. 1:10–11), saw these as signs of Yahweh's displeasure. His initial response is to call the people to repentance for the sin which has roused Yahweh's wrath.

> Sanctify a fast,
>> call a solemn assembly.
> Gather the elders
>> and all the inhabitants of the land
> to the house of Yahweh your God;
>> and cry to Yahweh. (1:14; cf. 2:12–17)

When that repentance is accomplished, Yahweh will respond graciously. The locust will be driven into the deserts and into the seas (2:20),[62] and there will be rain to restore the verdure to the land (2:23).

The concern of the prophet, however, is not limited to these natural disasters, for he sees in them symbols of a deeper significance, the coming of the Day of Yahweh. Perhaps the manner in which the hordes of locusts covered the sky, blotting out all light from sun, moon, and stars (2:10), is the sensation which jolts the prophet into the more profound train of thought.

> Blow the trumpet in Zion;
>> sound the alarm on my holy mountain!

---

[61] These sections are more clearly delineated in the chapter divisions of the Hebrew Bible than in those of English Bibles. In the Hebrew, chapter 3 corresponds with the English 2:28–32, while the Hebrew chapter 4 is identical to the English chapter 3.

[62] "Northerner" in 2:20 is probably a play upon words. In the first instance it seems to be a reference to the locusts, perhaps based on the direction from which they entered Judah. But it is also a more subtle allusion to the traditional enemies of the Jews (as in Jer. 1:15) and, by implication, to evil itself.

> Let all the inhabitants of the land tremble,
>   for the day of Yahweh is coming, it is near,
> a day of darkness and gloom,
>   a day of clouds and thick darkness!
> Like blackness there is spread upon the mountains
>   a great and powerful people;
> their like has never been from of old,
>   nor will be again after them
>   through the years of all generations. (2:1–2)

In the second section of the book, 2:28—3:21, the prophet's concern for the Day of Yahweh is predominant. As in the first section, this day is described in terms of frightening natural calamities: blood, fire, smoke, darkness (2:30–31). Yet there are to be two aspects to this day, the first of which is that it will witness an unprecedented outpouring of Yahweh's grace. The prophetic spirit will be rekindled, as in days of old (2:28–29), and those among the Jews who call upon the name of Yahweh will be gathered in safety to Jerusalem (2:32—3:1). There Yahweh will reign (3:16) while foreigners, who have been responsible for inflicting so much suffering upon Yahweh's people, will be excluded (3:17). And the land will become fruitful beyond measure.

> "And in that day
> the mountains shall drip sweet wine,
>   and the hills shall flow with milk,
> and all the stream beds of Judah
>   shall flow with water;
> and a fountain shall come forth from the house of Yahweh
>   and water the valley of Shittim." (3:18)

The other aspect of the Day of Yahweh will be that of terrible judgment. The nations which have oppressed Yahweh's people will be gathered into the Valley of Jehoshaphat (3:2, literal Hebrew: "Yahweh will judge," cf. 3:14 where the same location is referred to as the Valley of Decision),[63] and there will be a final conflict in which Yahweh confronts these nations and the evil which they represent (3:9–15). They will be destroyed while faithful Jews will be gathered into a Jerusalem where Yahweh reigns (3:19–21).

The Theology of Joel

The significance of Joel clearly lies in its apocalyptic elements. Although the prophet's interpretation of the locust plague and the drought (as a sign of

---

[63] It has become traditional (since the fourth century A.D.) to identify the Valley of Jehoshaphat with Jerusalem's Kidron Valley, but there is no firm basis for this identification in the text of Joel.

the need for repentance on the part of the people) is true to the traditions of classical Hebrew prophecy, it is in his application of these natural disasters as reminders of the coming Day of Yahweh that the importance of his oracles lies. We have noticed a tendency among some prophetic literature to make a place for apocalyptic, but no Hebrew prophet before Joel has produced a message in which the apocalyptic element has loomed so large. In this regard Joel thus becomes an important stage in the development of this genre of Jewish and Christian literature.

There are at least three ways in which the apocalyptic character of Joel is worthy of note. The first of these is that he utilizes the theme of the "peaceable kingdom," a theme already present in the prophetic tradition (e.g., Isa. 11:6–9), but he expresses it in a manner which is clearly "extra-historical." The mountains which drip wine and the hills which flow with milk are to have in their midst a temple from which flows a fountain of life-giving water (3:18; cf. Ezek. 47:1–12). The world of nature will be restored to its original state, and those over whom Yahweh presides will live in harmony with nature, with one another, and with Yahweh.

The second important aspect of Joel's apocalypticism, one which is related to the first, is that this "Golden Age" will witness a fresh outpouring of Yahweh's spirit (2:28–29). Some scholars have seen in this feature of Joel's prophecy a reference to an incident recorded in Numbers 11:29 in which Moses longs for the gift of prophecy to be conferred upon all of Yahweh's people. Such a condition will endure in the "times beyond time" when ecstasy, dreams, and visions will become the normal means of communication between the righteous children of Yahweh and their God.

A third significant aspect of Joel's apocalypticism is his use of oracles concerning the last cosmic battle. As noted above, Joel parodies a prophetic tradition recorded both in Isaiah 2:4 and Micah 4:3 where the defeat of Yahweh's enemies will usher in the "peaceable kingdom." Without denying that the "peaceable kingdom" is a vital aspect of the Day of Yahweh, Joel twists the traditional words to produce a contrasting impression.

> Proclaim this among the nations:
> Prepare war,
>   stir up the mighty men.
> Let all the men of war draw near,
>   let them come up.
> Beat your plowshares into swords,
>   and your pruning hooks into spears;
>   let the weak say, "I am a warrior." (3:9–10)

In this final battle the enemies of Yahweh and Israel will be subdued (3:11–15). Tyre, Sidon, Philistia (3:4), Egypt and Edom (3:19) are all mentioned by name, but the prophet's promise is directed not so much at those flesh-

and-blood peoples as at that cosmic evil of which they are the human representatives.

Because of its apocalyptic character, as well as for other reasons, the book of Joel deeply influenced the early Christian community, many of whose members felt themselves to be living in the Last Days described by the prophet (e.g., 1 Cor. 7:29–31). The most celebrated example of this influence is recorded in Acts 2, the account of the miracle on the Day of Pentecost, when the ecstasy experienced by the Christian disciples on that occasion is seen as the outpouring of God's Spirit promised in Joel 2:28–32, a text quoted in full in Peter's speech (Acts 2:17–21). The significance of this connection between Pentecost and Joel is that the spirit of ecstatic prophecy, so long dormant (see Zech. 13:1–6, discussed on p. 203), is now considered to be revived and flourishing, a fact interpreted by early Christians as one of the signs that the Day of Yahweh was near.

Another important manner in which the book of Joel, and Old Testament apocalyptic generally, influenced the New Testament is in the understanding of God's Last Judgment and the cosmic battle at the end of time. In the Gospels this understanding is expressed by Jesus' promise of a Final Judgment (Matt. 25:31–46) in which the "sheep" will be separated from the "goats" on the basis of their acts of human kindness (cf. Joel 3:19 where nations are condemned to destruction "for the violence done to the people of Judah"). The teaching of Joel is also to be detected in the so-called "Little Apocalypse" of Mark 13.

> "But in those days, after that tribulation, the sun will be darkened, and the moon will not give its light, and the stars will be falling from heaven, and the powers in the heavens will be shaken." (Mark 13:24–25; see Joel 2:30–31; Isa. 13:9–11)

But it is in the book of Revelation, the most extended example of apocalyptic writing in the New Testament, where Joel's vision of a cosmic battle is reproduced and expanded. The image of the sickle is recalled (Joel 3:13; Rev. 14:14–16), and war between God and evil, in this instance a war between "Michael and his angels" and the evil dragon, is described (Rev. 12:7–12). Finally, the portrait of the "Golden Age" to come, contained in Joel as well as in other prophetic literature, emerges in Revelation (chap. 21) as the Holy City, New Jerusalem.

A third important influence of the book of Joel upon the thought of the New Testament is to be seen in Joel's reference to the faithfulness of Yahweh's people. Those who are to be saved are those "who call upon the name of Yahweh" (Joel 2:32), a phrase quoted twice in the New Testament to refer to the faith which characterizes Christ's people (Acts 2:21; Rom. 10:13).

17
MALACHI

Date of Malachi's Work: c. 400 B.C.
Location: Jerusalem
Central Theological Concept: Yahweh loves the people of
   Israel, is in control of this world, in spite of what may
   seem to be contrary evidence, and demands faithfulness
   from the people.
An Outline of the Book of Malachi will be found on p. 190.

The Prophet and the Book

Nothing is known about the person(s) behind the oracles in the book of Malachi. The word itself is Hebrew for "my messenger" (or "my angel"), but since no ancestry is given for this prophet and no details are related concerning his personal life and circumstances (cf. Joel 1:1; Nah. 1:1), many scholars believe that "Malachi" is a title, rather than a personal name. The assumption is that an editor of this material composed 1:1 on the basis of an identification of the prophet with the messenger referred to in 3:1.

It is possible, however, to infer something of the time and circumstances under which these oracles were composed, and what we discover in this regard offers important insights into the life of postexilic Jerusalem. In 1:8 the Hebrew text contains a word (RSV: "governor") which was used during the Persian period and which establishes a postexilic date for Malachi's work. On the other hand, there is no urging, as in Haggai and Zechariah, that the Temple be rebuilt. To the contrary, the priestly offices associated with Temple worship are much in evidence (1:10; 3:1) and have, in fact, become so commonplace that the officiating priests have become bored with their rituals (1:13). There is no concern for the defenses of the city, a fact which would imply a date after Nehemiah's rebuilding of the walls about 444, but there is a concern on the part of the prophet over the foreign wives whom Jewish men have taken, in some cases after they had divorced Jewish wives whom they had married as youths (2:10–16). This was a concern of both Nehemiah (Neh. 13:23–27) and Ezra (Ezra 9—10) and if, as some scholars believe, the work of Ezra occurred after that of Nehemiah, the oracles of Malachi would fit the period of Ezra's reforms well (about 400 B.C.). One senses in the oracles of Malachi, therefore, that a "mature" postexilic community is being addressed. The grand visions of the Second Isaiah (Isa. 49:19–23) have not materialized as some expected, and even the promises of Haggai (Hag. 2:9) and Zechariah (Zech. 8:1–8) did not come true when, at their urging, the Temple was rebuilt. As a result, many Jews have begun to ignore their spiritual traditions in favor of accommodation to the pagan world, and even the priests go about their tasks halfheartedly. As for the teaching of the law and the prophets which declared that men and women of faith would prosper while the wicked would suffer, that view has become "old fashioned" and has ceased to be taken seriously (2:17; 3:14–15). Jewish men and women have looked at the relative poverty of their nation, which was still a province of the mighty Persian Empire, and found no correlation between the promises of faith and their present circumstances. It was in the effort to meet this crisis of the spirit and to rekindle the old zeal for the service of Yahweh that the prophet spoke.

Structurally, the book of Malachi falls into six oracles and an editorial conclusion.

A. An oracle concerning Yahweh's love for Israel: 1:2–5.
B. An oracle condemning false priests: 1:6—2:9.
C. An oracle concerning mixed marriages and divorce: 2:10–16.
D. An oracle concerning the justice of Yahweh: 2:17—3:5.
E. An oracle concerning the people's tithes: 3:6–12.
F. Another oracle concerning the justice of Yahweh: 3:13—4:3.
G. An editorial conclusion: 4:4–6.

The first oracle, 1:2–5, attempts to answer those Jews who point to the sorry plight of their nation. Ruled by a foreign power, their past experiences of tragic rebellion against Babylon had taught them the futility of armed revolt, and so they are instead tempted to revolt against the traditional understanding that they were in some manner a special people (Deut. 7:6). One can almost hear Malachi's contemporaries saying something like, "Yahweh must despise us, or else why are we treated so badly?" In reply, the prophet points to the recent experience of the Edomites (1:3) which has apparently left the land of that neighboring people in ruins. Many scholars see this as a reference to the Nabatean invasion of Edom[64] which caused many Edomites to flee to the region of Hebron. If Yahweh really despised Judah, so runs the prophet's logic, Judah would have been treated in the same manner as the descendants of Esau. Yahweh's continued favor of Judah is evidenced by

---

[64] See p. 181.

the promise not to allow the Edomites to rebuild their ruins (1:4). When Jews realize this, they will affirm, "Great is Yahweh, beyond the border of Israel!" (1:5).

The second oracle, 1:6—2:9, denounces those priests of Yahweh for whom the worship over which they preside has lost its meaning. The law instructed that only the very best animals of the flock should be sacrificed upon Yahweh's altar, and specifically prohibited the sacrifice of animals which were lame, blind, or otherwise blemished (Deut. 15:21). Yet these are the very animals which the cynical priests of Malachi's day accept for sacrifice to Yahweh (1:8), even as they profess the tedium of what they do (1:13). A son shows greater reverence than this to his father, and a slave to the master (1:6), while the gentiles are more faithful in their worship than these negligent priests (1:11). They have earned nothing but the contempt of Yahweh (1:14; 2:1–9).

The third oracle, 2:10–16, begins by condemning those Jews who have taken foreign wives and have thereby admitted the worship of foreign deities into the community of the people of Yahweh. The oracle's first words may seem to be an affirmation of the kinship of the entire human family, but the context in which they are placed indicates that they are probably an appeal to Jewish nationalism (the "father" of vs. 10 may be a reference to Abraham, instead of to Yahweh). It is Yahweh's wish that such persons be banished from the community of the people of Yahweh (2:12). The oracle then continues by pointing out that some Jews have divorced their wives, perhaps in order to marry the foreign women referred to above. Yahweh's attitude is unequivocal: "I hate divorce, . . . So take heed to yourselves and do not be faithless" (2:16).

The fourth oracle, 2:17—3:5, deals with the problem raised by the apparent delay of the enactment of Yahweh's universal justice, promised so long before (Isa. 11:1–5). The people parody the traditional answer concerning the seeming prosperity of the wicked and the suffering of the righteous (2:17, cf. Ps. 1), and ask instead, "Where is the God of justice?" The prophet's reply takes the form of a promise of a theophany, that is, an appearance of God. First, in language reminiscent of the Second Isaiah (Isa. 40:3) Malachi describes the coming of Yahweh's messenger who will prepare Yahweh's way. Then, Yahweh will appear in the Temple to execute judgment.[65] Yahweh is like "a refiner's fire" and "fuller's soap" (3:2) and will purify the Levitical priests (3:3) and sit in judgment upon those who have committed a variety of sins (3:5).

---

[65] The "messenger of the covenant" is perhaps a scribal gloss to warn against an expectation of a full self-revelation by Yahweh, since no flesh and blood could witness such an event and live (cf. Isa. 6:1–6).

The fifth oracle, 3:6–12, describes the true worshiper as one who faithfully pays tithes to Yahweh. The people have apparently complained because of drought and poor harvests (3:10), a complaint the prophet answers by saying that Yahweh is punishing the people because of their negligence in worship. Specifically, they have withheld their tithes (whose payment was doubtless made more difficult by the poor yield of their fields), so that it is they who have been unjust toward Yahweh, and not the other way round. When the people restore the payment of their proper offerings, Yahweh will restore the productivity of their fields and vineyards (3:11), so that all nations will honor Yahweh's people because of the beauty and fertility of their land (3:12).

The sixth oracle, 3:13—4:3, is similar to the fourth in that it speaks to the skepticism of those who watch the wicked prosper and Yahweh's own people grow more impoverished. Yahweh has heard their words by which they expressed their doubt of the traditional formulas of faith (3:14–15). Yet they should not lose hope, because Yahweh will yet sustain those who show reverence and will yet differentiate between the wicked and the righteous (3:16–18). Then in language which contains apocalyptic elements, a final judgment is described in which the wicked are burned leaving "neither root nor branch," and the righteous are blessed by the healing and redeeming presence of Yahweh (4:1–3). Interestingly, the manner in which Yahweh's presence is symbolized as a winged disc recalls similar emblems of the divine presence found in Egyptian and other ancient Near Eastern art. A further note of interest has to do with the "book of remembrance" of 3:16, echoes of which are found in the New Testament (Luke 10:20; Rev. 3:5).

The editorial conclusion, 4:4–6, promises that the prophet Elijah, who was translated (2 Kings 2:11), will return before the coming Day of Yahweh and will effect widespread human reconciliation in the spirit of the "peaceable kingdom" (cf. Isa. 11:6–9), a reconciliation which will mitigate the destructive aspects of Yahweh's judgment. This editorial addition to the oracles of Malachi was probably intended as a conclusion to the "Book of the Twelve" (see below) and resulted in the creation of an important place for the figure of Elijah in late Jewish apocalyptic. This, in turn, led to the early church's identification of John the Baptist with "Elijah returned" (Luke 1:17).

An impressive number of scholars feels that the material in the book of Malachi, together with similar (but later) material in Zechariah 9—14, constituted "independent" prophetic oracles which circulated in postexilic Judah and that the Malachi material was placed in its present position in the Jewish canon in order to round out the so-called "Book of the Twelve" (the twelve "Minor Prophets" of the English Bible, that is, the books of Hosea through Malachi). In the Hebrew Bible the "Book of the Twelve" is placed after Ezekiel and before Psalms. In most Christian Bibles however it, with Malachi as its final section, is placed at the very close of the Old Testament. The obvious reason for this arrangement is that it allows Malachi's promise of the return of Elijah to appear just before the Gospel of Matthew, that Gospel which places the most emphasis upon the Old Testament as a treasury of prophecies concerning the life and ministry of Christ.

The Theology of Malachi

The book of Malachi exhibits many of those features which, as we have seen, came to characterize Hebrew prophecy during the postexilic period. As with Joel and Obadiah, Malachi seems to see Yahweh's saving activity almost exclusively in terms of the Jewish people. The destruction of Edom for example (1:2–5) is identified as a positive sign of Yahweh's love for Israel. What is more, marriages with foreign women are viewed with alarm (2:10–12), although the prophet admits that many gentiles worship God in ways that are right and true, even if they may not know that they do so (1:11). But perhaps the nationalism of the prophet is most obvious not in what he says, but in what he does not say. There is no vision, such as that of the Second Isaiah (Isa. 42:6) or of the book of Jonah, in which Israel is seen as the vehicle by which Yahweh's knowledge is shared with the gentile world. Nor are the gentiles mentioned even in a subordinate role (as, for example, in Third Isaiah [Isa. 61:5]) as participants in the Golden Age to come.

Another characteristic of much postexilic prophecy which is also evident in Malachi is a preoccupation with the mechanics of the cult (cf. Hag. 2:10–13), a concern which Amos (Amos 5:21–24) and Jeremiah (Jer. 7:4), to name but two of Malachi's predecessors, would have found objectionable. Priests are condemned because they sacrifice inferior animals (1:8) and the laity because they withhold their tithes (3:8–9).

Finally, a number of scholars have pointed to the style of Malachi's oracles as reflecting a less elevated spirit. The self-confidence of a Jeremiah who could declare "thus says Yahweh" is diminished here, and an argumentative question-and-answer format is substituted in its place, as if the prophet somehow felt called upon to validate his message by means of a polemical logic (2:10).

To admit such features in Malachi's prophecy, however, is merely to call attention to the obvious fact that this prophet was, in some ways, a child of his time, a period in Israel's history when the nation felt itself isolated and defensive, fighting for its survival by withdrawing into the fortress of law and cult. What is surprising is not that Malachi exhibits characteristics of postexilic Judaism, but that in a number of ways he transcends them, as the following aspects of his message indicate.

A. *A loving Yahweh is still in control of the world*. In spite of the fact that Malachi's creation theology is not given a prominent place in his utterances (cf. Isa. 42:5), Yahweh is acknowledged as the Creator God (2:10). He is truly worshiped by many "good" gentiles (1:11), and wicked gentiles, such as the Edomites, feel his wrath (1:2–5). Israel's universal God is still in control of the processes of history, so that ultimately that which is evil will be destroyed (3:5; 4:1), while that which is good will be purified (3:2–4) and redeemed (4:2). Therefore, although appearances may be deceiving, Yahweh's justice and love will prevail.

B. *A holy and just Yahweh demands the utmost devotion from the people*. Although much of Malachi's concern for a right relationship between the individual and God is expressed in cultic and legal terms, rather than in terms of *mishpat* and *tsedheq*, at the center of this concern lies a determination that the heart of each person should be right. The priests' negligence in sacrificial matters masks an underlying skepticism and unbelief (1:6, 13), while the reluctance of the people to offer their tithes results from their lack of confidence in the providential care of Yahweh (3:6–12). When the Golden Age is finally ushered in, it will be characterized by *mishpat* and healing (4:2), as well as by human reconciliation (4:6). In the last analysis, it is these divine qualities which the prophet urges the people to incorporate into their lives.

C. *Those who represent God to the people are under special obligations of faith and practice*. There can be little doubt that this fundamental belief lies at the core of Malachi's attack on the lazy and skeptical priests (1:6–14). The prophet knew that, in spite of the external nature of the apparatus of worship, men and women are still moved and sustained by symbols. How can the ordinary person be expected to exercise faith and hope if those who are in a position to know Yahweh most intimately express their own relationship to God by offering less than their best?

D. *Marriage is a sacred relationship in which God is a partner and it is therefore not to be taken lightly.* "Yahweh was witness to the covenant between you and the wife of your youth" (2:14) and a man must not decide that he can cast off his wife because he has found a more beautiful woman or a more youthful partner for his own old age. In this respect, Malachi looks beyond the narrow provisions of ancient Hebrew law and anticipates the viewpoint of Jesus (Mark 10:2–12).

E. Finally, although this is not precisely a theological postulate of the prophet, *Malachi provides an important conceptual "tool" by which the early church, including Jesus himself, understood the work of John the Baptist.* We have noticed above how the promise of the coming of Elijah (4:5, in all likelihood an editorial addition in which a later writer equated Elijah with the "messenger" of 3:1) was interpreted by Jesus and certain New Testament writers as having been fulfilled in the ministry of John. This promise is an expression of the prophet's confidence that Yahweh will control the shape of human history, and it provided Jesus and his disciples with an important insight. If John was "Elijah returned," then Jesus himself was that Lord whose appearance would come suddenly, he was that "sun of righteousness" who would rise "with healing in its wings" (4:2). This prophetic promise then joins many others by which the early church understood that God was revealed in a distinct manner in Jesus of Nazareth.

18
JONAH

Date of the Writing of the Book of Jonah: some time in the
    postexilic period.
Location: unknown, but probably Jerusalem.
Central Theological Concept: Israel has a responsibility to
    share its knowledge of Yahweh with the nations of the
    world.
An Outline of the Book of Jonah will be found on p. 197

The Prophet and the Book

Jonah is unique in the prophetic literature of the Old Testament in that it
is not a collection of the oracles, visions, or sermons of a prophetic figure;[66]
but rather is a narrative story about an episode in the life of such a figure.
This uniqueness is more apparent than real, however, for in the Hebrew canon
such narratives as the books of Joshua, Judges, Samuel, and Kings were
included in the prophetic corpus because they told stories of important Hebrew prophets (Samuel, Elijah, etc.) and/or because they were considered to
contain a prophetic interpretation of Israel's history. It is in this sense that the
book of Jonah claims a place within the prophetic literature.

Jonah, the son of Amittai, is otherwise known to us only from a reference
in 2 Kings 14:25. There we learn that he was a native of Gath-hepher (in
northern Israel), that he was a contemporary of King Jeroboam II of Israel
(and therefore a contemporary of Amos and Hosea), and that he predicted
the success of certain of Jeroboam's military adventures. It should be noted
here that this is prior to the time of the Assyrian domination of Syria-Palestine
from about 725 to about 625.

According to the narrative of the book of Jonah, the prophet is commanded by Yahweh to preach repentance to Nineveh, the Assyrian capital,
but instead Jonah attempts to flee from the presence of Yahweh by boarding
a ship bound for Tarshish (perhaps on the Iberian peninsula). When the ship
encounters a storm, the sailors know that some deity has been offended and

---

[66]The only "sermon" of Jonah is the eight-word message of 3:4.

it is determined by the casting of lots that the guilty person is Jonah. Jonah confesses that he is fleeing from Yahweh and he proposes that the sailors throw him overboard in order to soothe Yahweh's anger. After some reluctance the men comply and the storm immediately subsides. Jonah, meanwhile, has been swallowed by a great fish and, following his cries for mercy from the belly of the fish, three days later he is vomited out upon the shore.

Again Yahweh commands Jonah to go to Nineveh to preach to the people. This time the prophet obeys only to discover that his words bring about the repentance of the citizens of that city, a success which leaves Jonah bitter since he had hoped that these wicked people would be destroyed by Yahweh. Fuming, Jonah retreats into the countryside to pout and brood. Yahweh then causes a plant to grow up over the prophet in order to shade him from the hot sun but then sends a worm which destroys the plant. Jonah's anger is made all the greater, and he expresses his indignation to Yahweh over what has just happened. Yahweh responds by saying that the welfare of a city of people is of far more importance than a plant to whose growth Jonah had contributed absolutely nothing. Curiously, the book ends with a question:

> "And should not I pity Nineveh, that great city, in which there are more than a hundred and twenty thousand persons who do not know their right hand from their left, and also much cattle?"

On this basis of the above narrative, an outline of the book of Jonah would take something like the following form:

A. Yahweh commands and the prophet flees: 1:1–17.
B. A psalm of thanksgiving: 2:1–10.
C. Yahweh commands again and the prophet reluctantly obeys: 3:1–10.
D. Jonah's dispute with Yahweh: 4:1–11.

There are several very strong reasons for concluding that the book of Jonah is not a record of historical events. Some of these have to do with the manner in which the Assyrian capital is referred to. In 3:3 the reader is told that Nineveh is so large that three days are required to travel from one side to the other, whereas archaeology has revealed that the diameter of the city walls was approximately two miles. Even if "greater" Nineveh (the city with its outlying towns and villages) is intended in 3:3, the description is still an overstatement. The Assyrian monarch is referred to as the "king of Nineveh" (3:6), an unlikely designation which neither Assyrian nor Hebrew historical records can sustain. And perhaps most importantly, we are told that the entire city, including the king, repented and turned to Yahweh (3:5–6), an event which, had it happened, would have received great attention in the Old Testament (cf. Nahum) and might also have been recorded by Assyrian scribes, neither of which is the case.

Other historical problems have to do with the chain of miraculous events surrounding the "great fish." The problem here is not that there could be a fish large enough to swallow a person (there is documented evidence that there are fish that large) but that the person could survive three days and nights in the stomach of the fish (1:17) and in the process compose a psalm in the style of a classical Hebrew psalm of thanksgiving (2:2–9). Other miracles cause problems also, such as the overnight growth of a plant large enough to provide shade for Jonah.

For these and other reasons (some of which are technical and have to do with the use of late Hebrew words and Aramaisms), most scholars conclude that the book of Jonah is either a parable or an allegory which borrowed the historical figure of Jonah, the son of Amittai, to be its protagonist and which was told in order to drive home a specific theological declaration (see below). Furthermore, although it is impossible to be sure about the date of the writing of Jonah, some time in the postexilic period seems most likely. This would account for the exaggerated description of a dimly remembered former political power, for the stylistic features in the Hebrew text of Jonah, and for the book's chief theological concern. It is unfortunate that during the last hundred years or so the question of the historical value of Jonah has become a point of controversy, some persons even going so far as to claim that belief in the historical nature of Jonah should be a test of one's religious orthodoxy. As such controversies often do, this one only serves to obscure the real issues raised by the text. Nevertheless, it may be stated with certainty that the narrative about the prophet Jonah is not a historical account and that its value for the modern reader lies not in its description of "events" within the prophet's life but in the theological message of the book. Jesus' reference to Jonah's three days and nights in the belly of the fish and to the repentance of the "men of Nineveh" (Matt. 12:39–41) should not be taken as evidence to the contrary. Different perspectives on the matter of historical accuracy characterized the thought of ancient men and women (including those to whom Jesus spoke), and one should not stumble over the problem of whether the book of Jonah is "historical" any more than one should stumble over whether Jesus' parables of the Good Samaritan and the Prodigal Son are "historical."

In light of the above considerations some scholars have suggested that the book of Jonah is an allegory in which Jonah represents the nation of Israel. According to this understanding the book assumes the form of a reading of Israel's history and of its obligations before Yahweh to the nations of the world. Jonah's unwillingness to obey Yahweh represents Israel's deafness to the prophetic word in the days before the Exile. The storm symbolizes the political turmoil caused by the Assyrian and Babylonian invasions of Syria-

Palestine, while Jonah's time in the belly of the great fish represents the Babylonian Exile. The vomiting up of the prophet is emblematic of the Judean restoration, and Yahweh's second call to Jonah is to be seen as the renewed opportunities for faith and obedience extended to the postexilic community. Jonah's bitterness over the task to which Yahweh has summoned him and over the success of his mission represent the narrow attitude of the postexilic Jerusalem community toward other nations.

Other scholars, however, see Jonah less as an allegory in which all the elements of the story represent some external reality, and more as a parable, a story with a single important meaning. According to this view the book of Jonah is a reading of the state of mind of the Jerusalem community during the years after the return from exile, a state of mind which one finds expressed in the books of Ezra and Nehemiah. Here is a community fearful of and hostile to the outside world with its walls (in both a literal and a spiritual sense) rebuilt and strengthened. In such an environment the election of Israel was viewed more in terms of privilege than in terms of responsibility. Any notion that Israel should reach out in compassion to share with the outside world its knowledge of Yahweh the God of love would have been met with the same vigorous denial which the prophet demonstrates when Yahweh first commands him to go to Nineveh to preach. This is the same nationalism demonstrated by the prophets Joel, Obadiah, and Malachi, a view of Israel's place in the world which was a far cry from the universal concern of the Second Isaiah (Isa. 42:6–7). This view of the nature of the book of Jonah holds that some anonymous Jewish writer told this story in order to combat the narrowness of outlook within the postexilic community and that the historical Jonah was used as the central personality in order to reinforce the prophetic character of the book.[67] The parabolic interpretation of Jonah is made all the more probable when one remembers that in the Old Testament the parable is often used to convey a message of judgment upon God's own people (2 Sam. 12:1–6; Isa. 5:1–7).

A Psalm of Thanksgiving: Jonah 2:2–9

A brief but separate word is in order concerning the psalm of 2:2–9. Even the casual reader of the book will realize that the poem does not fit smoothly in its present location within the text for, as it stands, the psalm describes how, at a time when he is still in the belly of the great fish, Jonah thanks Yahweh for having delivered him (vs. 6). The suspicion that the psalm is an

---

[67] Comparison may be made with the manner in which scholars view the circumstances surrounding the writing of the book of Daniel.

interpolation is strengthened by comparing 2:2–9 with other psalms of thanksgiving in the Old Testament (e.g., Pss. 30; 32), for here one finds the same literary and theological elements employed in similar ways. For these reasons the conclusion is drawn that 2:2–9 was a psalm from the liturgy of the Second Temple and that some editor, who found similarities between its language ("belly of Sheol," "heart of the seas," "all thy waves and thy billows passed over me") and the predicament of Jonah, inserted it at this place in the text of the book. We may be grateful that the editor did so, for otherwise this splendid expression of thanksgiving for God's saving mercy might not have been preserved for us.

The Theology of the Book of Jonah

There is a single overriding affirmation in the book of Jonah which has two dimensions: *Yahweh's compassion extends to all the nations of the earth, and Israel is under responsibility to be the vehicle by which that compassion is made known.* As noted above, this idea parallels a similar affirmation of the Second Isaiah, except that in Jonah the object of Yahweh's love (and therefore of Israel's obligation) is not "the nations" in some abstract sense (Isa. 42:6) but hated Nineveh (cf. Nah. 3:5–7). It is true that Yahweh's call to the prophet is couched initially in terms of Nineveh's wickedness (1:2), but it quickly becomes clear that Yahweh calls Jonah in order that the consequences of that wickedness (i.e., the destruction of the city) may be avoided. Yahweh loves Nineveh (4:11), a radical thing which the prophet cannot bring himself to do. Instead he resists going there in the first place and, when he finally goes and sees the marvelous results of his work, he grows bitter that Yahweh's grace has been exercised in such an expansive manner. The contrast between the attitudes of Yahweh and Jonah (Israel) could hardly be more sharply drawn. And it is in keeping with that ironic contrast that the whole story ends upon a question. The answer to that question is obvious, at least to those who are open enough to entertain it: Yahweh loves the Ninevehs of this world, and so should those within the community of faith.

19
THE SECOND ZECHARIAH

Date of the Second Zechariah's Work: unknown, but probably
   sometime during the Hellenistic period.
Location: unknown, perhaps Jerusalem.
Central Theological Concepts: The people of Yahweh will be
   vindicated, but Yahweh's enemies will be destroyed.
An Outline of Zechariah 9—14 will be found on p. 202.

For quite some time scholars have recognized that chapters 9—14 of the
book of Zechariah are not the work of the prophetic contemporary of Haggai
whose work is reflected in chapters 1—8. The setting in which this material
was composed, its language and stylistic features, and its theological outlook
all suggest a time much later than the late sixth century. Although scholarly
unanimity has certainly not been attained in the above matters, something
approaching a consensus sees the early Hellenistic period as the background
for Zechariah 9—14. This material is considered to be the work of two or
more writers and is composed of independent oracles similar to those in the
book of Obadiah. The manner in which they were collected and the reasons
for their attachment to the prophecies of Zechariah are unknown. These oracles
contain some of the most obscure and difficult passages in all of the prophetic
literature of the Old Testament, and even the task of determining the basic
literary units in Zechariah 9—14 is a matter of debate.

The Historical Context of Zechariah 9—14

Any student of the Old Testament who attempts a serious reconstruction
of the history of the Jerusalem community during the postexilic period is
doomed to a certain frustration because of the lack of reliable information
about conditions and events in Jerusalem after about 500 B.C. There are those
"windows" offered by the books of Ezra and Nehemiah, as well as by such
prophetic writings as Haggai, Zechariah, Joel, Obadiah, and Malachi. These
give us glimpses into the mood of the people but do not provide much infor-

mation about actual events in the Jerusalem which was now a Persian provincial capital. Nor are we given much assistance from the Persian records or from those of the other peoples of the area. The best we may do is to surmise that Jerusalem and all Judah lived peacefully and uneventfully as a part of the vast Persian domain and that as the grand promises of the Second Isaiah and others receded into the past, many people became less and less confident that Israel had a special relationship with Yahweh or that the old spiritual traditions of the people held any validity at all (cf. Mal. 1:13).

The ultimate downfall of the Persian Empire was accomplished by Greek armies under Alexander the Great who, in the fourth century B.C., led his troops across the face of western Asia in one of the most remarkable military campaigns in history. The Greeks and Persians had first engaged in hostilities during the days when Cyrus the Great was carving out the western reaches of his empire, but the climax of these armed encounters began when Alexander inflicted important defeats on the Persian king Darius III at Granicus in 334 and at Issus in 333 in what is now modern Turkey. In 332 the Phoenician city of Tyre fell to Alexander, and by 331 the Greek armies were in Jerusalem and in Egypt. By 326 Alexander was master of a vast kingdom which stretched from Greece to Egypt to Afghanistan, and he is reputed to have wept because he had no more worlds to conquer. Many scholars believe that it was during the Hellenistic period ("Hellas" is the Greek word for Greece) in Judah that the prophecies contained in Zechariah 9—14 were spoken and/or written.

The text is arranged according to two distinct divisions:

    A. The first collection of oracles: 9—11.
        1. Oracle concerning the messianic king: 9:1–13.
        2. Oracle concerning judgment and salvation in the last day: 9:14–17.
        3. Oracle concerning the overthrow of the false shepherds and the return of Yahweh's people: 10:1—11:3.
        4. Oracle concerning the true shepherd over Israel: 11:4–17.
    B. The second collection of oracles: 12—14.
        1. Oracle concerning the final battle and the grief over "him whom they have pierced": 12:1—13:9.
        2. Another oracle concerning the final battle and the Day of Yahweh: 14:1–21.

As stated above, it is not clear that these two major divisions or even the smaller units within the two divisions are from the same author.

The first section within the first collection of oracles, 9:1–13, is believed by many scholars to have been composed against the background of Alexander's victorious march into Syria-Palestine. The prophet views the political turmoil surrounding Alexander's invasion as a prelude to the coming of the messianic king (compare the manner in which Haggai viewed the political unrest which accompanied the rule of Darius, Hag. 2:6–7). There are some scholars who believe that the prophet had Alexander in mind in 9:9–10, but more likely is the suggestion that some unnamed Davidic king is intended. His entrance into the holy city will be humble, unlike that of the martial warrior-kings (9:9), but the extent of his kingdom is unlimited (9:10). The New Testament saw verses 9–10 as a reference to the Palm Sunday event in the life of Jesus (see Matt. 21:5).

The second section, 9:14–17, is difficult to interpret, especially with regard to its relation to 9:1–13. At some point in time, perhaps after the royal appearance of 9:9, Yahweh's (and Judah's) enemies will be destroyed and the people of Yahweh will be saved. Abundant grain and new wine will characterize the life of Yahweh's people in those days (9:17).

The third section, 10:1—11:3, again combines the themes of the destruction of Yahweh's enemies (vss. 3–5), in this case those who have apparently ruled Judah in evil and sinful ways, and of the redemption of Yahweh's people (10:6–12). Verses 8–12 describe the resettlement in Judah of those Jews and Israelites who have been scattered among the nations.

The fourth section, 11:4–17, describes an enigmatic shepherd of the doomed flock who kills "the three shepherds" (11:7–8). A great deal of work has been done by certain scholars in the effort to identify these shepherds as historical personalities, but to little avail. In this allegorical narrative the shepherd of the doomed flock shatters the staffs named "Grace" (meaning that Yahweh's grace is now at an end) and Union (perhaps a reference to the Samaritan schism of about 400 B.C.). In return for his services, the shepherd of the doomed flock is paid thirty shekels of silver, a sum of money which the New Testament relates to the "blood money" paid to Judas (see Matt. 27:9, where Zech. 11:12 is erroneously attributed to Jeremiah). It is interesting that the shepherd of the doomed flock speaks in the first person throughout this oracle.

The first section of the second collection of oracles, 12:1—13:9, describes the Day of Yahweh (12:3). On that day Jerusalem is attacked by "all the nations of the earth" (12:3), but these are routed by Yahweh who gives victory to Judah and to Jerusalem (12:7–9). Then an unnamed martyr is mourned by the people (12:10–14), and the nation repudiates idolatry and prophecy (13:1–6).[68] The final poem within this section (which may be a

---

[68] This negative description of the office of the prophet illustrates how greatly prophecy had declined in the late postexilic period.

separate oracle) describes the attack on Yahweh's shepherd and the scattering of the people, together with their final redemption (13:7–9; cf. Mark 14:27).

The second section within the second collection of oracles, 14:1–21, again describes the Day of Yahweh. The nations' assault upon Jerusalem causes the people to flee, but Yahweh intervenes to overthrow the evil powers and to institute a time of peace and prosperity. There is to be no cold or darkness in the Jerusalem over which Yahweh will be king. Living waters will flow from a Jersualem which is to be secure from all its enemies and which has become the center of the nations' worship of Yahweh. So thoroughly will humankind be committed to Yahweh that even the bells of the horses will be inscribed "Holy to Yahweh" (vs. 20). So many will come to Jerusalem to worship Yahweh that ordinary pots and pans will be pressed into this sacred service (vs. 21).

The Theology of Zechariah 9—14

As noted at the beginning of this chapter, the mood of postexilic Judaism during the late Persian and Hellenistic periods was characterized by a certain skepticism toward the great prophetic promises, especially toward those having to do with the coming glory of Jerusalem (as in Isa. 60:4–7). The continued domination by Persian and Greek authorities and the political insignificance of Jerusalem in the affairs of the civilized world caused many to turn from the hopes expressed in the traditions from the past and toward an accommodation with the culture and religion of the gentile world. The oracles of Zechariah 9—14 thus represent an expression of confidence that Yahweh's ancient plans for Jerusalem will yet be realized and that all nations will come to pay homage to the divine King who rules from the holy city (14:16–19).

As we have noticed, there is a difference in outlook among the various literary units of Zechariah 9—14 which leads many scholars to view these oracles as the collected work of more than one writer, but there is a certain theological affirmation which pervades all of this material: *Yahweh is still in control of the world and will demonstrate this sovereign rule by punishing all enemies and by exalting the people of Judah*. The final conflict in which the gentile enemies of Yahweh are overthrown is referred to on several occasions (12:1–9; 14:1–5) as is the ingathering of the dispersed Jews (10:8–12) and the final glory of Jerusalem (9:9–10; 13:1; 14:6–11). In spite of their mood of nationalism, however, the attitude of these oracles toward the gentiles is not that of total exclusion. Those "good" gentiles (that is, those who acknowledge the universal rule of Yahweh) will make the pilgrimage to Jerusalem where they will join the faithful among Yahweh's own people in the keeping of the feast of Booths (14:16–19). By this time in Israel's history apocalypticism had become the medium of hope for those faithful Jews who lived in a world which denied the very hopes that held their nation together, and thus it is in apocalyptic terms that this central theological affirmation is expressed in Zechariah 9—14. Jerusalem is more than the city of brick and mortar built upon Mt. Zion. It is an eschatological city in which there is neither cold nor darkness (14:6–8). Although the remainder of the land will be turned into a plain, Jerusalem will remain secure upon its lofty pinnacle (14:10–11), the eternal city from which Yahweh will rule all the earth (14:9).

We have already called attention to those texts in Zechariah 9—14 upon which writers of the New Testament drew in their portrayal of the life and ministry of Jesus Christ. The identification within several oracles of an individual who performs some special service helped to prepare the New Testament understanding of the ministry of Jesus. In this regard, the portraits of the humble ruler (9:9), the slain martyr (12:10), and the shepherd of Yahweh (11:4–17; 13:7–9) are significant. Beyond these texts, Zechariah 9—14 helped to shape the conceptual world of the New Testament by means of its apocalyptic imagery. By lifting the hopes of the people of God beyond their present oppressive conditions and by focusing their attention upon a reality which is beyond this world, Zechariah 9—14 joined other representatives of the apocalyptic tradition within the Old Testament in preparing the world for the ministry of One whose kingdom "is not of this world" (John 18:36).

20
THE ENDURING VALUE OF
THE PROPHETS' WORK

Any attempt to summarize the importance of the prophetic movement in Israel will inevitably come up short for the basic reason that the literature of the ancient Hebrew prophets possesses the surprising ability to speak in new ways to every age. Habakkuk's statement that "the righteous shall live by his faith" (2:4) contained a certain power in the sixth century B.C., it broke upon Paul (Rom. 1:17) with a renewed and somewhat different vigor in the first century A.D., and it possessed yet a third dimension of meaning for Martin Luther in the sixteenth century. Or again, Isaiah's statement to King Ahaz concerning the birth of a royal child (7:14) had one meaning for Judah's monarch (assuming that he listened to what the prophet was saying) but quite another for the early Christian community (Matt. 1:23). To acknowledge these many-splendored meanings of ancient Hebrew prophecy is not to suggest that, like Rorschach tests, prophetic utterances will bear whatever meaning a particular reader wishes to impose upon them. It is to affirm, however, that the ancient Hebrew prophets spoke truths about God and about human life which are not always immediately apparent, so that any effort to summarize the essential meaning of Old Testament prophecy will always be limited by the cultural and temporal context within which the interpreter of the prophets works.

Yet certain things stand out to the reader of the Old Testament prophetic literature, qualities which mark this material and the human individuals behind it as distinctive. It is true, as we discussed in the initial chapter of this book, that seers and charismatics were active in other ancient societies besides Israel. It is also true that other ancient societies were not without their social critics and/or those who attempted to call men and women back to basic spiritual ideals. The Pharaoh Amenhotep IV (Akhenaton), whom some have called the first true monotheist in history, would certainly rank high among such individuals whose memory has survived ancient times. Given the strenuous effort by the Pharaoh's hostile successors to blot out his work (cf. Jehoiakim's burning of the scroll containing Jeremiah's words, Jer. 36:23), we may only speculate what other reformers the ancient world produced whose memories have been erased forever by those who resisted their efforts. One thinks in this connection of the brief mention of the prophet Uriah (Jer. 26:20–23) and wonders how many others there were like him in ancient Israel and elsewhere whose words have been lost.

In spite of similar activity in other areas of the ancient world, however, no other ancient society witnessed the kind of sustained activity over many years which the Hebrew prophets carried on within Israel. The contribution of such individuals as Amos, Jeremiah, Ezekiel and the rest of those whose teachings we have examined is distinctive with regard to both its theological and its moral content. These qualities, plus the enduring ability of the Old Testament prophetic word to arouse and stimulate the human heart today, place the Hebrew prophets in a category of their own. Those elements which made the prophetic message distinctive and which contribute to its enduring worth we will attempt to outline below.

In the first place, the Hebrew prophets were consumed by the conviction that there is only one ultimate reality in human life: Yahweh, the God of Israel and of all humankind. All other realities are contingent upon this Primary Reality and depend upon it totally for their very existence. This sense of absolute reliance upon Yahweh is expressed in a number of ways. For the Second Isaiah, Yahweh is the Creator God who sustains human history and who shapes it according to a definite purpose (42:5). Being Lord, Yahweh may even do so scandalous a thing as apply to the pagan monarch Cyrus the title *mashiach* (messiah) and commission him to do the divine will (45:1). Those who argue with Yahweh about either the divine power or the divine intention do so in vain (Isa. 45:9–13).

For a number of the prophets this conviction concerning creation's utter dependence upon Yahweh is a feature of their call. For Amos, Yahweh's summons to speak the prophetic word is to be answered without hesitation:

> "The lion has roared;
>   who will not fear?
> the Lord Yahweh has spoken;
>   who can but prophesy?" (Amos 3:8)

Jeremiah's temperament was different and the prophet from Anathoth carried on an argument with Yahweh which may have lasted all his life. He bitterly and (one suspects) frequently resisted the responsibility Yahweh had laid upon him (Jer. 1:7; 20:7–8), yet in the end he consented to the prophetic vocation, not because he always found satisfaction in it but because to fail the prophetic calling was to deny the One Reality in life:

> If I say, "I will not mention him,
>   or speak any more in his name,"
> there is in my heart as it were a burning fire
>   shut up in my bones,
> and I am weary with holding it in,
>   and I cannot. (Jer. 20:9)

Still another expression of the prophetic commitment to Yahweh, the One Reality, may be found in Isaiah's political counsel to the Judean monarchs who were his contemporaries. The nation's security is not to be found in strong armaments or in alliances with powerful neighbors (Isa. 30:1–7) but in complete dependence upon and trust in Yahweh, the living God.

> For thus said the Lord Yahweh, the Holy One of Israel,
>   "In returning and rest you shall be saved;
>   in quietness and in trust shall be your strength." (Isa. 30:15)

In summary, however an individual prophet may have expressed it, the conviction of the absolute supremacy of God in human life is the foundation upon which the prophetic movement as a whole is based.

A second basic prophetic affirmation is this: Yahweh's love and judgment are expressions of the same fundamental nature of God. Although it was expressed in dramatically different ways by the various Hebrew prophets, belief in Yahweh's election of Israel to be a special people was characteristic of the teaching of all the Hebrew prophets. Jeremiah, for example, may have emphasized the covenant which Yahweh extended to the nation at Sinai (Jer. 31:32), whereas Amos may have ignored that theologically crucial word altogether. Yet even the prophet from Tekoa embraces the covenant idea when he declares these words of Yahweh:

> "You only have I known
>   of all the families of the earth;" (Amos 3:2)

Ezekiel's allegory of Israel as a waif rescued and raised by Yahweh (Ezek. 16:1–14), Hosea's symbolic declaration that Yahweh is Israel's husband (Hos. 2:16), Isaiah's poem in which the nation is portrayed as the vineyard of Yahweh, lovingly and carefully nurtured (Isa. 5:1–7), these and many other prophetic passages attest the central prophetic affirmation: Yahweh has loved Israel and has chosen it to be a special people. In spite of the fact that the prophetic belief in Yahweh's electing love became narrow and nationalistic among some of the later prophets, it nevertheless was a feature which shaped all of the prophetic teaching, especially that of the Second Isaiah and the author of the book of Jonah, whose views are anything but nationalistic.

With the above considerations in mind, it is very important to understand that the prophetic judgment upon Israel is a direct corollary of this prophetic belief in Yahweh's election of Israel. If the thundering denunciations of Israel's sinfulness which poured from the lips of Amos, Hosea, Jeremiah, and others is detached from the prophetic belief in election, it then appears to the modern reader of the prophets that Israel was, in a crucial sense, morally inferior to its neighbors and, for that reason, was singled out for judgment by Yahweh. But that is not the case. Yahweh's complaint against Israel, as expressed by the prophets, was that, because Israel enjoyed a *special relationship* to Yahweh, it was under a *special obligation*. If the student were to read each of the texts cited in the paragraph above, noting the larger context in which each one appears, it would become clear how closely election and judgment are linked. In each instance, Israel's wrongdoing is monstrous in the eyes of the prophet precisely because it has taken place against the background of a history of God's special love and self-revelation.

The prophets were not blind to the sinfulness of Israel's neighbors. The books of Amos (1:3—2:3), Isaiah (13:1—19:15), Jeremiah (46:1—51:64), and Ezekiel (25:1—32:32) contain catalogs of cruelty and moral turpitude on the part of other peoples in the ancient world. It is this very problem of the moral inferiority of the conquering Babylonians which vexes Habakkuk and causes him to wonder aloud about the seeming injustice of God's ways. Yet according to the prophetic vision, Israel's sinfulness was of a different order for the simple reason that its knowledge and experience of Yahweh, the God of all the nations, was more profound than that of any other nation. The importance of this link in the prophetic understanding between Yahweh's electing love and anger over Israel's sin cannot be emphasized too much. It is a feature which has often been overlooked especially by Christian readers of the Old Testament prophets, with the result that biblical Israel is believed to have been a moral cripple when, in fact, nothing could be further from the truth. After all, it was ancient Israel which nurtured the prophets and which preserved and transmitted their words, placing the rest of humankind in its debt. What is more, this connection between election and judgment is one of the features which has made the prophetic message a living thing in every age, for it reminds us all that those who have received the most light are expected to reflect it in the manner of their lives.

A third feature of the prophetic theology is that the threat of judgment was almost always linked to a call for repentance. Furthermore, the prophets were quite specific as to how repentance was to be accomplished. It is true that, in some of the prophetic utterances, there is the kind of pessimism which leaves the impression that the time for repentance is past and that there is now no course left to the people but to await the withering judgment of Yahweh. If one assumes with many scholars that those passages in the book of Amos which promise restoration are later additions, then such pessimism is certainly characteristic of the prophet from Tekoa. And it certainly seems true that, toward the end of his ministry, Jeremiah spoke less and less of repentance and more and more about the coming judgment. But these are exceptions to the rule. Hosea, for example, could employ his favorite metaphor as a call to repentance as effectively as he could make of it a description of the nation's sin.

> "Plead with your mother, plead—
>   for she is not my wife,
>   and I am not her husband—
> that she put away her harlotry from her face,
>   and her adultery from between her breasts;" (2:1)

Isaiah (1:18–20) and young Jeremiah (3:12–14) both stress the need to repent and to change the ways of the nation and of the individual, and even gloomy Zephaniah calls for a change of heart (Zeph. 2:3).

Nor was this summons to repentance a vague abstraction. It was usually couched in the most concrete terms and was expressed by means of a group of Hebrew words which were basically relational in their meaning. Over and again throughout this book we have encountered the prophets' call for *mishpat, ts^{e}dhaqah* (or *tsedheq*), *'^{e}meth, '^{e}munah, chesedh,* and the like.[69] Amos 5:21–24; Hosea 6:6; and Jeremiah 7:5–7 are all cases in point, but in the matter of repentance no prophetic passage surpasses the moving question and answer of Micah.

> "With what shall I come before Yahweh,
>   and bow myself before God on high?"
>
> He has showed you, O man, what is good;
>   and what does Yahweh require of you
> but to do justice, and to love kindness,
>   and to walk humbly with your God? (Mic. 6:6, 8)

There may be some debate about the prophetic attitude toward the cult and about whether individual prophets felt the sacrificial system to be a necessary means by which Israel responded to Yahweh. Ezekiel and Haggai, to name but two examples, certainly viewed the cult as important, whereas Amos and Jeremiah seem to have scorned it. But there can be no debate over the central position of faith and right relationships in the prophetic view of the human response to God's love. Without trust in Yahweh and a commitment to live

---

[69] See pp. 40ff.

justly and compassionately, all of the sacrifices and prayers in the world are of no avail.

A fourth proclamation of the prophets is that not even the destructive power of human sin is able ultimately to frustrate Yahweh's love for Israel and for all humankind. This belief in the sovereign power of Yahweh's love receives many different expressions among the prophets. In some instances it is narrowly nationalistic, in others it is universal in scope. Some prophets speak as if Yahweh's redemptive love is to be expressed within the context of human history, in some cases, immediately. Other prophetic utterances seem to describe Yahweh's ultimate redemptive work in a setting that is beyond time. But almost all of the prophets[70] declare that, no matter how reprehensible the people's sin, beyond these acts of judgment the people will be restored to Yahweh. Jeremiah's words are especially significant in this regard:

> "Behold, the days are coming, says Yahweh, when I will make a new covenant with the house of Israel and the house of Judah, not like the covenant which I made with their fathers when I took them by the hand to bring them out of the land of Egypt, . . . But this is the covenant which I will make with the house of Israel after those days, says Yahweh: I will put my law within them, and I will write it upon their hearts; and I will be their God, and they shall be my people. And no longer shall each man teach his neighbor and each his brother, saying 'Know Yahweh,' for they shall all know me, from the least of them to the greatest, says Yahweh; for I will forgive their iniquity, and I will remember their sin no more." (Jer. 31:31–34)

The prophetic declaration of redemption contains two elements which have been especially important for Christians. The first of these is the hope for a Messiah. We have noted from time to time passages which speak of Yahweh's saving activity in terms of the Davidic royal house and in terms of a future representative member of that house. Important texts in this regard are Isaiah 7:14–17; 9:1–7; 11:1–9; Ezekiel 34:20–24; Haggai 2:20–23; and Zechariah 6:12–14. It is very important to take note here that these texts, although they gave rise to the Christian hope for a messianic figure and helped to affirm that Jesus of Nazareth is that Messiah, are not entirely unambiguous. As we have discussed, there is reason to believe that Isaiah's immediate concern may have been with a contemporary Davidic ruler and that he was doubtless disappointed that no ruler of his time fulfilled his high expectations. And it is certainly true that both Haggai and Zechariah anticipated that their great hopes would be consummated in the person of the Davidic figure Zerubbabel. This is not to suggest that these and similar messianic texts from the Old Testament should not be applied to Jesus of Nazareth. It is, however,

---

[70] Amos, as mentioned above, may be an important exception. Cf. Zephaniah 1:2–3.

to point out that the prophetic description of the Messiah was partial and fragmentary, and it is not until the messianic promises of the prophets are combined with other Old Testament images and symbols that they have full validity. When Jesus accepted the disciples' affirmation that he was the Christ (the Greek translation of the Hebrew *mashiach*), he immediately began to talk not of kingly glory, but of his suffering and death (Mark 8:27—9:1). In other words, the prophetic vision of the Messiah, when it was finally realized, more nearly approximated the model of the Suffering Servant (Isa. 52:13—53:12) than the splendid regal hopes of Haggai and Zechariah.

Another element in the prophetic declaration of redemption which is important for Christians is the affirmation, found both in the literature associated with the Second Isaiah and in the book of Jonah, that Yahweh's redemptive intention is that the people of faith share their knowledge of Yahweh's love with those who do not know about it. To be sure, this was a minority voice among the prophets and was sometimes unheard in the midst of other prophetic voices which describe Yahweh's hatred of Israel's enemies (Nahum) or which depict Yahweh's salvation in terms of the exaltation of Israel alone (Obadiah). Yet this prophetic affirmation of the universal love of God serves as a continuing reminder to God's people across the centuries that the redemptive work is incomplete until those who have received it have shared it with others.

One last observation to be made here is not so much a description of a prophetic principle as it is a conclusion to be drawn from the preceding discussion. This is that, contrary to much popular opinion, the prophets were not primarily predictors of the future but were individuals who were deeply concerned about how life before Yahweh should be lived in the present moment, both *their* present moment and *our* present moment. To be sure the prophets often had crucially important words to speak about the future, but fortune-tellers they were not, and any effort to reduce the prophetic books into mere windows into the future is to distort the nature of the prophetic literature and to misunderstand the prophetic office. In the first place, when the prophets spoke of the future their promises were often couched in conditional terms: "Yahweh will destroy the nation *if* the people do not repent," or "Israel will inherit the land *if* they obey and love Yahweh," and so on. Modern readers of the prophets have sometimes made the mistake of accepting as final and ultimate something which the prophets meant to be only provisional. In the second place, there are occasions on which the prophets' expectations, *narrowly conceived*, proved to be wrong. Perhaps the most dramatic case in point is, as referred to above, the expectation by Haggai and Zechariah that Zerubbabel would mount the throne of David and inaugurate a new and magnificent era in Israel's history. No such thing happened. Nor did

Jerusalem ever become the political and financial center of human life as some of the later prophets anticipated it would.

This leads to the consideration that when the prophets' promises were fulfilled, it was quite often in a manner which they themselves might have least imagined. To return to the messianic expectation, it is probably true that no Old Testament prophet anticipated the fulfillment of the messianic promises in precisely the way in which they came about. It was Jesus' unique contribution to understand messiahship in terms of humility (Zech. 9:9) and suffering (Isa. 52:13—53:12; Zech. 12:10) rather than in terms of temporal power. Peter and the other disciples were outraged that Jesus should juxtapose such apparent opposites, and there is every reason to believe that such a juxtaposition would have been just as offensive to certain Old Testament prophets who first envisioned a Messiah to come.

None of this is to propose that the Old Testament prophets were wrong. On the contrary, they were right, as the continuing power of their message proves. What it does suggest, however, is that God is not bound even by the inspired words of the prophets and even less by our interpretation of those words. When God ultimately fulfills the prophetic promises, it is often in ways that surprise and joyfully astonish us all. If one remembers this, one is guarded against the danger of using the prophetic teachings in ways for which they were never intended.

21
Appendix:
DANIEL

Date of the Writing of the Book of Daniel: about 165 B.C.
Location: probably Jerusalem.
Central Theological Concepts: God is still in control of the
forces of history, although there is much that seems to
suggest the contrary. In the end time God will overthrow the
forces of evil and establish a righteous rule. Therefore,
God's people must persevere in their faith.
An Outline of the Book of Daniel will be found on p. 215.

The book of Daniel is not prophetic literature nor is its hero to be counted among the prophets of the Old Testament tradition in spite of the inclusion of the book of Daniel within the body of prophetic writings in most Christian Bibles. Originally the Palestinian Jewish canon (in the Hebrew language, the canon upon which modern editions of the Hebrew Old Testament are based) included the book of Daniel in the so-called *kethuvim* (the "Writings"), that portion of the Old Testament which also contains such widely differing books as Psalms, Ecclesiastes, and 1—2 Chronicles. The Greek speaking Jews of Egypt, who in the third and second centuries B.C. translated the Old Testament into Greek (the Septuagint), are responsible for (1) placing Daniel in the body of prophetic literature (immediately after Ezekiel) and (2) including in the text of Daniel a number of later additions which, in many English Bibles, are considered to be part of the Apocrypha. These additions include The Song of the Three Holy Children, Susanna, and Bel and the Dragon. Since the Septuagint translation was, to a much greater degree than the Hebrew text, the Old Testament of the early church, the practices of including the book of Daniel among the prophetic writings and of considering the man Daniel to have been a Hebrew prophet of the late exilic period gained a wide acceptance among the first Christians, a viewpoint which continued into the modern era. More recently, however, literary and historical research has established the true nature of the book of Daniel and, while this has assisted us in understanding the origin and purpose of this literature, it has by no means detracted from its moral and spiritual value.

The Contents and Nature of the Book of Daniel

The structural components of the book are quite carefully drawn, so that the following outline can clearly be identified.

A. Stories about Daniel and his friends: 1:1—6:28.
   1. The fidelity of the four young men in the matter of the king's food: 1:1–21.
   2. Daniel interprets Nebuchadnezzar's dream: 2:1–49.
   3. The three friends in the fiery furnace: 3:1–30.
   4. Daniel prophesies Nebuchadnezzar's madness: 4:1–37.
   5. Belshazzar's feast: 5:1–31.
   6. Daniel and the lions' den: 6:1–28.
B. The four visions of Daniel: 7:1—12:13.
   1. The vision of the four beasts: 7:1–28.
   2. The vision of the ram and the he-goat: 8:1–27.
   3. The vision of the seventy weeks: 9:1–27.
   4. The vision revealed by the angel: 10:1—12:13.

Concerning the first section, 1:1—6:28, it may be observed that each of the six stories is a self-contained narrative. In the first story, 1:1–21, Daniel and his three companions, all of whom are exiled Jews living in the court of Nebuchadnezzar, distinguish themselves by their obedience to the traditional Jewish laws concerning clean and unclean food. Although they refuse the ritually unclean food from the king's table in favor of their clean, traditional fare, their health and physical appearance become much better than that of those who do eat the royal food. The king himself takes note of their behavior and, upon inspection, finds them all, especially Daniel, to be far superior in "wisdom and understanding" to his own courtiers.

In the second story, 2:1–49, Daniel correctly interprets Nebuchadnezzar's dream and promises a series of four kingdoms (including Nebuchadnezzar's own) which will precede God's establishment of an everlasting kingdom at the end of time.

The third story, 3:1–30, concerns Daniel's three friends, Shadrach, Meshach, and Abednego (Daniel himself being absent from the narrative). Because the three young men will not worship the golden image which Nebuchadnezzar has erected, they are thrown into a fiery furnace which is so hot that those who throw them in are killed. To the king's amazement, however, the three friends are not harmed but are seen walking about in the furnace accompanied by a fourth individual whose appearance is "like a son of the gods" (3:25). The three young men are brought out of the furnace and given positions of great responsibility within the kingdom.

The fourth story, 4:1–37, relates the manner in which Daniel correctly interprets another dream of the king. Just as Daniel reveals, so Nebuchadnezzar grows mad and lives in the out-of-doors like a beast. But at the end of his period of madness Nebuchadnezzar recovers his faculties and praises Daniel's God.

In the fifth story, 5:1–31, Daniel is present at a banquet given by King Belshazzar, Nebuchadnezzar's son. Daniel accurately reads the mysterious handwriting which appears on the wall and, true to Daniel's prophecy, the city of Babylon falls that very night to the army of "Darius the Mede" (5:31).

The sixth story, 6:1–28, tells how Daniel is betrayed by jealous officials who resent his success and power at Darius' court. Because of Daniel's piety and faithfulness to his God, Darius is forced against his will to commit Daniel to a den of lions. But God prevents the lions from attacking Daniel so that, when the king anxiously goes to the lions' den the next morning, he is relieved to find Daniel safe and sound.

In the second major section, 7:1—12:13, four visions of Daniel are recounted. In the first, 7:1–28, Daniel sees a series of four beasts, the last of which is so terrible that it, unlike the other three, does not compare to any known variety of animal life. The final beast produces ten horns and an additional horn bearing "the eyes of a man." Finally, "one like the Ancient of Days" is seen reigning in splendor upon a throne. Daniel is told that the four beasts represent four kingdoms, the last of which will oppress the "saints" until the intervention of the Ancient of Days, a period of "a time, two times, and half a time" (7:25), or presumably three and one-half years. Then the fourth beast will be overthrown and the kingdom of the saints will be established as an everlasting kingdom.

In the second vision, 8:1–27, a ram with two horns is attacked and destroyed by a he-goat, which then "magnified himself exceedingly" (8:8). The horn of the he-goat is broken and replaced by four other horns which produce, in turn, a little horn which succeeds in disrupting the regular offering of sacrifices by the people of God for a period of "two thousand three hundred evenings and mornings," a figure which computes to eleven hundred and fifty days, or slightly more than three years. When the vision is interpreted to Daniel by the angel Gabriel, the two-horned ram is identified as the kingdom of Media-Persia and the he-goat as Greece, whereas the four secondary horns which grow out of the he-goat symbolize the four kingdoms which arise out of Greece. The final little horn represents "a king of bold countenance" (8:23) who will cause great destruction. However, "by no human hand, he shall be broken" (8:25).

The third vision, 9:1–27, is a reference to Jeremiah 25:11–12 in which the duration of the Exile is said to be seventy, or ten times a Sabbath of, years (cf. Lev. 26:43 which also describes the Exile in terms of the Sabbath, in this instance a Sabbath rest for the land). In response to Daniel's prayer for God's intervention, Gabriel appears in order to foretell an end of the Exile. According to the scheme which he enunciates, Jeremiah's seventy years are actually seventy weeks of years (or four hundred and ninety years). From the declaration of the word (of Cyrus? [see Ezra 1:2–4]) concerning the rebuilding of Jerusalem to the coming of "an anointed one, a prince" (9:25) seven weeks will elapse. The city will then live for sixty-two weeks "in a troubled time," after which an anointed one will be "cut off and have nothing." The city will be destroyed by the army of a coming prince. He will then "make a strong covenant with many for one week" and for half of a week he will put a stop to the regular offering of sacrifices. In addition, he will bring desolation upon "the wing of abominations" (9:27) before his decreed end.

The final vision, 10:1—12:13, is the longest of the four and its symbolism the most intricate and obscure. By means of an angelic revelation Daniel is told of the end of the Persian Empire and the establishment of the Greek Empire. A bitter rivalry between the "king of the south" and the "king of the north" is then described, a confrontation which is climaxed by the defeat of the king of the south and the conquest of the lands of the south, including Egypt. The evil, victorious king who with his lieutenants has perpetrated many atrocities, including the setting up of "the abomination that makes desolate" (11:31), will finally be overthrown through the agency of Michael, "the great prince who has charge of your people" (12:1). This time of great suffering, which will last for "a time, two times, and half a time" (12:7), will culminate in the vindication of the righteous and the final conquest of the wicked.

In terms of chronology, the first four stories are set in the reign of Nebuchadnezzar, the fifth story in the reign of Belshazzar, and the sixth in the reign of Darius the Mede. Of the visions, the first two are set in the reign of Nebuchadnezzar, the third in the reign of Darius the Mede, and the fourth in that of Cyrus the Persian. Thus in the scheme of the writer(s) of the book of Daniel, the events of the stories and those of the visions are roughly contemporary.

There are two additional features of the structure of the book worthy of note, the first of these having to do with language. The book begins in Hebrew and continues thusly until 2:4 where, with the first words of the Chaldeans, the language becomes Aramaic. The Aramaic continues until the end of chapter 7, where the Hebrew resumes (8:1) and continues until the end of the book. A second structural division is between those parts which treat Daniel in the third person and those in which the first person is employed. Basically, the stories refer to Daniel in the third person, whereas in the visions Daniel himself is the speaker.

There has been a great deal of scholarly discussion concerning the authorship of the book of Daniel and its literary history. Many scholars have suggested that the book is the work of more than one individual, and some scholars have attributed the stories to one set of authors and the visions to another. Other scholars have attempted to distinguish strata of literary composition on the basis of linguistic or other considerations, while certain scholars have attempted to defend the literary unity of the book and to attribute all of it to a single writer. This latter viewpoint is perhaps the most widely held today and is a subject to which we will return.

Another debate has centered around the question of which language was prior, the Hebrew or the Aramaic. Some scholars have argued that the entire book was originally written in the Aramaic language, with some sections later being translated into Hebrew in order to make them more acceptable to pious Jews. Other scholars, however, have maintained the contrary position that the Hebrew sections were in that language from the beginning, whereas the Aramaic section is a translation from the Hebrew, made for reasons unknown. A third position is that the book was originally written in precisely the form in which we have it today, with an Aramaic section sandwiched between two sections of Hebrew. This last view is often associated with those who hold to the literary unity of the book. In truth, the reason for the two languages is a mystery which has thus far defied solution.

Problems in the Book of Daniel

For most of the period of Christian history the nature of the book of Daniel, as understood by the Septuagint translators, was unchallenged. That is, it was considered that Daniel was a Hebrew prophet living in Babylon during the time of the Exile, a man prominent in courtly circles who predicted future events some of which were to transpire within his own lifetime and others in more distant times.[71] It was occasionally noted by some commentators, both Jewish and Christian, that Daniel's concerns were very different from those of other prophets such as Amos and Jeremiah with their great burden over the sin of God's people. But this was usually attributed to a difference in the time and circumstances under which the prophet worked rather than to a difference in the nature of the literature associated with Daniel.

However, when the new tools of literary and historical research which had been developed in the seventeenth and eighteenth centuries were applied to Daniel, certain questions were raised about the nature of this literature which the traditional interpretation was quite unable to answer. Such intellec-

---

[71] One notable exception to this consensus was the Neo-Platonist scholar Porphyry (A.D. 232–303) who maintained the Maccabean origins of the book.

tual giants as Baruch Spinoza (1632–1677) and Sir Isaac Newton (1642–1727, who, incidentally, devoted a great deal of his time to the scholarly study of the Bible) were among the first to question the traditionally accepted view of the book. When, in the nineteenth and twentieth centuries, archaeologists produced materials which enabled scholars to reconstruct that world in which the prophet Daniel is supposed to have lived, the evidence became overwhelming that the book was not the product of the sixth century B.C., but of the second century B.C.

It is not possible here to catalog all of the literary and historical problems which are raised by the book of Daniel, but it is in order to list two or three of the more obvious. First, there is the matter of King Belshazzar. In the book of Daniel this monarch is described as the son and successor of the great Nebuchadnezzar (5:2, 18), and it is his lot to preside over the Babylonian kingdom at the time of its conquest by Darius the Mede. We now know from contemporary records that the historical Bel-shar-usar was, in fact, the son of the last Neo-Babylonian king, Nabonidus. Although he was left in command of the city of Babylon during the extensive absence of his father and may even have enjoyed the status of co-regent, he never ruled Babylon as its sole monarch as the book of Daniel suggests. With respect to his being Nebuchadnezzar's son, the dynasty represented by Nebuchadnezzar came to an end six years after Nebuchadnezzar's death when Nabonidus seized control of the empire in about 556. Not only was Nabonidus, and therefore Belshazzar/Bel-shar-usar, of no kin to Nebuchadnezzar, but also the contemporary record hints that Nabonidus was not even a Chaldean.

A second historical difficulty has to do with Darius the Mede. In the book of Daniel this monarch is identified as the conqueror of Babylon, and we are even told that at the time of Babylon's fall Darius the Mede was sixty-two years old (5:31). It is now possible to demonstrate that Darius the Mede never existed. To be sure, Cyrus, whom we now know to have been the conqueror of Babylon in 538, was of Median descent (through his mother), and he had previously united his father's Persian kingdom with the Median kingdom of his grandfather Astyges. It is also true that a succession of monarchs who bore the name Darius were later to rule the Persian empire. But the simple fact is that contemporary records, which are now somewhat extensive, record no historical person named Darius the Mede and, in fact, clearly indicate that the conqueror of Babylon was Cyrus the Persian.

A third difficulty is related to the second. If there was no Darius the Mede, there was also no Median empire prominent between the Babylonian and Persian periods. Yet the sequence of empires recorded in both chapters 2 and 7 of the book of Daniel is clearly Babylonian, Median, Persian, and Greek. During the seventh century, a Median empire had flourished in the region of modern Iran and had, in fact, been allied with the Babylonians under Nabopolassar (Nebuchadnezzar's father) in the destruction of the old Assyrian capital city of Nineveh in 612. But, as mentioned above, the Medes had been incorporated into the Persian empire by Cyrus about 550 and did not exist as an independent political/military force at the time of the fall of Babylon in 538.

Under the weight of these and other, less obvious difficulties, the conclusion is inevitable that the author(s) of the book of Daniel wrote about a distant past which was only imperfectly understood and, therefore, imperfectly described. However, if the book is not a sixth-century document about a Hebrew prophet who had been active during that same period, when was it written and what does a later date of composition have to say about the book's central figure?

The Date and Circumstances of the Writing of Daniel

The Persian empire, whose founder (Cyrus) had been responsible for the conquest of Babylon in 538 and the liberation of the Jews, ultimately fell victim to the armies of Alexander the Great. This brilliant young warrior from Macedonia established Greek domination over the ancient world, as we have observed above, as far east as Afghanistan and as far south as Egypt by 326. When Alexander died in 323, his empire was divided among a number of his generals, two of the most important of whom were Seleucus, who inherited Syria and the Tigris-Euphrates valley, and Ptolemy, who gained control over Egypt. The descendants of Alexander's generals, in spite of their common Greek culture, often fought bitterly with one another, and Judah, lying on the way between western Asia and Egypt, became a frequent battleground between the Seleucids and the Ptolemies. In 199 B.C. the Seleucids administered a shattering defeat to the Ptolemaic forces, with the result that Jerusalem and Judah came permanently under Seleucid control. Many Jews welcomed this turn of events, especially those who were favorably drawn toward the Hellenistic way of life, because they felt that it would bring peace and security to their region. And, as long as other Jews were free to reject Hellenistic manners in favor of their own spiritual and cultural traditions, life could be lived with a minimum of ferment.

However, tensions within the Jerusalem community and between the Seleucid authorities and those Jews who were opposed to the Hellenistic way of life came to a head in the years after 175. As the result of the assassination in that year of the Seleucid ruler Seleucus IV, Antiochus IV, his brother, came to the throne. In order to thwart the rising power of Rome, which he greatly feared, Antiochus (who was also called Epiphanes because he considered himself the incarnation or epiphany of the supreme Greek god, Zeus) attempted to consolidate his power by two means. First, he tried to wrest control of Egypt from the Ptolemies, and second, he attempted to unify his dominions by imposing upon the people various forms of Greek culture, including the worship of the Greek gods. Perhaps because he was frustrated in his first objective, he pursued the second with a vicious intensity. Returning from Egypt, he passed through Jerusalem where he desecrated the Temple and caused a number of the enemies of his regime to be killed. When groups of Jews resisted this tyranny, he imposed it all the more harshly by forbidding the practices of Jewish worship and commanding that Greek forms of worship be followed instead. An altar to Zeus was set up in the Temple and various practices which pious Jews considered blasphemous (including the sacrifice and eating of pork) were commanded. Many within the upper classes were willing to acquiesce to Antiochus' demands, but the poorer Jews and those who lived in the countryside spoke of revolt. On a day in 167 when Antiochus' officers came to the village of Modein to enforce the new regulations concerning worship, an uprising resulted in which a group of Jewish nationalists, led by an elderly priest named Mattathias, routed the Seleucid soldiers and those Jews who wished to cooperate with them. This event marked the beginning of the Maccabean rebellion (also called the Hasmonean revolt, both terms deriving from family names of Mattathias and his descendants).

The period of warfare that followed, which is detailed in the first and second books of Maccabees and in the writings of the Jewish historian Josephus, was cruel and bloody. Although Mattathias died within a year of the incident at Modein (and Antiochus some four years later), the struggle continued and was taken up by Mattathias' sons, of whom the most famous was Judas (the first member of the family to whom the name Maccabee, perhaps meaning "the hammerer," was applied). Fighting against vastly superior Seleucid forces with a ferocity born out of deep spiritual conviction, the Jewish forces under the Maccabees succeeded in winning Judah's independence, an independence which was not crushed until the Roman army of Pompey marched through Syria-Palestine and, in 63 B.C., captured Jerusalem, turning Judah into the Roman province of Judea with which we are familiar from the writings of the New Testament.

There is now a large scholarly consensus that the book of Daniel grew out of this struggle and that it was an effort by some unknown writer(s) to call the Jews of the second century to faith in their ancient traditions and to kindle within them the courage necessary to wage successful warfare against an alien and cruel oppressor. There are several reasons for concluding this. The first has to do with the historical motif of the four kingdoms, a theme which is prominent in 2:36–45 and 7:2–18. In both passages the kingdoms represented are Babylon, Media, Persia and Greece. In both passages the Greek kingdom receives special attention, 7:7–8 being particularly interesting. Here the fourth beast (kingdom) was "different from all the beasts that were before it," for it grew ten horns and after that "another horn" (Antiochus Epiphanes) which had eyes and "a mouth speaking great things." In both passages the final kingdom is overthrown by the power of God who, after a period of warfare, sets up "a kingdom which shall never be destroyed" (2:44, cf. 7:14). Such a motif bears all of the characteristics of having been written to promise the eventual overthrow of Antiochus' rule and the victory of the people of God. In the same vein, the struggles between "the king of the south" and "the king of the north" as related in the fourth vision (11:11) strongly suggest the rivalry between the Seleucids and the Ptolemies.

Other details corroborate this conclusion. Under Antiochus pious Jews were forced to eat foods which they considered ceremonially unclean, whereas Daniel and his friends are subjected to the same pressures but successfully resist (1:1–21). Antiochus caused an image of Zeus to be set up in the Jerusalem Temple and all Jews were expected to reverence it, whereas Nebuchadnezzar fashions a golden image and orders his subjects to worship it. In the latter case, when Daniel's three friends refuse to do so, they are cast into the fiery furnace but remain unharmed, a fact which causes Nebuchadnezzar to worship their God (3:1–30). Again, although Antiochus proclaimed himself to be a god, others, including some Greeks, believed him to be mad; Nebuchadnezzar is condemned to madness by God because of his royal pride (4:1–37). Antiochus desecrated the Jerusalem Temple, whereas Belshazzar, who had violated the Temple treasures (5:2–4), is destroyed (10:1—12:13). Finally, Antiochus' claims to divinity are similar to those of Darius the Mede (6:7). These are denied by Daniel, and he is cast into a den of lions but is miraculously delivered by God (6:1–28).

The list of such parallels is considerably longer, but the examples above strongly suggest that it was in order to meet the threat imposed by Antiochus that the book of Daniel was written. To men and women who resisted the Seleucid oppression, often at the cost of their lives, the message was clear: do not compromise or capitulate, for the God of Israel is on your side, as was the case with Daniel and his friends, and will ultimately bring victory to this present generation of faithful, beleaguered people, as was the case long ago. Even death itself should hold no terrors for those who are faithful to the ancient ways of Israel, for after the last battle has been won "many of those who sleep in the dust of the earth shall awake" (12:2), one of the earliest references in the Bible to belief in a personal resurrection.

The promise of resurrection (see also 12:13) is one of at least two important apocalyptic elements in Daniel, the other being the expectation of the imminent end of the age, a climax which will be characterized by the final conquest of evil and the establishment of the eternal kingdom of God. The author(s) of Daniel even dates this final climax to three and one-half years after the forcible end of the offering of sacrifices in the Jerusalem Temple (the "time, two times, and half a time" of 7:25 and 12:7).

Another interesting feature of the book of Daniel is its relation to the wisdom movement in Israel and in the ancient Near East. In the Ugaritic literature unearthed at Ras Shamra there is a cycle of stories which scholars have termed "The Tale of Aqhat"[72] and which tell of a certain Daniel (a name which means "God judges") whose special concern is the administering of justice to widows and orphans. In Ezekiel 28:3 (cf. 14:14) Daniel is referred to as a wise man. In the book of Daniel itself, Belshazzar tells Daniel that "light and understanding and excellent wisdom are found in you" (5:14). Like Joseph (the narratives about whom also exhibit characteristics associated with the wisdom movement), Daniel's powers of interpretation cause him to be installed as an administrator over the kingdom and "chief prefect over all the wise men of Babylon" (2:48). The significance of these wisdom elements in the book of Daniel is a matter of debate among scholars, but one possibility is that the author(s) of our book of Daniel took over a traditional tale well-known (perhaps in several versions) among Semitic peoples and wove it into a narrative containing apocalyptic and other elements in order to fashion a dramatic tale which would strike a note of courage and endurance during the difficult days of the Maccabean revolt. (Cf. the manner in which some scholars believe the book of Job is based on an older tale about a folk figure of that name.)

The Theology of the Book of Daniel

It should not be concluded that the moral and spiritual values of the book of Daniel are in any manner weakened by the modern understanding of the origin and nature of this literature. The attitudes toward authorship which prevail in our world were not shared by men and women in ancient times, partly because of our laws (made necessary by the invention of the printing press, the photocopier, and the word processor) regarding publication and copyright but primarily because the entire matter of the relationship between the individual and society were so different in the ancient world. As we have noticed in connection with material in the books of Micah and Isaiah, later writers or scribes could claim their own words to be those of a figure from the past when speaking or writing in the spirit of that figure. When Jesus refers to "the desolating sacrilege spoken of by the prophet Daniel" (Matt. 24:15), he is speaking in the language of the men and women of his time, and such a statement by no means detracts from his authority or from the

---

[72] ANET, pp. 149–55.

value of the book of Daniel. This literature played an important role in shaping the thought of New Testament writers (see, for example, 2 Thess. 2:1–12; Rev. 13) and continues to strengthen the faith and resolution of men and women today.

The theological principles enunciated in the book of Daniel include the following:

A. *God is the sovereign Lord of the creation and controls all things, including human history.* It is not unusual for men and women of faith, especially those who live in circumstances where evil seems to flourish unchecked, to question either the goodness of God or God's power over the world. Even some of the greatest of Israel's prophets indulged in such questioning, for we have heard Jeremiah curse the day of his birth (Jer. 20:14–18) and Habakkuk wonder, in the face of the Babylonian invasion, if God were still a vital force for good in the world (Hab. 1:2–4). Even Jesus cried out in his despair from the cross that God seemed to be a distant and alien Being (Matt. 27:46; Mark 15:34). We may be sure that many Jews of the second century B.C. were driven to similar expressions under the weight of the cruel pressures imposed by Antiochus.

In response, the book of Daniel answers with the assurance that God has not abandoned the divine principles of grace and justice nor does God ever abandon the faithful people who look for divine deliverance. And whatever historical problems the book may contain, its basic theological orientation is correct. God has saved the people in the past from Babylonian captivity and, before that, from Egyptian bondage and will do so again, as the survival of the Jews under Antiochus' cruel oppression attests.

B. *Because God is still in control of this world, men and women who trust God must have courage when faith and moral integrity are threatened.* The history of the Judeo-Christian community is filled with examples of human courage which, sustained by faith in God, has carried God's people, both Jewish and Christian, through very dark days. And because this courage has often been the only human instrumentality which permitted the community of God's people to endure, it has become an important means by which God's sovereignty over creation has been expressed. In part, this courage is based upon the promise of the book of Daniel (12:2), a promise echoed by Jesus (John 14:3) and by the writers of the New Testament (1 Cor. 15:12–19) that death is not the end of the human experience. It is the promise that, although this world is an important arena for living out the faith of the community of God's people, there is another world beyond this from which tyranny and death have been banished.

Index of Subjects